D⋅⋅

EMPLOYMENT EXPANSION AND POPULATION GROWTH

A PUBLICATION OF THE
INSTITUTE OF INDUSTRIAL RELATIONS
UNIVERSITY OF CALIFORNIA

EMPLOYMENT EXPANSION AND POPULATION GROWTH

The California Experience: 1900-1950

By

MARGARET S. GORDON

UNIVERSITY OF CALIFORNIA PRESS
BERKELEY AND LOS ANGELES
1954

UNIVERSITY OF CALIFORNIA PRESS

BERKELEY AND LOS ANGELES

CALIFORNIA

◇

CAMBRIDGE UNIVERSITY PRESS

LONDON, ENGLAND

PRINTED IN THE UNITED STATES OF AMERICA

BY THE UNIVERSITY OF CALIFORNIA PRINTING DEPARTMENT

FOREWORD

DR. GORDON's monograph, "Employment Expansion and Population Growth, The California Experience: 1900–1950," focuses its attention upon the special employment problems associated with rapid growth in population. The study should be of unusual interest to all who are concerned with California's economic development and the long-run trends influencing employment in this state in relation to the.nation as a whole. It also will provide profitable and enjoyable reading for those who have a general interest in the problems emerging from the rapid rise of a complex modern industrial society on the Pacific Coast of the United States.

In 1952, Davis McEntire's monograph on a closely related subject, "The Labor Force in California," was published by the Institute of Industrial Relations. In his foreword to the McEntire volume, Clark Kerr, then Director of the Institute, referred to Dr. Gordon's study which was in its formative stage at that time. It is our hope and belief that the Gordon and McEntire studies will be authoritative sources for specific data and basic analysis, as well as the inspiration for further investigations.

E. T. GRETHER, *Director*

PREFACE

THIS STUDY was originally suggested by Clark Kerr, Chancellor of the University of California (Berkeley) and formerly Director of the Institute of Industrial Relations (Northern Division). Dean E. T. Grether of the School of Business Administration, who succeeded Dr. Kerr as Director of the Institute, has given me valuable advice and encouragement.

The manuscript has profited greatly from the many constructive suggestions and critical comments of those who read the first draft. They include Varden Fuller, Walter Galenson, and Harvey Leibenstein of the Institute reading committee; M. E. Gershenson, Chief of the Division of Labor Statistics and Research of the California State Department of Industrial Relations; Frank L. Kidner, Director of the Bureau of Business and Economic Research, University of California (Berkeley); Herbert F. Ormsby, Director of the Research Department, California State Chamber of Commerce; George S. Roche, Chief, Research and Statistics, California State Department of Employment; Harry S. Schwartz, Head, Research Department, Federal Reserve Bank of San Francisco; Richard C. Singleton of the Stanford Research Institute; Professor William A. Spurr of the Graduate School of Business, Stanford University; Van Beuren Stanbery, formerly of the San Francisco regional office of the United States Department of Commerce, whose many earlier studies of California's economic problems have been of invaluable assistance to the author; and Warren S. Thompson, who is currently directing a study of California's population growth for the John Randolph Haynes and Dora Haynes Foundation. William Goldner of the Institute staff checked the footnotes and made some useful suggestions. Richard Osborne and Alice Lundin gave valuable assistance in the compilation of statistical series.

For all matters of interpretation, and for any defects or errors which may have crept into the final version of the manuscript, I alone am responsible.

May, 1951   MARGARET S. GORDON

CONTENTS

LIST OF TABLES

TABLES IN STATISTICAL APPENDIX

LIST OF FIGURES

I. INTRODUCTION

AN UNUSUALLY rapid rate of population growth has been a striking feature of California's development ever since the days of the Gold Rush. Between 1850 and 1950, the nation's population increased more than sixfold, whereas California's population increased about sixty-four-fold.[1] It need scarcely be pointed out that most of this growth has come about through in-migration. The Gold Rush was merely the first of a series of waves of migration from other states and from abroad. Between 1860 and 1950, nearly 80 per cent of the growth in population of the state, on the average, came about through a net influx of persons born outside of California.

Throughout the decades, the rate of employment expansion has tended to keep pace with the growth in population, but the process of adjustment has not always been smooth, and there have been periods of severe unemployment, particularly in the 'thirties. During World War II, the opinion was widely held throughout the state that there would be a serious unemployment crisis following the cessation of hostilities, since the volume of employment under peacetime conditions was expected to fall far short of the level required to provide jobs for all the war workers who had migrated to the state to work in the Bay Area shipyards and the aircraft plants of southern California.[2] Actually, no serious crisis ever developed, although many war workers remained in the state and in-migration continued after the war. Unemployment increased from V-J Day to an estimated peak of 485,000 in April, 1946,[3] but from that point on there was steady improvement, and, on the whole, the level of economic activity was high throughout the postwar period.

Even so, although there was no postwar unemployment *crisis*, California did not escape an unemployment *problem* after the war. Throughout the months from V-J Day to the outbreak of the Korean War, the unemployment rate in California was considerably higher than the rate for the nation as a whole. From 1946 to 1949, average annual unemployment in the

---

[1] The increase was actually a hundred-fold on the basis of the official 1850 Census figure for the population of the state, but this figure clearly understated California's population in 1950 by a wide margin. Cf. table 1, n.a.

[2] For varying forecasts of postwar unemployment, see California, Reconstruction and Re-employment Commission, *Estimates of Wartime and Postwar Employment in California* (Sacramento, 1944), and *Second Report on Postwar Employment in California* (Sacramento, 1945). See also S. C. May and A. G. Norris, *Estimates of California Employment and Unemployment: 1946–1947* (mimeographed report, Bureau of Public Administration, University of California, Berkeley, 1946).

[3] California, Department of Industial Relations, *Handbook of California Labor Statistics: 1951–1952* (San Francisco, 1953), p. 75.

state was estimated to have varied from 6.7 to 9.2 per cent of the civilian labor force, whereas the corresponding unemployment rate for the nation varied from 3.9 to 5.9 per cent.[4] With the onset of the Korean crisis, unemployment rates dropped to lower levels in both state and nation, though there was still some tendency for the California rate to exceed the nationwide rate by a slight margin.

The postwar situation gave rise to considerable speculation about future population and employment trends in the state. It was recognized that a serious crisis had been averted in part because substantial postwar employment gains were to be expected in the trade and service industries and in construction, in which employment expansion during the war had been held back by man power shortages and by government controls. But in the long run, would underlying employment trends continue to provide jobs for a rapidly growing population, or would in-migration and a higher birth rate than formerly lead eventually to periodic unemployment crises and a reduced level of per capita income in the state compared to the national average?

Pessimists could point to the fact that California's natural resources did not seem as abundant, in relation to growing needs, as they had ten or twenty years earlier. Petroleum reserves were showing some signs of depletion,[5] and a pipeline was constructed to bring in natural gas from Texas. Inadequate supplies of water might well prove a serious limiting factor in the long run, although large-scale multiple-purpose water projects were being carried out. The lack of easily accessible deposits of such important raw materials as coal and iron was frequently mentioned as a factor limiting the scope of potential industrialization.

If, as a recent estimate indicates, the population of California is likely to reach a level somewhere between 13,400,000 and 14,900,000 people in 1960,[6] the state's labor force at the end of the present decade may be expected to include roughly 5,500,000 to 6,250,000 persons. Will there be jobs enough for all these people, after allowing for a modest amount of frictional unemployment? This is the type of question that is frequently asked about the state's economic future.

---

[4] See California, Department of Employment, *A Sourcebook on Unemployment Insurance in California* (Sacramento, 1953), p. 60. The United States data (based on Census Bureau estimates) have been adjusted to comparability with the California data by including in the number unemployed those not working because of bad weather or temporary layoffs. Even so, the California estimates may tend to produce a slightly higher apparent rate of unemployment than the U.S. Bureau of the Census method would give. For further discussion of the differences in methods used in preparing the two sets of estimates, see pp. 128–129, below.

[5] For an informative discussion of the postwar petroleum supply and demand situation in California, see Federal Reserve Bank of San Francisco, *Monthly Review* supplement, "Western Power and Fuel Outlook," November, 1950.

[6] See chapter ii, footnote 2.

It is not the purpose here to attempt a technical appraisal of the adequacy of California's resources to support a growing population, but rather to examine historical trends and fluctuations in the growth of population and employment, in the expectation that the findings may shed some light on probable future trends. Such questions as the following will be important:

1. Are there indications of a long-run downward trend in the *rate of increase* of population, employment, or both? Is population growth likely to "outrun" the expansion of employment?

2. What has been the nature of the relationship between population growth and the rate of expansion of employment in individual industries or groups of industries? Have certain industries reached a stage of maturity in which further growth of employment is unlikely or an actual decline has set in?

3. Is there evidence that, with increasing industrialization, employment is becoming less stable in the state? Is there any discernible relationship between fluctuations in the rate of population growth and in unemployment?

4. Why has the rate of population growth and of net in-migration shown marked fluctuations? In what way or ways have these fluctuations been related to changes in economic conditions and in the rate of employment expansion?

These all are important questions, but there is one serious obstacle that besets the path of an investigator who would like to answer them. The available statistical information is inadequate to the task at hand. Except for some series relating to factory employment, there are almost no monthly or annual data on employment or unemployment in California for years before 1939. For an analysis of long-run trends, census data are, of course, extremely valuable, but even here changes in definitions and in methods of classification have seriously impaired the comparability of the figures.

In spite of these obstacles, the task is by no means hopeless. In the absence of adequate monthly or annual employment data, certain limited inferences can be drawn as to what was probably happening to employment through a careful study of available data relating to income, wage rates, production, department store sales, building permits, and other economic variables. The present study has by no means exhausted the possibilities in this direction. It is to be hoped that one of its contributions will lie in pointing to areas in which further useful work of this type might be done.

II. POPULATION GROWTH

POPULATION GROWTH DURING THE DECADES

NOT ONLY has California grown rapidly during the last hundred years, but the number of people added in each ten-year period has tended to rise, reaching a peak in the last decade with an increase of more than 3,500,000 persons (see table 1). In percentage terms, however, the highest rate of increase occurred in 1850–1860, when the effects of the gold discovery were still at work and the level from which the increase occurred was very low.[1] Except for this early inrush of population, the peak rate of growth occurred in the 1920–1930 decade. This was also the decade in which the ratio of California's rate of increase to the national rate reached its maximum point.

TABLE 1

POPULATION GROWTH OF CALIFORNIA AND THE UNITED STATES,
BY DECADES, 1850–1950

Census year	California			United States			Ratio of California's rate of growth to U.S. rate of growth
	Population (in thousands)	Increase in each decade		Population (in thousands)	Increase in each decade		
		Number	Per cent		Number	Per cent	
1850	93ᵃ	....	....	23,192	.....	...	...
1860	380	287	310.4	31,443	8,251	35.6	8.7
1870	560	180	47.4	39,818	8,375	26.6	1.8
1880	865	304	54.3	50,156	10,337	26.0	2.1
1890	1,213	349	40.3	62,948	12,792	25.5	1.6
1900	1,485	272	22.4	75,995	13,047	20.7	1.1
1910	2,378	892	60.1	91,972	15,978	21.0	2.9
1920	3,427	1,049	44.1	105,711	13,738	14.9	3.0
1930	5,677	2,250	65.7	122,775	17,064	16.1	4.1
1940	6,907	1,230	21.7	131,669	8,894	7.2	3.0
1950	10,586	3,679	53.3	150,697	19,028	14.5	3.7

SOURCE: U.S. Bureau of the Census, *Statistical Abstract of the United States: 1952*, p. 12. All computations are based on unrounded data.
ᵃThe 1850 Census figure is considered to be too low, owing to inadequacies in census-taking procedures in California that year, and has been estimated at 165,000. See Commonwealth Club of California, *The Population of California* (San Francisco, 1946), p. 3. This report, prepared by Davis McEntire, is a valuable source of information on the state's population growth.

Although California's rate of population growth, like that of the nation, has fluctuated from decade to decade, the fluctuations have been considerably more pronounced in California. Detailed discussion of this question will be found in chapter vi, but it is worth observing at this point that the lowest rates of increase occurred in the two severely depressed decades of the 1890's and the 1930's.

[1] But see the note to table 1, on the undercount in 1850.

The percentage rate of population growth for the nation as a whole has shown a clear-cut tendency to decline (disregarding decade-to-decade fluctuations), but it is not certain that California's rate of growth has passed its peak. The fact that the rate of growth was materially smaller in the 'forties than in the 'twenties suggests, but does not prove, that the state has entered a period of secular decline in the rate of growth. More will be said on this point when the relative importance of net migration and natural increase as sources of growth are considered. In the meantime, it is interesting to observe that the ratio of California's rate of growth to that of the nation has been considerably higher during the present century than in the period from 1860 to 1900. This change appears to reflect chiefly a marked rise in the flow of internal migration to California from about the turn of the century onward.

There have been a number of attempts in recent years to forecast the future population growth of California. Most of these forecasts have taken the form of estimating, within a range between upper and lower limits, the probable size of the population of the state in 1960. According to an estimate recently published by the United States Bureau of the Census, the population of California in 1960 is likely to fall within a range between a low of 13,380,000 and a high of 14,919,000.[2] These figures would imply a rate of growth in the 1950's (27 to 42 per cent) considerably less than that attained in the decade of the 'forties (53 per cent). A lower rate of growth in the 'fifties is also indicated by the other available forecasts.

An independent estimate of California's population growth will not be attempted here, but it will be useful to analyze some of the changes which have occurred in the characteristics of California's population during the decades.

---

[2] U.S. Bureau of the Census, *Current Population Reports*, Series P-25, No. 56, January 27, 1952. The method used in these projections is one variation of the so-called "ratio" method. In the California projection, this method involved: (1) extrapolating the ratio of California's population to that of the Pacific Coast states on the assumption that the rate of change in this ratio would decrease linearly from the average annual rate of change in the 1930–1950 period to zero in the year 2000–2001, (2) extrapolating the ratio of the population of the Pacific Coast states to that of the United States on the basis of the same assumption; (3) applying the projected ratios for the year 1960 to the projection (low, medium, and high) of the population of the United States as published in *ibid.*, No. 43, July 1, 1949. The estimates relate to the civilian population plus those members of the armed forces who resided in the state at the time of their entry into military service.

For an informative summary of other forecasts of California's population in 1960, see Pacific Coast Board of Intergovernmental Relations, *People, Jobs, and Income on the Pacific Coast, 1949–1960* (San Francisco, 1950), p. 50.

Recently, the California State Department of Finance has published an estimate of the total resident population (12,950,000) of the state in 1955. California, Department of Finance, *Estimated Population of California, 1950–1953: With Projections to 1955* (Sacramento, 1953), p. 1.

NET IN-MIGRATION AS A FACTOR IN GROWTH

As has been seen, most of California's population growth has occurred through net in-migration rather than through natural increase. Indeed, as table 2 indicates, net in-migration has been an even more important factor, relatively, during the present century than it was between 1860 and 1900.[3] It is interesting to observe, however, that the rate of net in-migration, measured as a percentage of the state's population, reached a peak in the 1920's whereas the rate of natural increase was higher in the decade of the

TABLE 2

POPULATION GROWTH OF CALIFORNIA BY NATURAL INCREASE AND
NET IN-MIGRATION (ESTIMATED), 1860–1950

Decade	Total increase (in thousands)	Increase in population during decade						
		Estimated natural increase			Estimated net in-migration			
		Number (in thousands)	Per cent of total increase	Per cent of population at beginning of decade	Number (in thousands)	Per cent of total increase	Per cent of state's population at beginning of decade	Per cent of nation's population at beginning of decade
1860–1870	180	71	39.5	18.6	109	60.5	28.6	0.3
1870–1880	308	135	43.9	24.1	173	56.1	30.7	0.4
1880–1890	349	93	26.7	10.7	256	73.3	29.4	0.5
1890–1900	273	94	34.4	7.7	179	65.6	14.7	0.3
1900–1910	890	115	12.9	7.7	775	87.1	52.0	1.0
1910–1920	1,051	170	16.2	7.1	881	83.8	37.0	1.0
1920–1930	2,253	371	16.4	10.8	1,882	83.6	54.8	1.8
1930–1940	1,228	178	14.5	3.1	1,050	85.5	18.5	0.9
1940–1950	3,679	1,021	27.8	14.8	2,658	72.2	38.5	2.0

SOURCE: Estimates for period from 1860 to 1940 from U.S. Department of Agriculture, Bureau of Agricultural Economics, Population Committee for the Central Valley Project Studies, *California Migration*, Statistical Memorandum No. 6, by C. N. Reynolds and S. Miles (mimeographed report, Berkeley, California, July, 1944), p. 107. In the preparation of these estimates, the census population figures were corrected for underenumeration of young children (according to minimum estimates of underenumeration by the U.S. Bureau of the Census). For this reason, the figures for the total increase in each decade do not always agree precisely with those in table 1.
Estimates for the 1940–1950 decade are from U.S. Bureau of the Census, *Current Population Reports*, Series P-25, No. 72, May, 1953. The net movement of persons into the armed forces between 1940 and 1950 (65,000 persons) is included.

---

[3] Until comparatively recently, no systematic attempt was made to collect statistics on internal migration in this country. From census data for years before 1940, it is possible to arrive at estimates of migration between the decennial censuses through use of the information on place of birth. (See table 2.) The 1940 Census included the question, "Where did this person live in April, 1935?" the replies to which yield a wealth of data on internal migration between April, 1935, and April, 1940. Since 1940, the Census Bureau has been conducting quite frequent sample surveys of internal migration, which yield information on nation-wide migration but not on migration to or from particular states or regions. The 1950 Census included the question, "Where did this person live a year ago?" the replies to which, when fully tabulated, will yield a great deal of information on internal migration between April, 1949, and April, 1950.

1940's with its high birth rates, than in any previous decade since the 1870's.[4]

If the rate of net in-migration to California is computed as a percentage of the nation's rather than of the state's population, it is found that this percentage has displayed a long-run tendency to increase, though apparently at a declining rate since the 1920's. Here again, however, the upward tendency was interrupted in the depressed 1890's and 1930's. As California's population gains in proportion to the nation's population, it will require relatively more out-migration from other states to maintain a given rate of growth in California through net in-migration. It is possible that this requirement will be met, that is, that the proportion of the nation's residents migrating to California will rise sufficiently during the course of the next several decades so that the rate of population growth through net in-migration in California will not show a secular decline. This might conceivably happen if the propensity of Americans to participate in internal migration were to show a marked tendency to rise secularly. It is interesting to notice in this connection that the percentage of native-born Americans living in states other than that in which they were born has tended to rise since 1900, in spite of the disappearance of the frontier, and has attained in 1950 the highest level (25.2 per cent) reached in a century.[5]

It must be remembered, however, that if the nation's rate of population growth continues its secular decline, the number of persons participating in internal migration may not increase very much, even if such persons continue to represent a rising percentage of the total population. Furthermore, as the ratio of population to resources becomes more nearly equalized in the various parts of the nation, we may anticipate a decline in the proportion of persons participating in internal migration. In any event, the rate of population growth in California through net in-migration declined substantially between the 'twenties and the 'forties, even though net in-migration in the latter decade represented a slightly higher percentage of the nation's population than it had in the 'twenties. All things considered, it seems unlikely that the proportion of the nation's residents migrating to California will tend to increase *enough* in future decades to prevent a decline in California's rate of growth through in-migration.

REGIONAL SOURCES OF IN-MIGRATION

During the latter part of the nineteenth century and the first decade of the

---

[4] For purposes of analyzing long-run trends, it would be preferable to compute percentage rates of increase on the basis of the population at the mid-point of the decade rather than at the beginning of the decade. When this method was tried, however, it was found that the results did not differ sufficiently from those in table 2 to lead to different conclusions.

[5] See *United States Census of Population: 1950*, Special Report, P-E, No. 4A, p. 11.

present century, a substantial but decreasing proportion of the in-migrants to California were foreign-born.[6] The rapidly diminishing importance of such in-migration in recent decades reflects the effect of immigration restrictions imposed by the federal government. Internal migration of native-born Americans has become the predominant influence in California's population growth. Indeed, the proportion of California residents who were born in other states has shown a steady rise during the present century, with the 1950 Census indicating that more than half of the state's residents had been born in other parts of the United States.

The sources of internal migration to California have been shifting westward during the decades.[7] In 1860, more than half of the American-born residents of California who had been born in other states came from the Eastern seaboard. By 1950, 60.7 per cent had been born in states west of the Mississippi, that is, in the West North Central, West South Central, Mountain, and Pacific areas.

The reasons for this trend are rather obvious. The population center of the country has been gradually shifting westward, and, as this has occurred, the areas west of the Eastern seaboard have given birth to increasing numbers of potential migrants to the Pacific Coast. In addition, the pattern of early migration to California was something of an exception in the populating of the West. Most western states increased their population as a result of the gradual pushing westward of agricultural settlers. Partly because of the tremendous impact of the discovery of gold and partly because of its accessibility by sea, California drew people from all over the world and from all parts of the United States. The overland trip presented great difficulties until the completion of the transcontinental railroad in 1869, but after that California was brought within relatively easy reach of the Middle West.

During the depressed decade of the 'thirties, there was a sharp rise in the relative proportion of migrants who had been born in the West South Central states. This is brought out clearly in Appendix table A-3, which shows the proportions by which each geographic division contributed to the increase in each decade in the number of California residents born in other states.[8] In fact, the only two geographic divisions which contributed

---

[6] See Appendix, table A-1, on the place of birth of California residents. From the data on place of birth, it is possible to compute the net change in foreign-born residents each decade (not shown in the table).

[7] See Appendix, table A-2.

[8] The increase per decade in the number of residents born in other states does not, of course, provide an accurate measure of net in-migration during the decade, since it makes no allowance for the death or out-migration during the decade of former in-migrants. As to the geographical sources of in-migration, moreover, these data may be somewhat misleading, since an individual may not have migrated directly to California from the state in which he was born. They do, however, provide an approximate measure of long-run shifts in geographical sources of in-migration.

a higher percentage of this increase during the 'thirties than in the previous decade were the West North Central and West South Central states, many of which were affected in the middle 'thirties by the severe and prolonged drought in the Great Plains. In large part, this movement during the 'thirties was distress migration, influenced more by "push" than by "pull" factors. Even after the drought had subsided, the more prolonged effects of the displacement of sharecroppers by tractors and other mechanized equipment helped to account for continued migration to California.[9] The two states of Oklahoma and Texas alone contributed 18.5 per cent of the in-migrants of the 1935–1940 period.[10] Steinbeck's *Grapes of Wrath* immortalized the plight of the Dust Bowl refugees, but, as will be seen when the economic characteristics of the in-migrants of this period are considered, it was not only the farmers of the drought areas who sought refuge in California, but also the shopkeepers and other economic groups who had been dependent on the trade of the displaced farmers.

The changes in sources of in-migration during the 'forties, as indicated by state-of-birth data, represented, in some respects, a reversal of previous trends. There was a rise in the relative importance of all areas east of the Mississippi, at the expense of western areas. This shift probably reflected the comparatively greater importance of long distance migration in the 'forties.[11] How much of the change was attributable to the higher income and employment levels of the 'forties, how much to the marked production shifts that occurred during and after the war, and how much to the wartime movements of members of the Armed Forces and their families is not entirely clear.[12] Each of these factors played a role. There is little doubt,

[9] Cf. Commonwealth Club of California, *The Population of California* (San Francisco, 1946); L. V. Fuller, *The Supply of Agricultural Labor as a Factor in the Evolution of Farm Organization in California*, printed as Exhibit 8762 A in Hearings, U.S. Senate Committee on Education and Labor, 76th Congress, 3d Sess., Part 54, *Agricultural Labor in California* (Washington, 1940), pp. 19777–19898; and C. MacWilliams, *Factories in the Field* (Boston: Little, Brown, 1939).

[10] See *Sixteenth Census of the United States: 1940, Population, Internal Migration in the United States, 1935–1940: Color and Sex of Migrants*, pp. 96, 113–114, and 118.

[11] The Six-City Occupational Mobility Survey, conducted by the U.S. Bureau of the Census in early 1951, in coöperation with seven university research centers and the Social Science Research Council, indicated that larger percentages of the migrants who had entered the six cities during the 'forties had come from long distances than had been true in the late 'thirties. The six cities included in the survey were Chicago, Los Angeles, New Haven, Philadelphia, St. Paul, and San Francisco. For an analysis of the results of the survey, see G. L. Palmer, *Labor Mobility in Six Cities* (New York: Social Science Research Council, 1954). The San Francisco data will be analyzed in a forthcoming monograph to be published by the Institute of Industrial Relations, University of California, Berkeley.

[12] It is generally known, of course, that many service men who visited California during the war were attracted by the area and decided to move here after the war, as a result.

also, that the spread in the ownership of the automobile has facilitated long-distance migration of workers and their families and may continue to encourage increased long-distance migration in future decades.[13] At present, however, there is no basis for sound prediction as to whether sources of migration to California in future decades will shift in the direction indicated by long-run trends or by the changes that occurred in the 'forties.[14]

URBAN CONCENTRATION OF THE POPULATION AND URBAN SOURCES OF MIGRATION

A surprisingly large proportion of California's population has lived in the cities from very early days, and this proportion has grown rapidly.[15] There has been a particularly heavy and growing concentration of people, moreover, in the two big metropolitan areas of San Francisco and Los Angeles, which together accounted for 62.4 per cent of the state's population in 1950.[16] This high degree of urban concentration is somewhat surprising in a state that was long regarded as primarily agricultural, but it will seem less surprising after the analysis of the industrial distribution of the state's labor force in the next chapter.

The census data summarized in table A-4 suggest that the trend toward increasing urbanization was greatly slowed down in the nation and reversed in California after 1930. Actually, except for a temporary back-to-the-farm movement in the Great Depression of the early 'thirties, the proportion of the population living on farms has continued to decline appreciably, both in the United States and in California. Meanwhile, with the increasingly widespread ownership of automobiles, more and more people have moved to suburban and semirural communities. Many of these com-

[13] In his study of migration to the Seattle area in 1940–1942, Clark Kerr points out that the automobile provided a cheap means of transportation for most migrants regardless of their place of origin. About three out of every four new workers arrived in automobiles, and nearly half of them spent less than ten dollars in cash to get to the Seattle area. *Migration to the Seattle Labor Market Area, 1940–1942*, University of Washington Publications in the Social Sciences, Vol. 11, No. 3 (Seattle: University of Washington Press, 1942), p. 160.

[14] It must be recognized that state-of-birth data may not provide a completely accurate picture of shifts in sources of migration in the 'forties, in view of the fact that some migrants may not have moved to California directly from their states of birth. The state-of-birth data for the most part, however, are consistent with such migration data as are available. If, for example, the 1950 Census data on migration in the year, 1949–1950, are compared with the 1940 Census data on migration in the 1935–1940 period, similar evidence is found of a rise in the relative importance of migration from the East during the 'forties. In certain other respects, however, the shifts indicated by the two sets of data are inconsistent, but in this connection it should be recognized that distribution of sources of in-migration in the single year 1949–1950 may have differed somewhat from that which prevailed over the entire decade of the 'forties.

[15] See Appendix, table A-4.

[16] Computed from *United States Census of Population: 1950*, Vol. II., Part 5, p. 51.

munities, particularly in the West, were classified by the census as rural nonfarm from 1920 to 1940, and, in California, two-thirds of the "rural" population lived in such areas in 1940. Under the new 1950 Census definition, with suburbs of sizable cities classified as urban,[17] more than 80 per cent of California's population resided in urban areas in 1950, as compared with 64 per cent of the population in the nation as a whole.

Although this study is concerned primarily with state-wide problems rather than with problems of particular regions of the state, it is important to recognize that throughout most of the period, the southern part of the state accounted for a substantial percentage of the population growth. This had not been true during the decades immediately following the Gold Rush, when most of the growth occurred in the northern part of the state, but after a direct rail route to Los Angeles was opened up in the 1880's, southern California began to develop rapidly. By 1940, 55.7 per cent of the population of the state lived in southern California.[18] During the following decade, although both sections of the state grew rapidly, northern California's percentage of the total population rose slightly.

Not only have the migrants largely been settling in urban areas in recent decades, but most of them have come from urban, rather than rural, areas of other states. Of the 1935–1940 in-migrants from other states, nearly two-thirds had come from urban areas, and more than half of the remainder had come from rural nonfarm areas.[19] The Six-City Occupational Mobility Survey, conducted in early 1951, indicated that only a small proportion of the migrants living in San Francisco and Los Angeles were sons or daughters of farmers.[20]

AGE AND SEX CHARACTERISTICS OF IN-MIGRANTS

The fact that California's population has grown so largely through inmigration has had important effects on its age and sex composition. Retired Iowa farmers have certainly played a role among migrants to California, but the statistics do not indicate that it has been a dominant one. The people who predominate in large migrations are usually young and are often preponderantly male. The migration to California has been no

---

[17] Urban areas are now defined to include (a) places of 2,500 inhabitants or more, incorporated or unincorporated, and (b) the densely settled urban fringe, incorporated or unincorporated, around cities of 50,000 or more. California was one of the states most affected by the change in definition. Cf. *ibid.*, p. v.

[18] See Appendix, table A-5. A list of the counties which are included in southern California may be found in the footnote to the table.

[19] *Sixteenth Census of the United States: 1940, Population, Internal Migration in the United States: 1935–1940, Color and Sex of Migrants*, p. 4.

[20] For a definition of "migrants," see the note to table 4. See the reference to the Six-City study in footnote 11.

exception to this rule. The typical pioneer of the Gold Rush days was a young, unattached male, and for several decades thereafter there was a marked scarcity of women in the population. The Census of 1870 revealed a sex ratio of 165.8 men to 100 women, but, as time went on and the process of moving to California became less arduous, the preponderance of men among the migrants gradually became less marked, and the sex distribution of babies born within the state was characterized, of course, by the normal balance between the sexes. Meanwhile, several factors were contributing to a gradual shift in the sex composition of the nation as a whole. One of these was the lower death rate among the women. Another, which became important about the middle of the 1920's was the sharp drop in immigration from abroad, which had been predominantly male. By 1950, the nation-wide sex ratio was 98.6 men to 100 women, and California's ratio was 100.1 men to 100 women. There is some evidence that during the 'forties, women predominanted among the in-migrants to the state, but on this point we do not have conclusive figures.[21]

Although the ratio between the sexes has shifted, young adults have continued to form the largest group among the migrants (see table A-6).[22] Were it not for this tendency, California's population would have become heavily weighted with older people as a consequence of the relatively low rate of natural increase. The preponderance of young adults among the migrants tended to diminish somewhat between 1880 and 1940,[23] although persons in the age brackets from 20 to 39 (as of the end of the decade) accounted for far more than 50 per cent of net in-migration in every decade before 1940. Meanwhile, the proportion of persons forty years and older among the migrants tended to increase somewhat up to 1920 and then to decline. It is significant that the decades 1900–1910 and 1920–1930, both of which were characterized by unusually heavy in-migration, showed a relatively low proportion of in-migrants in both the ten-to-nineteen and

---

[21] The Six-City Occupational Mobility Survey indicated that a majority of the migrants (those who had lived in the metropolitan area less than twelve years) in both San Francisco and Los Angeles, as well as in the other cities of the survey, were women, but the survey was conducted in early 1951, when a good many relatively recent male migrants may have been already in the armed forces. See Palmer, *op. cit.*, pp. 16 and 24. Place-of-birth data indicate that the number of women born outside the state increased slightly more than the number of such men between 1940 and 1950, but the 1940 data would have to be adjusted for deaths and out-migration during the decade to permit the drawing of definite conclusions on the sex composition of in-migrants between 1940 and 1950.

[22] For a detailed statistical analysis of these trends, see Commonwealth Club of California (*op. cit.*). The Six-City Occupational Mobility Survey showed that migrants to San Francisco and Los Angeles, in the decade of the 'forties, as well as to the other cities in the survey, tended to include a substantially larger percentage of young adults than did the nonmigrant population. See Palmer, *loc. cit.*

[23] Comparable data for the 1940–1950 decade are not available.

more-than-sixty categories. The explanation for this becomes apparent when the numerical, rather than percentage, figures for the various age groups are examined.[24] The fluctuations between decades of relatively heavy or light migration have been widest in the age brackets comprising adults of working age, whereas the youngest and oldest age brackets have shown a relatively steady increase in numbers from decade to decade. This is not surprising, in view of the evidence which will be discussed in later chapters that the periods of heaviest in-migration have been those in which employment opportunities have expanded most rapidly and have attracted in-migrants of working age.

OCCUPATIONAL CHARACTERISTICS OF IN-MIGRANTS

If the impact of in-migration on the California labor market is to be understood, it is necessary to know something about the occupational characteristics of in-migrants. Are the persons who migrate to California from other states primarily unskilled or semiskilled workers, or are they broadly representative of all occupation groups? The 1940 Census data on internal migration yielded, for the first time, comprehensive statistical information bearing on this question.

TABLE 3

MAJOR OCCUPATION GROUP OF IN-MIGRANTS AND ALL EMPLOYED WORKERS, CALIFORNIA, 1940, IN PER CENT

Major occupation group	In-migrants from other states[a]	All employed[b] workers
Total employed...........................	354,357	2,525,281
Per cent................................	100.0	100.0
Professional and semiprofessional workers.........	8.8	9.6
Farmers and farm managers...................	1.0	4.0
Proprietors, managers, and officials, except farm....	7.7	11.2
Clerical, sales, and kindred workers..............	18.2	20.8
Craftsmen, foremen, and kindred workers.........	12.6	12.8
Operatives and kindred workers.................	15.4	15.2
Domestic service workers......................	6.0	3.5
Service workers, other than domestic.............	16.3	10.6
Farm laborers and foremen....................	7.1	5.6
Laborers (except farm and mine) and occupation not reported................................	6.9	6.7

SOURCE: *Sixteenth Census of the United States: 1940. Population, Internal Migration in the United States, 1935–40: Economic Characteristics of Migrants*, pp. 72–73.
[a] In-migrants from other states were defined as persons living in California in 1940 who had lived in other states in 1935.
[b] Excluding those employed on public emergency work.

Probably the most striking conclusion that emerges from these data (see table 3) is that the in-migrants who were employed in the state in 1940

___
[24] The numerical data are not shown in table A-6.

were distributed occupationally, on the *whole*, in much the same manner as California's employed workers in general. Yet there were some important differences. Farmers and managerial workers represented a smaller proportion of the in-migrants than of all employed workers, as did clerical and sales workers. On the other hand, a comparatively large percentage of the in-migrants were employed as service workers (including domestic) and as farm laborers. All in all, approximately 64 per cent of the in-migrants, as compared with 54 per cent of all employed workers, were engaged in manual occupations in 1940, and it was in relatively unskilled manual occupations that the migrants were found in unusually large numbers.

One aspect of these results which is rather surprising is the fact that, in the light of what is known of the problem created by the Dust Bowl refugees of the period, the percentage of farm laborers among employed in-migrants in 1940 was not higher. Actually, although large numbers of the Dust Bowl refugees were farmers and many of them did seek employment as farm laborers in California, the majority of in-migrants, *even from the Dust Bowl areas*, came from the towns and cities rather than from the farms. Of the in-migrants from the states of Nebraska, Kansas, Oklahoma, Texas, and Colorado (all of which were affected by drought conditions and sent large numbers of migrants to California), 60.2 per cent had lived in urban areas of these states in 1935, 16 per cent in rural nonfarm areas, and only 23.8 per cent in rural farm areas.[25] Furthermore, the great majority (75.1 per cent) of these in-migrants were living in urban areas of California in 1940, with the remainder almost equally divided between rural farm and rural nonfarm areas. Of course, many farm laborers in California, particularly in the off-season,[26] live in areas classified by the census as urban or rural nonfarm and might have been temporarily employed in some other industry or classified as unemployed in the 1940 Census. But such persons would not account for a large percentage of the in-migrants who were employed in 1940. It is probable that many of the farmers and farm laborers who migrated to California between 1935 and 1940 had either returned to their former states by 1940 or had become employed in other occupations in California.

Unfortunately, we have no state-wide data on the occupational char-

---

[25] Of the total in-migrants from Oklahoma, the home of the "Okies" and the largest single source of migration to California in this period, 35.1 per cent were from rural farm areas and 18.8 per cent from rural nonfarm areas. These percentages and those cited in the text are computed from data in *Sixteenth Census of the United States: 1940, Population, Internal Migration in the United States, 1935–1940: Color and Sex of Migrants*, pp. 106–115.

[26] April, the month in which the 1940 Census was taken, is a month of relatively low agricultural employment in California.

TABLE 4

MAJOR OCCUPATION GROUP OF WORKERS BY MIGRATION STATUS, CITIES OF LOS ANGELES AND SAN FRANCISCO, 1940 AND 1951

Major occupation group	Los Angeles 1940[b] Migrants	Nonmigrants	1951[a] Migrants[c]	Nonmigrants	San Francisco 1940[b] Migrants	Nonmigrants	1951[a] Migrants[c]	Nonmigrants
Total workers[d]	137,683	447,344	383,635	388,498	47,657	220,844	130,509	201,619
Per cent	100	100	100	100	100	100	100	100
Professional, technical, and kindred workers	11	11	14	15	13	9	10	10
Managers, officials, and proprietors, incl. farm	10	13	15	21	9	12	11	18
Clerical and kindred workers	25	26	16	12	29	29	22	18
Sales workers			8	8			9	8
Craftsmen, foremen, and kindred workers	12	13	14	15	8	12	13	13
Operatives and kindred workers	16	16	17	16	10	15	12	13
Private household workers	6	4	2	1	5	3	2	1
Service workers, exc. private household	14	11	9	9	22	13	17	13
Laborers	6	6	5	3	4	7	4	6

SOURCES: *Sixteenth Census of the United States: 1940. Population, Internal Migration in the United States: 1935 to 1940, Economic Characteristics of Migrants*, pp. 170 and 176; and U.S. Bureau of the Census, Six-City Occupational Mobility Survey, 1951 (unpublished tables).

[a] Since the 1951 data are based on a sample survey, they are subject to sampling variability.

[b] According to the 1940 Census definition, migrants were persons who had lived in another county (or quasi county) in 1935. Immigrants were originally classified separately, but they are included here with migrants, as was the case in the 1951 survey.

[c] In the Occupational Mobility Survey, migrants were defined as persons who had lived in the Standard Metropolitan Area (of Los Angeles or San Francisco, respectively) less than 12 years.

[d] Totals for 1940 include all employed workers except those on public emergency work and those whose migration status was not reported; totals for 1951 include all persons aged 25 years and older (in the civilian noninstitutional population) who had worked fulltime for pay at least one month during 1950 (excluding those whose occupation or migration status was not reported).

acteristics of migrants who entered the state[27] during the decade of the 'forties, but, for the cities of Los Angeles and San Francisco, the results of the Six-City Occupational Mobility Survey, conducted in early 1951, yield information on the occupational characteristics of workers in these cities who had moved from other areas since the beginning of 1940 (see table 4). The majority of these migrants had come from outside the state, although in both cities, and particularly in San Francisco, there was a substantial minority of migrants who had come from other parts of California.

For comparative purposes we have included in table 4 the 1940 Census data relating to the occupational characteristics of migrants and nonmigrants in the two cities.[28] The tendency for relatively fewer migrants to be employed as managerial workers showed up in both cities in 1940. In part, this difference reflected the comparative youth of the migrants; managerial workers tend to be somewhat older, on the average, than workers in other occupation groups. In part, it may also have reflected the more limited opportunities available to migrants to enter self-employment or to secure executive positions. So far as the 1940 situation was considered, the differences in occupational characteristics between migrants and nonmigrants were considerably more marked in San Francisco than in Los Angeles. Professional workers were more heavily represented among the migrants, and at the other end of the occupational scale, San Francisco migrants were found in service jobs to a considerably greater extent than were the nonmigrants. On the other hand, comparatively few San Francisco migrants were employed as craftsmen, operatives, or laborers in 1940. These differences were much less marked, and, for some occupation groups, did not show up at all in the Los Angeles data.

In 1951, relatively fewer migrants were found in managerial jobs and relatively more in clerical jobs in both cities, whereas service workers were again somewhat more heavily represented among the migrants than among the nonmigrants in San Francisco, though not to as marked an extent as in 1940. In other respects the occupational differences between migrants and nonmigrants cannot be considered statistically significant.

The chief conclusion that emerges from analysis of these data is that migrants to California and to the largest cities in the state are not heavily concentrated at any particular level of skill but contribute to the growth of the labor force at all levels of skill. Partly because so many of them are young and partly, probably, because of the handicaps under which they suffer as newcomers to the area, they are less likely to be found in mana-

---

[27] Tabulations on the occupational characteristics of 1949–1950 migrants have not yet been published by the Census Bureau.

[28] In comparing the two sets of data, the difference in coverage, as well as in the definition of a migrant, as explained in the footnote to the table, should be kept in mind.

gerial occupations than are employed workers in general. The state-wide data relating to the 1935-1940 period indicate that migrants were more heavily concentrated in manual occupations than were employed workers in general, but we have no conclusive evidence that this pattern prevailed during the 'forties.

There is some evidence that the occupational characteristics of migrants who enter the major cities of the state may be affected, to some extent, by conditions prevailing in the labor market at the time they migrate. When the migrants living in San Francisco in 1951 were classified by years of residence in the area, it was found that those who had entered during the war years, when the shortage of manual workers was acute, were much more heavily concentrated in manual occupations than were those who had entered in the postwar period.[29] This difference showed to a less marked degree for Los Angeles, probably because there was a less sharp contraction of job opportunities for manual workers in Los Angeles in the immediate postwar period.

Thus far, the question has not been discussed as to whether or not the migrants who come to California tend to find jobs in the same occupations in which they were employed before migration. So far as can be judged from the available data, the majority of workers who migrated to California's major cities during the decade of the 'forties did experience a shift in occupational affiliation at the time of migration. Such shifts were much more common, however, among workers who lacked specialized skill or training than among professional workers or skilled craftsmen. Furthermore, although many individual workers experienced occupational shifts, it was found that the occupational distribution of migrants *after* migration did not differ markedly from their occupational distribution *before* migration.[30]

RACIAL CHARACTERISTICS OF IN-MIGRANTS

Although nonwhites have tended to represent a small minority of California's population throughout the state's history, there have been some interesting shifts in the racial composition of the nonwhite population. California history, moreover, has been highlighted by intense controversy over the in-migration of nonwhite workers. Since this story, particularly as it bears on the history of migratory farm labor in the state, has been fully set forth by others,[31] I shall deal only briefly with the changing racial com-

---

[29] These differences will be more fully analyzed in a forthcoming Institute monograph, which will be based on the Occupational Mobility Survey data for San Francisco.

[30] Here again, the results of the Six-City Occupational Mobility Survey, and particularly the San Francisco data, will be more extensively discussed in forthcoming publications of the Institute of Industrial Relations, University of California (Berkeley).

[31] See the references cited in footnote 9.

position of the state's population and with certain recent trends which, if they continue, are likely to have an important bearing on the California labor market in the next few decades.

As Appendix table A-7 indicates, nonwhites represented an important element (15 per cent) in the population of the state in 1860, with Chinese and native California Indians predominating among the nonwhites. As time went on, and indeed until 1940, the white population grew more rapidly than the nonwhite. Chinese immigration was prohibited in 1882, and entry of the Japanese was restricted by administrative regulations in 1907 and was prohibited in 1924.[32] The proportion of nonwhites had fallen to 4.5 per cent by the time of the 1940 Census.

Until 1940, the Negro population of the state grew quite slowly. In fact, writers on internal migration had commented on the surprisingly small flow of Negro migration to California in relation both to total migration to the state and to migration of Negroes from the South to Northern industrial cities.[33] By and large, except for temporary shortages from time to time, the demand for "cheap labor," particularly in the farm areas of the state, was satisfied by the successive influxes of Chinese, Japanese, Mexicans, and "Dust Bowl" refugees. It was not until World War II that the labor market situation was such as to encourage a large-scale movement of Negroes to California. The Negro population of the state grew from 124,306 in 1940 to 462,172 in 1950, an increase of 272 per cent.[34] Representing only 1.8 per cent of the total population in 1940, it amounted to 4.4 per cent ten years later. Other nonwhite groups grew more slowly and, as a proportion of the total population of the state, fell from 2.8 per cent in 1940 to 2 per cent in 1950.[35]

It seems reasonable to suppose that, with the larger Negro population now residing in California, there will be an increased tendency for Negroes to move to the state to join relatives or friends already living there. In other words, now that there is a well-established pattern of Negro migration to California, the Negro population may be expected to grow appreciably during the next several decades, though there is every reason to suppose that in-migration of Negroes will vary with fluctuations in economic conditions, together with other types of migration.[36]

[32] Under the Immigration and Nationality Act of 1952, aliens from Asiatic countries, who were barred from the quota system by the 1924 Immigration Act, now have small quota allotments. See U.S. Public Law 414, *The Immigration and Nationality Act*, June 27, 1952.

[33] See, for example, C. W. Thornthwaite, *Internal Migration in the United States* (Philadelphia: University of Pennsylvania Press, 1934), p. 12.

[34] See *United States Census of Population: 1950*, Vol. II, Part 5, p. 57.

[35] See Appendix, table A-7.

[36] See chapters vi and viii.

The Role of Natural Increase in Population Growth

Earlier sections have pointed out that most of California's population growth during the decades has come about through net in-migration rather than through natural increase. This relationship might have prevailed even if the birth rate had not been unusually low in California throughout much of the state's history, but a comparatively low birth has tended to keep down the rate of natural increase and has probably helped to create conditions favorable to a high rate of net in-migration. In other words, if California's native population had been increasing at a more rapid rate, native-born residents would have been entering the labor force in larger numbers from year to year, and fewer job opportunities might well have been available for in-migrants.

In the last few decades, on the other hand, the birth rate in California has tended to approach the nation-wide rate. Does this mean that the era of a *relatively* low birth rate in California is over? This question cannot easily be answered, but in order even to attempt to answer, it is necessary to understand why the birth rate was relatively low in the state in earlier decades and has moved closer to the national rate in the last few decades.

Reliable birth rate statistics for the state are available only from 1919 on, but differential fertility rates for earlier periods have been computed by the Bureau of the Census for various groups of women. In addition, an analysis of changes in the proportion of children less than five in the population provides a rough indication of birth-rate trends.

The relatively low proportion of children in California throughout the latter half of the nineteenth century and the early decades of the present century was attributable in part to the comparatively high sex ratio in the state. This was true of whites and even more strikingly true of nonwhites,[37] since a very large proportion of the Chinese workers who migrated to California in the early decades of the state's history and a substantial proportion of the Japanese who came later were single men. As time went on, however, the high sex ratio gradually disappeared, and, in any event, it did not fully account for the small proportion of children. The fact that fertility rates, which measure the ratio of children of specified ages to women of specified ages in the population, were also relatively low, indicates that we must look to other factors for a full explanation of the low birth rate.[38] Since the nonwhite population of the state has been too small to affect trends in fertility rates appreciably, the analysis will be confined to the white population.

During the period from 1860 to 1920, the average fertility rate for white women—defined in this case as the number of children less than five per

---

[37] See Appendix, table A-8.
[38] See Appendix, table A-9.

1,000 women fifteen to forty-nine years of age—declined much more rapidly in California than in the nation. A number of factors were apparently responsible. In the first two decades of this period, urbanization was proceeding more rapidly in California than in the nation. (In this period, as in more recent years, fertility rates tended to be substantially lower in urban than in rural areas.) Second, although the proportion of foreign-born persons in California's population exceeded that in the United States throughout this period, it declined substantially in the state but not in the nation after 1860, so that the difference between state and nation in this respect steadily narrowed. Third, as a consequence of the low birth rate, the age distribution of California's population shifted in an elderly direction as the decades passed. By 1900, the proportion of persons aged forty-five and more was substantially higher in California than in the nation.[39]

After World War I, the ratio of the average fertility rate for white women in California to that in the nation tended to rise. This change in relationship reflected the fact that the California rate fell less rapidly than the national rate until the bottom of the Great Depression and rose more rapidly thereafter. The timing of the change (which can be determined only approximately on the basis of the available data) and the behavior of age-specific fertility and birth rates for urban and rural women provide a clue to what was probably the most important factor in the changing relationship.

Between 1910 and 1940, average fertility rates for young white women in California rose, although the corresponding rates in the nation declined. Fertility rates for older women in California declined somewhat less than those in the nation during this period, particularly in urban and rural nonfarm areas. If the ratio of the fertility rate in the state to that in the nation for each age group of women in urban and rural areas is computed, it is found that nearly all the ratios rose. The ratios for women in urban and rural nonfarm areas, however, rose more sharply than for those in farm areas, and the most marked increases applied to the youngest age groups. They scarcely rose at all for older women in farm areas.

These changes began to occur at a time when net in-migration was ceasing to be an important factor in the population growth of the United States but was a substantially more important factor, relatively, in the population growth of California than had been true in the latter part of the nineteenth century. Furthermore, the changing relationship affected primarily those female age groups among whom the largest percentages of in-migrants would be found. But was there any reason for supposing that the in-migrants to California, who were drawn from all parts of the United

[39] See Appendix, table A-11.

States, would tend to have higher fertility rates than native California women? There is no direct evidence on this point, but it is known that the regions which were rising markedly in relative importance as sources of in-migration to California during this period—the West South Central and Mountain states—were regions of comparatively high fertility rates.[40] In-migration from the West North Central states, in which fertility rates were somewhat above the national average, was also comparatively important during this period. During the years from 1910 to 1930, moreover, a very substantial influx of Mexicans occurred. In the 'twenties alone, the number of persons of Mexican birth residing in California rose by 111,000 and represented more than a third of the total increase in foreign-born residents between 1920 and 1930.[41] If the fluctuations in the crude birth rate in California and the United States since 1919 are examined, moreover, it is found that the ratio of the California rate to the national rate tended to rise during periods of rising net migration to California and to decline during periods of falling migration.[42] In large part, this fluctuating relationship was probably attributable to the fact that the proportion of young adults of child-bearing age tended to rise as net migration rose and perhaps to fall somewhat as net migration fell. But it is likely, also, that it reflected the fact that a large proportion of the migrants who entered the state, particularly in the 'thirties, came from areas and from social and economic groups in which relatively high birth rates were prevalent.

Another factor which may well have had a more pronounced impact on birth and fertility rates in California than in the nation as a whole in recent decades has been the movement to the suburbs. Just as urbanization played an important role in the long-run decline of the birth rate during many decades, so suburbanization of the population has undoubtedly been a factor in the rise of the birth rate in the last few decades. There is some evidence that the movement to the suburbs got under way somewhat earlier in California and had proceeded further by 1950 than in the country as a whole. The 1950 Census showed that 31.1 per cent of California's population lived in "urban fringe" areas, as compared with 13.9 per cent of the nation's population.[43]

Finally, the shifting relationship between birth rates in California and

---

[40] See the useful table providing historical data on fertility rates by region in U.S. Bureau of the Census, *Forecasts of the Population of the United States: 1945–1975* (Washington, 1947), p. 16.

[41] See U.S. Bureau of Agricultural Economics, Population Committee for the Central Valley Project Studies, *California Migration*, Statistical Memorandum No. 6, by C. N. Reynolds and S. Miles (mimeographed report, Berkeley, California, July, 1944), pp. 5 and 10.

[42] See Appendix, table A-12.

[43] *United States Census of Population: 1950*, Vol. II, Part 1, p. 5, and Part 5, p. 7.

the United States in recent decades must be attributed in part to the more rapid rise in the proportion of the older age groups in the population of the nation. In 1920, the proportion of persons aged forty-five and older was substantially smaller in the nation (21.9 per cent) than in California (26.6 per cent). By 1950, the proportion in this age bracket was almost as high in the nation (28.8 per cent) as in the state (29.8 per cent).[44] The drop in net immigration and the factors, already discussed, contributing to a decline in the *relative* height of the birth rate in the nation had gradually brought about this change. By 1950, the differences in age composition between California and the nation were narrower than ever before.

On the whole, it seems likely that birth rates and fertility rates in California will remain closer to those in the nation than in the early decades of the present century. The fact that the age and sex distribution of the state's population now closely resembles that of the nation will contribute to this end. But the crude birth rate in the state may be expected to rise or fall somewhat in relation to the corresponding national rate as the rate of net migration to the state rises or falls. Shifts in regional sources of in-migration may also affect the relationship between state and national birth and fertility rates. Furthermore, even though regions with relatively high birth rates continue to be comparatively important as sources of in-migration to California, their birth rates may move closer to the national average as they become more urbanized and industrialized. Finally, although the rest of the nation may have lagged behind California, to some extent, in suburbanization, the movement to the suburbs is now clearly a nation-wide movement, which is undoubtedly encouraging a tendency all over the country toward raising larger families. Thus, though there are grounds for predicting that the birth and fertility rates in California in the next several decades are likely to deviate less widely from nation-wide rates than they did in 1910 or 1920, it would be extremely hazardous to make any prediction as to precisely what their relationship to national rates will be in 1960 or 1970.

The annual excess of births over deaths in California in 1952 amounted to 172,800, the highest total for any year since such data have become available. This annual gain was almost as large as the total ten-year natural increase achieved in the decade of the 'thirties (see table 2). The change reflected the combined effects of the rise in the birth rate, the slow long-run decline in the death rate, and the increase in the size of the population. Whether the annual gain will continue at this level will depend primarily on nation-wide developments affecting the birth rate, since, as we have seen, the California rate has been close to the national rate in recent

---

[44] See Appendix, table A-11.

years. Both in California and in the nation, the percentage of persons aged fifteen to twenty-four was smaller in 1950 than at any previous time since 1870, as a result of the decline in the birth rate in the late 'twenties and early 'thirties. Since it is in this age group that would doubtless be found the most prolific parents of the 1950's, there is some reason to expect a decline in the birth rate in the late 'fifties, followed by an increase from about 1960 on, when the generation that was born in the 'forties reaches child-bearing age. But the age structure of the population is by no means the only factor that will affect the course of the birth rate in the next few decades. A thoroughgoing analysis of the complex factors that will determine its course would take us far beyond the scope of the present study.[45]

TABLE 5

GROWTH OF POPULATION AND LABOR FORCE, BY DECADES,
CALIFORNIA, 1870–1950

Census year	Total population		Population of working age[a]		Labor force[b]		Labor force as per cent of population of working age
	Number (in thousands)	Percentage increase in preceding decade	Number (in thousands)	Percentage increase in preceding decade	Number (in thousands)	Percentage increase in preceding decade	
1870	560	....	430	....	239	....	55.4
1880	865	54.3	681	58.2	377	57.8	55.3
1890	1,213	40.3	990	45.3	544	44.5	55.0
1900	1,485	22.4	1,120	23.5[c]	642	18.4[c]	57.4
1910	2,378	60.1	1,870	67.0	1,090[d]	72.1	58.3
1920	3,427	44.1	2,660	42.2	1,511	38.6	56.8
1930	5,677	65.7	4,466	67.9	2,499	65.4	56.0
1940	6,907	21.7	5,642	26.3	2,948	18.0	52.3
1950	10,586	53.3	8,108	43.7	4,411	49.6	54.4

SOURCES: *Ninth to Seventeenth Censuses of the United States.* Data for the years 1870 to 1910 have been compiled from the appropriate census volumes, except for the adjusted 1910 figure for gainful workers, which is from D. McEntire. *The Labor Force in California* (Berkeley: University of California Press, 1952), p. 77. Data for 1920 to 1950 are from *United States Census of Population: 1950,* Vol. II, Part 5, p. 67. All percentages have been computed from unrounded data.

[a]Includes all persons aged 10 years and older, 1870 to 1890, and all persons aged 14 years and older, 1900 to 1950.

[b]Data for 1870 to 1890 refer to "gainful workers", aged 10 years and older; for 1900 to 1930 to "gainful workers", aged 14 years and older; and, for 1940 and 1950, to persons in the "labor force", aged 14 years and older.

[c]In computing these percentages, persons aged 10–13 were included in the 1900 figure, as well as in the 1890 figure.

[d]Adjusted for census overcount of agricultural workers in 1910. See source reference above.

---

[45] For some recent population projections and discussion of the problem, see U.S. Bureau of the Census, *Current Population Reports,* Series P-25, No. 43, August 10, 1950; P. K. Whelpton and J. V. Grauman, "Population: Prospects and Problems in 1960," *Dun's Review,* January, 1952; H. F. Dorn, "Pitfalls in Population Forecasts and Projections," *Journal of the American Statistical Association,* LXV (1950), pp. 311–334; J. S. Davis, *The Population Upsurge in the United States,* Stanford University, Food Research Institute, War-Peace Pamphlet No. 12, December, 1949; and J. S. Davis, "Our Changed Population Outlook and Its Significance," *American Economic Review,* XLII (1952), pp. 304–325.

GROWTH OF THE LABOR FORCE

Since the growth of California's labor force has been analyzed in detail in an earlier Institute study, it will be dealt with only very briefly here.[46] Changes in the age distribution of the state's population, as well as changes in the labor force participation rates of various groups in the population, have meant that the proportion of the total population in the labor force has fluctuated to a certain extent. With increasing industrialization and urbanization, moreover, there has been a long-run decline in the labor force participation rates of children and older men and a rise in the percentage of women in the labor force.

These changes, however, have not materially affected the proportion of the total population of working age in the labor force (see table 5). Furthermore, the decline in this proportion between 1930 and 1940 was attributable in part to the shift by the Census Bureau from the "gainful worker" concept to the "labor force" concept. Before 1940, census data referred to "gainful workers," that is, persons who *usually* worked at gainful labor, regardless of whether they were working or seeking work at the time of the census. The labor force, as defined in the 1940 Census, included all persons who were employed or who were seeking work or on public emergency work during a specific week (in this case, March 24–30, 1940).[47] This concept, with only minor modifications, has been used by the Census Bureau ever since.

For purposes of this study, the important point is that the growth of the labor force has, on the whole, tended to keep pace with the growth of the population. Decades of relatively rapid population growth have also been decades of rapid growth of the labor force, and *vice versa*. Minor variations in labor force participation rates have affected the growth of the labor force but little from decade to decade; fluctuations in the rate of population growth have been the decisive influence.

CONCLUSIONS

Although net in-migration was by far the most important component of California's population growth during the first half of the present century, there is at least a possibility that it will gradually become somewhat less important, relatively, in the second half of the century. As California's population comes to represent a larger proportion of the nation's population, it will require an ever-increasing percentage of out-migrants from

[46] See D. McEntire, *The Labor Force in California* (Berkeley: University of California Press, 1952).

[47] For an excellent discussion of these problems see *Sixteenth Census of the United States: 1940, Comparative Occupation Statistics for the United States: 1870 to 1940*, by A. M. Edwards (Washington, 1943), especially chapter iii.

other states to maintain a given rate of growth through migration in California, and, as has been discussed, this requirement is unlikely to be fulfilled. It may also be true that a rising ratio of population to resources in California will gradually tend to decrease the net economic advantage to be gained by migrating to the state; however, as I shall show in subsequent chapters, the evidence on this point is not at all conclusive.

Meanwhile, experts are by no means in agreement as to what is likely to happen to the birth rate during the second half of the century, although a temporary decline in the second half of the 'fifties is generally expected. Unless the secular tendency is toward a substantial decline in the birth rate below present levels, the rate of natural increase in California will tend to be considerably higher than it had been for many decades before the 1940's.

A long-run decline in the relative importance of net in-migration as a factor in growth would mean that California's rate of population growth would move closer to the nation-wide rate. It would also mean, as will become apparent in the discussion in later chapters, that fluctuations in California's rate of growth would become somewhat more moderate. But perhaps the most important point is that these changes will probably come about very slowly. Because the ratio of California's ten-year rate of growth to that in the nation has been at least three to one since 1910, and even higher in the 'twenties and 'forties, it seems likely that the state's rate of growth will remain substantially above that in the nation for some decades. I shall reserve discussion of short-run fluctuations in the rate of growth to chapter vi and turn now to an analysis of employment trends.

III. LONG-RUN EMPLOYMENT TRENDS

THIS CHAPTER is concerned with the long-run pattern of employment expansion in California. In what industries have the newcomers to the state found jobs from decade to decade? Does an analysis of employment expansion in the past shed any light on what is likely to happen in the future?

As already indicated, a major difficulty in connection with the analysis of employment trends in California is the lack of adequate statistical data. A long-run historical study must rely almost entirely on the decennial

TABLE 6A

PERCENTAGE DISTRIBUTION OF GAINFUL WORKERS BY MAJOR INDUSTRY GROUP,
CALIFORNIA AND UNITED STATES, SELECTED CENSUS YEARS, 1870–1930

Major industry group in California	1870	1890	1910	1930
Total gainful workers..........................	100.0	100.0	100.0	100.0
Commodity producing industries...............	66.5	58.5	48.9	40.9
Agriculture.................................	29.5	28.9	17.9	13.3
Forestry and fishing........................	1.5	1.7	1.2	0.5
Extraction of minerals......................	15.5	4.5	2.9	1.6
Building trades workers.....................	5.7	6.5	9.0	7.5
Manufacturing and mechanical workers (exc. building trades)..........................	14.3	16.9	17.9	18.0
Distributive and service industries..............	32.7	38.6	44.9	49.1
Transportation and communication...........	6.9	7.4	9.6	8.0
Trade......................................	9.4	10.9	13.9	17.5
Public service (n.e.c.)......................	1.4	1.3	2.2	2.4
Professional service........................	3.1	5.1	6.4	9.4
Domestic and personal service...............	11.9	13.9	12.8	11.8
Clerical workers.............................	0.8	2.9	6.2	10.0

census figures, but frequent changes in definitions and in classification methods have seriously impaired the comparability of census data from decade to decade. In addition, it was not until 1940 that the Census Bureau began to publish data on the industrial and occupational distribution of persons who were actually *employed* on the census date. Before 1940, census data referred to "gainful workers." These workers, moreover, were not separately classified by occupation and industry, as they are at present, but were classified by occupation within a broad industrial framework.[1]

---

[1] In many cases, the classification system was hybrid in character. All telephone and telegraph operators, for example, were classified in the telephone and telegraph industry, although some of them were employed in other industries. Thus, the broad industrial categories are not precisely comparable with those used from 1940 on. See *Sixteenth Census of the United States: 1940, Comparative Occupation Statistics for the United States: 1870 to 1940*, by A. M. Edwards (Washington, 1943), p. 31.

After undertaking a considerable amount of reclassifying and adjusting, I believe that a reasonably comparable set of data has been developed on the distribution of gainful workers, by major industry groups, for California and the United States for the period 1870–1930.[2] In addition, for 1930, adjusted figures on employment by major industry groups have been developed, which are approximately comparable with employment data for 1940 and 1950. But the limitations of the data for purposes of analyzing long-run trends are still serious and should be kept in mind by the reader throughout the present chapter. On the other hand, comparisons between

TABLE 6B

PERCENTAGE DISTRIBUTION OF GAINFUL WORKERS BY MAJOR INDUSTRY GROUP, CALIFORNIA AND UNITED STATES, SELECTED CENSUS YEARS, 1870–1930

Major industry group in United States	1870	1890	1910	1930
Total gainful workers..........................	100.0	100.0	100.0	100.0
Commodity producing industries..............	75.3	67.9	62.9	52.8
Agriculture................................	52.1	41.2	31.1	21.4
Forestry and fishing........................	0.4	0.7	0.6	0.5
Extraction of minerals......................	1.5	1.9	2.6	2.0
Building trades workers.....................	5.1	5.8	6.2	6.1
Manufacturing and mechanical workers (exc. building trades).........................	16.2	18.3	22.4	22.8
Distributive and service industries..............	24.0	29.9	32.5	39.0
Transportation and communication..........	4.5	6.3	7.1	7.9
Trade.....................................	6.2	8.3	9.7	12.5
Public service (n.e.c.).....................	0.7	0.9	1.2	1.8
Professional service.......................	2.7	3.9	4.5	6.7
Domestic and personal service..............	9.9	10.5	10.0	10.1
Clerical workers............................	0.7	2.2	4.6	8.2

SOURCE: See Appendix table A-13. Percentages have been adjusted to add to 100.0, and, in the case of California, have been computed on the basis of unrounded data.

California and the United States for any given census year are for the most part reasonably reliable, since the data have been treated in a uniform manner for both areas.

DISTINGUISHING CHARACTERISTICS OF CALIFORNIA'S EMPLOYMENT STRUCTURE

The industrial distribution of employment in California has differed markedly from the national pattern ever since 1870, and probably earlier (see tables 6 and 7).

---

[2] For a description of these adjustments, see Appendix B.

Throughout the nation as a whole, in 1870, more than half of all workers were engaged in the extractive industries. Together with those who were in the building trades or in manufacturing, they made a total of about three-fourths of all workers engaged in commodity-producing industries. The remaining fourth was found in distributive and service industries.[3]

As productivity and real incomes increased, people spent a smaller proportion of their incomes on the basic essentials, particularly food, and a larger percentage on more elaborate goods and services. At the same time, many activities which formerly had been carried on at home came to be carried on outside the home—in factories, in service establishments, in hospitals and professional offices, and in places of public entertainment. On the supply side, increasing agricultural productivity made it possible for a smaller proportion (and after 1910, a declining absolute number) of the nation's workers to furnish an adequate food supply for both domestic consumption and export. All this meant a gradual decline in the relative importance of agriculture as an occupation, a decline that was offset in *part* by a growth in manufacturing, but to a much greater extent by an increase in distributive and service activities.

In California, the shifts that have occurred since 1870 have been similar, but the distributive and service industries have been far more important from the beginning. A third of California's workers in 1870 were engaged in the distributive and service industries, as compared with about a fourth of the nation's workers. By 1950, California still had a considerably larger percentage of her workers engaged in these industries (63.2 per cent) than did the nation (52.4 per cent). Furthermore, each major industry group within the distributive and service sector of the economy was represented by a larger percentage of workers in California than in the nation, and this, too, had been true since 1870.

The reasons for the predominance of distributive and service industries in California are worth exploring, especially in view of the fact that this situation has prevailed for so long a period and extends back to the days when agriculture and mining were the leading commodity-producing industries in the state. A clue to one of the most important reasons is found by considering what other states have long had employment patterns resembling that of California, at least in this respect. The one state that has consistently had as high, or nearly as high, a proportion of distributive and service workers as California is New York.[4] The distribution of New York's

---

[3] "Clerical workers," as shown in table 6, represent an occupational, rather than an industrial category, but no satisfactory method of distributing these workers among industry groups could be devised. For further discussion of this problem, see Appendix B.

[4] See tables on the industrial distribution of employment in the various states in the decennial census reports from 1870 on.

workers among the various major industry groups within the distributive and service sector, moreover, has been quite similar to that in California.

TABLE 7

PERCENTAGE DISTRIBUTION OF EMPLOYED WORKERS BY MAJOR INDUSTRY GROUP
CALIFORNIA AND UNITED STATES, 1930–1950

Major industry group	California			United States		
	1930[a]	1940	1950	1930[a]	1940	1950
Total employed workers.............	100.0	100.0	100.0	100.0	100.0	100.0
Commodity producing industries......	39.9	35.9	35.7	53.1	49.0	46.1
Agriculture......................	13.7	10.7	7.3	22.1	18.7	12.2
Forestry and fisheries.............	0.5	0.3	0.3	0.5	0.2	0.2
Mining.........................	2.1	1.9	0.8	2.3	2.0	1.7
Construction....................	6.5	6.2	7.7	5.6	4.6	6.1
Manufacturing..................	17.0	16.8	19.6	22.6	23.5	25.9
Durable goods.................	....	8.3	10.8	....	11.4	13.8
Nondurable goods..............	....	8.3	8.6	....	11.7	11.9
Not specified..................	....	0.2	0.1	....	0.4	0.2
Distributive and service industries......	57.6	62.6	63.2	44.7	49.2	52.4
Transportation, communication, and other public utilities............	8.1	8.0	8.2	7.4	6.9	7.8
Transportation.................	....	5.2	5.0	....	4.9	5.2
Telecommunication.............	....	1.2	1.5	....	0.8	1.1
Utilities and sanitary services.....	....	1.7	1.7	....	1.2	1.4
Trade..........................	17.4	22.3	22.4	13.1	16.8	18.8
Wholesale trade.................	....	4.4	4.7	....	2.7	3.5
Retail trade....................	....	17.9	17.7	....	14.1	15.2
Finance, insurance, and real estate...	5.2	4.8	4.6	3.0	3.3	3.4
Service industries.................	23.8	23.7	21.7	18.6	19.1	18.6
Business and repair services.......	} 13.4	2.8	3.3	} 11.3	2.0	2.5
Personal services...............		9.6	6.7		8.9	6.2
Entertainment and recreation services......................	2.2	2.6	2.0	0.9	0.9	1.0
Professional and related services....	8.2	8.7	9.7	6.4	7.3	8.3
Public administration.............	3.1	3.8	6.3	2.6	3.1	4.4
Industry not reported..............	2.5	1.4	1.2	2.2	1.6	1.5

SOURCE: See Appendix, table A-14.
[a] 1930 data have been adjusted but are not precisely comparable with 1940 and 1950 data.

There is nothing surprising about these resemblances in employment structure between New York and California.[5] New York City is by far the largest port on the Atlantic Coast. California includes the two largest ports (San Francisco and Los Angeles) on the Pacific Coast. This has meant that

[5] Outside of the distributive and service sector of the economy, the similarities are not so marked. A larger percentage of New York's workers have been engaged in manufacturing than has been the case in California, and, as might be expected, New York has had relatively fewer workers in agriculture.

New York and the two California cities (particularly San Francisco) have
been shipping centers, with substantial numbers of sailors, longshoremen,
and other workers directly or indirectly connected with ocean transportation in their populations. It has also meant continuous arrivals in these
centers of large numbers of foreign tourists and immigrants, who have
stayed for varying periods and required hotel and other services.

Partly because of their convenient access to sea routes, partly for other
reasons, the two major California cities have become the commercial and
financial centers of the West, just as New York is the commercial and financial center of the East.[6] According to the 1950 Census, New York and New
Jersey were the only two states with a higher proportion of workers employed in finance, insurance, and real estate than California, and Florida
was the only state with a larger percentage of workers in wholesale trade.[7]
One reason for the relative importance of wholesale trade in Florida and
California is the fact that it includes packing of fresh fruits and vegetables.

In addition, New York and California are meccas for internal tourists as
well as for foreign tourists. This again tends to encourage considerable employment in the various branches of the service trades that cater to tourists'
needs.[8] In short, we may attribute California's high percentage of employment in the distributive and service industries in large part to the fact that
its two major cities have been, and continue to be, the leading commercial,

---

[6] Carey MacWilliams has pointed out that, early in the history of San Francisco, substantial fortunes were accumulated which became available for investment and for the
establishment of financial institutions. See *California: The Great Exception* (New York:
A. A. Wyn, 1949), p. 229.

[7] *United States Census of Population: 1950*, Vol. II, Part 1, p. 135. If we consider
total value of wholesale sales in 1948, New York, with $43,140,000, and Illinois with
$18,137,000, were the only states which exceeded California, with $13,271,000. In total
bank deposits, at the end of 1950, California, with $14,018,000 ranked second only to
New York, with $44,393,000. U.S. Bureau of the Census, *Statistical Abstract of the United
States: 1952*, p. 395.

[8] There has been a tendency, in economic literature, to expect a high rate of tertiary
employment only in areas with relatively high incomes and in a mature stage of industrialization. Thus Colin Clark refers to Japan's proportion of tertiary workers as "in-
explicably high," in view of her low income level and relatively high percentage of
workers in primary industries. He also expresses surprise that Holland and Great Britain,
"with their highly compact populations," employed larger proportions of transport
workers than the United States. See *The Conditions of Economic Progress* (London: Macmillan, 1951), p. 182. In all these cases, the chief explanation of the high ratio of tertiary employment would appear to be the heavy foreign trade and tourist activities of
these countries.

It has been recently pointed out that a high rate of tertiary employment has been
found to prevail in certain underdeveloped areas with low income and wage levels.
Rottenberg attributes this to the fact that in such areas, where the population is large
relative to resources (particularly capital), self-employment in the service trades offers
an opportunity for numerous workers to eke out a precarious existence. See S. Rottenberg, "Note on 'Economic Progress and Occupational Distribution,' " *Review of Economics and Statistics*, XXXV (1953), 168–170; and P. T. Bauer and E. S. Yamey, "Economic Progress and Occupational Distribution," *Economic Journal*, LXI (1951), 741–755.

financial, foreign trade, and tourist centers of the West. But there have been other factors as well which have helped to account for the predominance of the distributive and service industries. Of these, probably the most important are the following:

1. The relatively high income level which has prevailed in California throughout its history as a state has tended to stimulate the development of tertiary industries. Per capita incomes have been especially high, relative to those in the nation, in the extractive industries. Thus, persons engaged in agriculture and mining, in particular, have undoubtedly been in a position to spend larger amounts on services than has been true in other parts of the nation.

2. Because manufacturing was slow to develop in the state, at least before 1900, and because some branches of manufacturing have never been very well represented, there always has been a need for an unusually large number of wholesale distributors and eastern manufactures' representatives.

3. The regional offices of many federal government agencies are located in California. In addition, there are large military and naval installations in various parts of the state.[9]

4. The fact that California's population has grown so largely through in-migration has meant that substantial numbers of newcomers entering the state, especially in periods of heavy in-migration, have required the services of transportation companies, moving companies, tourist camps, and the like. Furthermore, Californians tend to do a good deal of moving about within the state, perhaps, in part, because many of those who are relative newcomers have not established strong ties to particular jobs or to particular localities.[10] Undoubtedly, a mobile population requires more services than does a stationary population.

5. As has been pointed out, California has had a relatively large percentage of adults in her population and, until recently, a disproportionately large percentage of men. Such a population tends to spend a relatively large share of its income on services.

6. In recent decades, the movie industry has been primarily responsible for the relatively high proportion of workers found in the amusement and recreation industry in California.

Thus far, attempt has been made to explain the relatively high proportion of workers in the distributive and service industries, rather than the comparatively low proportion found in agriculture, manufacturing, and

---

[9] Members of the Armed Forces were included among gainful workers by the Census Bureau before 1940. Since 1940, they have been excluded from data relating to the civilian labor force and thus are not included in tables relating to employment by major industry groups. Civilian workers employed in military and naval installations are, however, included in the civilian labor force.

[10] The 1940 Census data on internal migration between 1935 and 1940 show that the percentage of California residents who had moved between counties (or quasi counties) within the state between 1935 and 1940 was considerably higher (11.6 per cent) than the corresponding percentage for the nation (7.0 per cent) or for any other state except Texas (13.8 per cent). See *Sixteenth Census of the United States: 1940, Population, Internal Migration in the United States, 1935 to 1940: Color and Sex of Migrants* (Washington, 1943), p. 8. The Six-City Occupational Mobility Survey yields evidence that the frequency with which workers change jobs tends to vary indirectly with the length of time they have resided in a given area. See G. L. Palmer, *Labor Mobility in Six Cities* (New York: Social Science Research Council, 1954) pp. 42–43.

other commodity-producing industries. As tables 6 and 7 indicate, construction is the only industry outside of the distributive and service group which has consistently employed a larger percentage of California's workers than of those in the nation, and this exception is certainly to be expected in a state with a rapidly growing population. The mining industry accounted for an unusually large proportion of California's workers in the early decades of the state's history, but after the heyday of the gold-mining era, the more rapid growth of other branches of California's economy gradually resulted in the displacement of mining as a leading source of employment. Although the petroleum industry eventually became far more important than gold mining as a producer of income, the production of crude petroleum does not require much man power.

But what about the fact that both agriculture and manufacturing have consistently employed relatively fewer workers in California than in the nation? Is this merely a reflection of the fact that, since the share of the distributive and service industries in total employment has been so high, the share of most other major industry groups must inevitably have been relatively low? Or are there independent explanations of the comparatively small percentages of workers to be found in agriculture and manufacturing?

So far as agriculture is concerned, it is recognized at the outset that California agriculture differs in a great many characteristics from the national pattern. The degree of commercialization and specialization in agriculture is much greater than in most other states, as is the wide variety of products grown and the relative importance of fruit and vegetable production. Farms are somewhat larger, on the average (266.9 acres in 1950), than in the country as a whole (215.3 acres in 1950),[11] but there are relatively few moderate-sized farms, a great many small farms, and a comparatively large proportion of giant farms. The dominant importance of large-scale farming is indicated by the fact that, although farms of 1,000 acres and more represented only 4.4 per cent of the total *number* of farms in 1950, they accounted for 70.7 per cent of all land in farms. Throughout the nation as a whole, farms of this size accounted for only 42.6 per cent of all land in farms.[12]

That California farms rely heavily on seasonal labor is well known. Probably less familiar is the fact that even in the off-season, the ratio of hired labor to farm owners is relatively high. The 1950 *Census of Population* showed that 52 per cent of all employed workers in agriculture were paid farm laborers, as compared with 22 per cent for the United States.[13] The census, moreover, was conducted in a period of relatively low seasonal employment.

---

[11] *United States Census of Agriculture: 1950*, Vol. II, *General Report*, p. 799.

[12] *Ibid.*, pp. 842–843.

[13] *United States Census of Population: 1950*, Vol. II, Part 1, pp. 261 and 265, and Part 5, pp. 278 and 280.

California agriculture has differed from the national pattern throughout the state's history. Specialization has always been present to an unusual degree, though its direction has gone through a series of important changes. The huge cattle ranches of the Mexican and early American days gave way, in part, to the large wheat farms of the 'sixties and 'seventies, and these in turn gave way to the more intensive types of production which came to play an increasingly important role from the 'eighties onward. As more and more lands were brought under irrigation, there was a tendency to shift to higher value crops which could better meet the heavy costs of irrigation. But the high degree of specialization and commercialization, the relatively high productivity, and the heavy reliance on seasonal labor have characterized California agriculture throughout almost the entire period since 1850.[14]

Because of differences between California and the country as a whole in the seasonal pattern of variation in agricultural employment, decennial census data tend to exaggerate the relative underrepresentation of agricultural workers in California. In 1950, census employment data referred to the week preceding the enumerator's visit, which usually was during the first two weeks in April. The seasonal low point in agricultural employment occurs somewhat later in California (about March 15) than in the nation as a whole (January). Thus, by the time census interviewers are making their rounds, agricultural employment has risen above its seasonal low point somewhat more, relatively, in the nation than in California. According to Census Bureau estimates, April employment on the nation's farms represented about 95 per cent of average annual employment in agriculture during the period from 1947 to 1950.[15] On California farms in the same period, April employment represented only about 85 per cent of average annual employment.[16] Furthermore, the available estimates suggest that seasonal variations in agricultural employment tend to be somewhat wider in California than in the nation.[17]

---

[14] Cf. M. R. Benedict, "The Economic and Social Structure of California Agriculture," in C. B. Hutchison, ed., *California Agriculture* (Berkeley: University of California Press, 1946), pp. 399–406; and L. V. Fuller, *The Supply of Agricultural Labor as a Factor in the Evolution of Farm Organization in California*, printed as Exhibit 8762A in Hearings, U.S. Senate Committee on Education and Labor, 76th Congress, 3d Sess., Part 54, *Agricultural Labor in California* (Washington, 1940).

[15] The actual percentages varied slightly from year to year; on an average, for the four years, 1947–1950, April agricultural employment represented 95.4 per cent of average annual agricultural employment. Computed from the estimates in U.S. Bureau of the Census, *Current Population Reports*, Series P-50, Nos. 13, 19, and 31 (February 16, 1949, March 2, 1950, and March 9, 1951).

[16] Computed from monthly estimates of agricultural employment supplied by the California State Department of Employment.

[17] On an average, in the years from 1947 to 1950, according to California Department of Employment estimates, employment on California farms varied seasonally from

On an average annual basis, about 9.7 per cent of California's workers were employed in agriculture in the 1947–1950 period.[18] In the nation as a whole, agriculture accounted for about 13.5 per cent of average annual employment in the same period. In other words, on an annual average basis, employment in agriculture in both state and nation represents a somewhat larger percentage of total employment than the 1950 Census figures indicate. Furthermore, the percentage employed in agriculture in California, though well below that in the country as a whole, is somewhat closer to the nation-wide percentage if computed on an average annual basis. In evaluating these comparisons, however, it must be recognized that monthly employment estimates for California are prepared by quite a different method from that used in preparing the estimates cited for the country as a whole.[19] Furthermore, because of differences in the way agricultural employment is defined, the California method would tend to yield a higher estimate of agricultural employment in the state than the method used by the Census Bureau. In April, 1950, for example, agricultural employment in California, according to the estimate prepared by the State Department of Employment, was 352,000, whereas the 1950 Census figure was 287,000.

The important point is that even after allowance has been made for differences in seasonal patterns of variation, it remains true that agriculture employs relatively fewer people in California than in the nation. The state accounts, however, for a substantially larger percentage of total farm income and of the value of farm products in the nation than of the nation's farm workers. Thus, in 1950, with only 5.4 per cent of the farm workers, California was producing 8.8 per cent of total agricultural income in the nation and 8.0 per cent of the total value of farm products.[20]

These comparisons do not necessarily indicate that output per worker is higher in California than in the nation as a whole. As is quite generally

---

79.9 per cent of the annual average, in March, to 125.8 per cent in September or October, or 45.9 percentage points. In the United States, according to Census Bureau estimates, farm employment varied, in the same period, from 82.6 per cent of average annual employment in January or February to 121.2 per cent in June, or 38.6 percentage points.

[18] The percentage cited in the text represents an average, for the years 1947–1950, of estimated average annual employment in agriculture as a percentage of estimated average annual total employment in the state.

[19] For further discussion of this point, see chapter vii.

[20] The percentage of agricultural workers is computed from the estimates of average annual employment prepared by the California Department of Employment and the United States Bureau of the Census. (See the references in footnotes 15 and 16.) The percentage of agricultural income is computed from Department of Commerce income estimates published in *Survey of Current Business*, August, 1951, p. 16. For value of farm products, we have used the estimates in United States Bureau of Agricultural Economics, *The Farm Income Situation.*

known, fruit and vegetable production accounts for a much larger percentage of total farm production in California than in the nation, and there are other important differences as well. Meaningful comparisons of output per worker could be made only on a product-by-product basis. Furthermore, although the value of many California specialty crops is quite high in relation either to acreage used or to labor employed, farm expenses are also high.

Even so, California farmers tend to enjoy a relatively high income level. According to 1950 Census data, the median income of California male farmers and farm managers in the experienced civilian labor force was $2,409, or 66 per cent higher than the corresponding figure for the nation as a whole. The comparison for male farm laborers and foremen (excluding unpaid family workers) was somewhat less favorable. For this group, the median income in California in 1949 was $1,401, or 49 per cent higher than the corresponding nation-wide figure.[21] The analysis of income differentials in chapter v will show that these differences are much wider than those prevailing between state and nation in most other industries.

Thus the conclusion is that the comparatively small proportion of workers employed in agriculture in no way suggests that California agriculture is in a relatively disadvantageous position. Rather, it reflects (1) the differences in seasonal pattern between state and nation, (2) the distinctive characteristics of farm production in the state, and (3) the predominance of the trade and service industries, which were emphasized in the early part of this chapter.

The importance of agriculture in California's economy is understated, however, if only the proportion of the state's workers employed in agriculture itself is considered. The food-processing and-packing industries, together with many industries producing such varied items as tin cans, boxes, and irrigation equipment, are obviously highly dependent on the maintenance of California's agricultural output, as are many workers in transport and distribution.

California agriculture has clearly reached a mature stage of development. The next section points out that there is very little likelihood of further substantial growth of employment in agriculture in the state, even if output continues to increase.

The situation in manufacturing is quite different. Although California manufacturing has developed rapidly in the last fifty years, its development

---

[21] See *United States Census of Population: 1950*, Vol. II, Part 1, pp. 280–281, and Part 5, pp. 362–363. The median income of California male farm laborers and foremen, as shown in table 11, differs somewhat from the figure cited in the text, since it includes unpaid family workers. The inclusion of these unpaid workers, moreover, alters the comparison with the United States substantially.

has not reached the point at which it is comparable with that in the leading industrial states of the northeastern and north central regions of the country: Massachusetts, New York, New Jersey, Pennsylvania, Ohio, Michigan, and Illinois. In these states, employment in manufacturing ranged from 30 to 41 per cent of total employment in 1950.[22] Probably the most important factor that has hampered the growth of manufacturing in the state has been the inadequate size of the western market. Although population growth on the Pacific Coast has been extraordinarily rapid and has been a major factor in stimulating the growth of manufacturing, the population center of the country still lies east of the Mississippi River, and there are vast stretches of sparsely settled territory between the Pacific Coast states and the states lying just west of the Mississippi. Relatively "foot-loose" industries do not necessarily find it advantageous to locate in California, nor do those which are characterized by substantial economies of large-scale production.[23] Indeed, it is interesting from a historical point of view to point out that the history of California manufacturing after the Civil War might have been somewhat different had it not been for the development of mass production methods in eastern manufacturing centers during that period.[24] As it was, a number of infant industries which got a start in the state during the war, when eastern manufacturers were not in a position to supply the California market, were unable to withstand the renewed competition from the East after the war. Most of the industries which have flourished in California are either "market-oriented" or owe their locational advantage to the state's natural resources, including her climate.

There is no question that California manufacturing will continue to grow as her population increases, and as the entire western market grows. This does not necessarily mean, however, that manufacturing will eventually employ as large a percentage of the state's workers as is now the case in the leading industrial states. This point will be considered more fully in the next chapter. Suffice it to say, at this point, that the relatively small percentage of employed workers in manufacturing in the state reflects not only the influence of all those factors which have accounted for the predominance of the trade and service industries, but also of a set of factors which have tended, over the decades, to hold back the growth of manufacturing.

---

[22] Computed from *1950 Census of Population: Advance Reports*, Series PC-14, No. 10, March 13, 1953, p. 4.

[23] For an excellent discussion of locational factors affecting California manufacturing, see California, Reconstruction and Re-employment Commission, *The Steel and Steel-Using Industries of California*, by E. T. Grether and others (Sacramento, 1946), chapter iv.

[24] On the growth of mass production methods, see S. Rezneck, "Mass Production since the War between the States," in H. F. Williamson, ed., *The Growth of the American Economy* (New York: Prentice-Hall, 1944), pp. 496–520.

TRENDS IN EMPLOYMENT EXPANSION BY MAJOR INDUSTRY GROUPS

The changes in the industrial distribution of employment in California between 1870 and 1950 reflected the results of markedly different rates of growth in the various branches of California's economy.[25] During the eighty-year period as a whole, the highest rates of growth were displayed in public administration and in wholesale and retail trade, in both of which the number of workers increased, percentagewise, substantially more than did the total number of workers in all industries. Intermediate rates of growth were displayed by the service industries, building trades, manufacturing, and the transportation group, in all of which the number of workers increased, in the period as a whole, somewhat more rapidly than the total number of workers. Agricultural employment increased comparatively slowly, and the number of workers in other extractive industries not at all, in these eight decades of rapid population growth.

The rates of increase in each industry division have fluctuated markedly from decade to decade.[26] To some extent, employment expansion in many of the industry groups has varied with the rate of population growth, but there have been important exceptions to this pattern. This question will be discussed in more detail at a later point. For the moment, an analysis of long-run changes in rates of growth in the various industry divisions is essential.

In view of the inadequacies in the basic statistical data, sophisticated methods of measuring changes in rates of growth, for example, the fitting of trend lines, do not seem appropriate. Furthermore, since changing rates of population growth have been accompanied, to a considerable extent, by changing rates of growth in the various industry groups, the interesting question is whether there have been secular changes in the ratio of employment expansion in each industry division to population growth. On the whole, the most satisfactory method is the one used in table 8, which presents the ratio of percentage changes in number of workers in each major industry group to percentage changes in population for three periods: 1870–1900, 1900–1930, and 1930–1950.[27]

---

[25] Actually, of course, the data for 1870 to 1930 apply to gainful workers rather than to employed workers, but this difference would not markedly affect the broad comparisons of rates of growth which concern us at the moment.

[26] See Appendix, table A-15.

[27] The question may be raised as to why ratios of employment expansion to population growth have been used rather than ratios of employment expansion to the growth of the labor force. The main reason was that the primary interest was in the effect of the growth of the size of the California market, as measured by the rate of population growth, on the expansion of employment in the various industry divisions. Actually, since variations in the rate of population growth were very similar to the variations in the rate of growth of the labor force from decade to decade, the two types of ratios would differ very little.

Before commenting on trends in the various industry divisions, the fact should be mentioned that, whereas the total number of gainful workers increased at almost the same percentage rate as the total population from 1870 to 1930, both the civilian labor force and the total number of employed workers increased only about four-fifths as rapidly as the population from 1930 to 1950. There appear to have been a number of reasons

TABLE 8

RATIO OF PERCENTAGE CHANGE IN NUMBER OF WORKERS IN EACH MAJOR INDUSTRY GROUP TO PERCENTAGE CHANGE IN POPULATION, CALIFORNIA, 1870–1900, 1900–1930, AND 1930–1950

Major industry group	1870–1900	1900–1930	1930–1950
Gainful workers[a].....................	1.03	1.02	....
Civilian labor force.....................	....	....	0.82
Employed workers[a].....................	....	....	0.79
Agriculture.....................	0.78	0.38	−0.12
Other extractive industries..................	−0.02	0.13	−0.37
Building trades workers.....................	1.12	1.35	....
Construction employment..................	....	....	1.13
Manufacturing and mechanical workers........	1.41	1.05	....
Manufacturing employment..............	....	....	1.08
Transportation and communication workers....	1.38	0.95	....
Transportation, communication, and other public utilities.....................	....	....	0.81
Trade.....................	1.76	1.41	1.16
Service industries.....................	1.45	1.19	0.62
Public administration.....................	1.28	1.76	2.73
Clerical workers.....................	5.16	4.41	....

SOURCE: Text table 1 and Appendix tables A-13 and A-14.
[a]Number of gainful workers 10 years of age and older, 1870–1930, and number of employed workers, 14 years of age and older, 1930–1950.

for the relatively more moderate increase in the size of the civilian labor force and of employment in the two most recent decades: (1) the change in the age distribution of the population, with an increase in the relative importance of young children and of "senior citizens" (those sixty-five years of age and older) at the expense of adults of working age, [28] (2) a moderate decline in the labor force participation rate, and (3) a rise in the percentage of the population in the Armed Forces. In addition, the change from the "gainful worker" to the "labor force" concept between 1930 and 1940 had the effect of excluding from the figures a number of workers, particularly in the older age groups, who would have been reported as gainful workers in 1930 but were not actively participating in the labor force under the 1940 definition. It was impossible to "correct" for this factor in adjusting the 1930 data.

The evidence of a declining rate of growth in agricultural employment

---

[28] See Appendix, table A-11.

over the course of the eighty-year period from 1870 to 1950 is clear and requires little comment. The only interesting question here is whether agricultural employment is likely in the next few decades to continue a very slow rate of increase, similar to that of the 1940's, or to decline, as it has in the country as a whole since 1910. An intelligent guess on this point would depend on a careful analysis of such interrelated problems as future government policy toward the importation of Mexican labor, the rate of mechanization of farm operations, the outlook for large-scale irrigation projects, and trends in the size distribution of California farms. Furthermore, census data give the level of agricultural employment at approximately the seasonal low point and fail to reflect the increase in seasonal variation in farm employment which took place between the late 'thirties and late 'forties, in considerable part as a result of the growth in cotton production. Thus a thorough analysis would have to consider what is likely to happen to agricultural employment at both the seasonal high and low points.[29] The point to be stressed here is that California agriculture is not likely to contribute appreciably to the expansion of employment opportunities in the state in the decades to come, though it may well continue to contribute substantially to the growth of income.

The situation in the other extractive industries also requires only brief comment. The number of workers attached to these industries has failed to show any appreciable net gain throughout the entire eighty-year period. There was a moderate increase from 1900 to 1930, associated chiefly with the growth of the petroleum industry, but this was followed by a decline in the next two decades. Here again, no appreciable contribution to the expansion of employment opportunities in future decades can be expected.

The building industry presents an entirely different picture. Employment in this industry, so far as can be judged from the somewhat unsatisfactory data, has tended to increase at a more rapid rate than total population. In view of the fact that the data for the two most recent decades apply to employment in the construction industry, whereas those for the first six decades apply to the number of gainful workers in the building trades, it would be hazardous to attach much significance to changes in the ratios. Yet there are grounds for believing that the ratio of employment expansion in the construction industry to population growth may show some tendency toward secular decline in future decades. If the percentage of the population employed in the construction industry is a function of the rate of population growth—a relationship which would be expected to prevail

---

[29] For further discussion of these problems, see *Migratory Labor in American Agriculture*, Report of the President's Commission on Migratory Labor (Washington, 1951).

both on theoretical grounds[30] and in the light of the empirical evidence—
it follows that, if California's rate of population growth shows a tendency
toward secular decline over the course of the next several decades, as the
preceding chapter indicated may well happen, the percentage of the population employed in the construction industry is also likely to decline. This
is equivalent to saying that the ratio of the rate of employment expansion
in the construction industry to the rate of population growth is likely to fall.

Other grounds exist, also, for anticipating a decrease in this ratio. There
are numerous possibilities for more efficient utilization of labor in the important residential building sector of the construction industry, which are
not as yet being fully utilized but which may gradually bring about important changes in the not too distant future. Improved power tools
and new materials which are slowly being introduced may well be more
extensively utilized if profit margins recede from the high levels which have
characterized the building boom of the last eight years.[31] Furthermore, although industrial construction is less closely associated with population
growth than either residential or commercial construction, there is no
reason to anticipate a rise in the rate of expansion of industrial construction
activity if the rate of population growth declines—in fact, the reverse is
more likely to happen.

It must be emphasized that we have been discussing probable secular

[30] If E represents employment in the construction industry and P, total population,
then $\frac{E}{P} = \frac{k \Delta P}{P}$, where ΔP is the annual numerical increase in population and k is a
constant, representing the ratio of construction employment to the increase in popula-
tion. Thus if the rate of population growth $\frac{\Delta P}{P}$ should decline, then $\frac{E}{P}$ would also decline
unless k should rise. Actually, as is pointed out later, k is likely to decline.

Since construction employment is highly sensitive to what many writers designate as
"population investment"—that is, that part of total investment which is attributable
to population growth—the above formulation is consistent with the position taken by
Barber, who shows that the ratio of population investment to total national income will
vary with the rate of population growth. Cf. C. L. Barber, "Population Growth and the
Demand for Capital," *American Economic Review*, XLIII (1953), 133–139. The argument is essentially similar, as Barber points out, to that advanced by a number of economists who have shown that a constant proportionate (not absolute) rate of growth in
output is necessary to call forth the amount of capital investment required to offset the
amount of saving that would be forthcoming at a full-employment level of income. Cf.,
in particular, E. D. Domar, "Expansion and Employment," *American Economic Review*,
XXXVII (1947), 34–55; R. F. Harrod, *Towards a Dynamic Economics* (London: Macmillan, 1948); and W. Fellner, "The Capital-Output Ratio in Dynamic Economics,"
in *Money, Trade, and Economic Growth* (New York: Macmillan, 1951), pp. 105–134.

[31] A more efficient utilization of labor in the construction industry would mean, of
course, a decline in k in the formula presented in the preceding footnote.

For an interesting discussion of the possibilities for improved efficiency in housebuilding, see S. J. Maisel, *Housebuilding in Transition* (Berkeley: University of California Press,
1953).

tendencies. As will be considered at a later point, the rate of employment expansion in the construction industry is likely to be highly variable from decade to decade, depending on the course of the building cycle.

On the whole, in the eighty-year period which has been considered, *manufacturing* employment has increased at a somewhat more rapid rate than population, but the data here assembled do not provide a basis for arriving at any clear-cut conclusion as to what is happening to the long-run trend. Since the *Census of Manufacturers* data which will be analyzed in the next chapter are somewhat more satisfactory for this purpose, no comment will be made on the long-run outlook for manufacturing employment at this point.

Employment in *transportation, communication, and other public utilities* increased more rapidly than population on the average, during the last three decades of the nineteenth century, largely because of the growth of the railroad industry. Since the turn of the century, its average rate of growth has been approximately equal to the rate of population growth. The more detailed decade-to-decade ratios in figure 1 suggest a moderate upward trend from 1910–1920 on, reflecting in all probability a rapid increase of employment in trucking, air transportation (after 1930), communications, and public utilities. Whether this upward trend is likely to continue is problematical. Unfortunately, it is extremely difficult to develop reliable historical series on the growth of employment in the various subdivisions of this broad industry group in California, and without such series there is little basis for making any sort of prediction.

Certain considerations suggest, however, that employment in the transportation group may increase somewhat less rapidly, on the average, than population in the decades to come. Nearly a fourth of total employment in this group of industries is represented by railroad employment, which has been in a phase of slow, secular decline in the country as a whole since World War I, although there have been temporary periods of substantial gains in employment during World War II and after the outbreak of the Korean War.[32] Although railroad employment in California showed a moderate increase between 1930 and 1950, the contrast between California's experience and that of the country as a whole in this twenty-year period was primarily attributable to the fact that railroad employment in California increased, percentagewise, more markedly in World War II than

---

[32] On December 31, 1920, slightly more than 2,000,000 workers were employed by the railroads (including Classes I, II, and III). By the end of 1950, the total had fallen to 1,237,000. See U.S. Bureau of the Census, *Statistical Abstract of the United States: 1952*, p. 505 (data compiled by the Interstate Commerce Commission). Comparable data are not available for individual states.

For an analysis of nation-wide trends in transportation, see H. Barger, *The Transportation Industries, 1889–1946* (New York: National Bureau of Economic Research, 1951).

was true in the nation as a whole.[33] This is not surprising, in view of California's role, not only as a war production center, but also as a shipping center. After the war, railroad employment in the state declined slowly but quite steadily until the outbreak of the Korean War. If a secular decline in railroad employment should set in, it would probably slow down the rate of employment expansion in the transportation group as a whole.

A marked change in the outlook for expansion of foreign trade with the Far East would, of course, affect all branches of transportation in California, particularly the maritime trades.[34] At present, however, there appears to be little likelihood of a marked secular increase in trade with other countries in the Pacific Basin.

In *wholesale and retail trade*, employment has increased considerably more rapidly than population, on the average. Nevertheless, the ratios in table 8 show a tendency to decline, although they remain above 1.00 right to the end of our period. On the whole, taking into account the striking improvements in labor productivity in retail trade which have recently been occurring, the declining relative importance of foreign trade to the California economy, and the tendencies toward greater self-sufficiency in the state, it would not be unreasonable to expect that, whereas employment in wholesale and retail trade will continue to grow and to grow as rapidly as population, the expansion relative to population growth will not be as great as it was in the early decades of the period.

There is little doubt about the downward trend in the ratio of employment expansion to population growth in the *service* industries. This appears to reflect primarily a decline in the rate of growth in the industries supplying personal services, which has been related not only to price and wage trends, but to other developments as well.[35] Employment in entertainment and recreation services increased comparatively slowly in the 'forties, reflecting chiefly the maturing of the movie industry. On the other hand, employment in business and repair services gained as a percentage of total

[33] For California data, see California, Department of Industrial Relations, *Handbook of California Labor Statistics: 1949–1950* (San Francisco, 1951), pp. 23–30. Railroad employment in 1930 can be roughly estimated from 1930 Census data.

[34] For interesting data on recent trends in the Pacific Coast shipping industry, see W. Gorter and G. H. Hildebrand, *The Pacific Coast Maritime Shipping Industry: 1930–1948*, Vol. I, (Berkeley: University of California Press, 1952). The second volume of their study, which includes an analysis of the reasons for the declining trend in the period they studied, will appear shortly.

[35] An analysis of nation-wide trends in employment between 1910 and 1948 shows a decline of 26 per cent in employment per 10,000 population in the personal service industries. See G. L. Palmer and A. Ratner, *Industrial and Occupational Trends in National Employment: 1910–1940, 1910–1948*, Research Report No. 11, Industrial Research Department, University of Pennsylvania (Philadelphia, 1949), p. 11. See also, G. J. Stigler, *Trends in Output and Employment* (New York: National Bureau of Economic Research, 1947), pp. 37–40.

employment between 1940 and 1950, and employment in professional and related services continued the increase in relative importance which had characterized its expansion in earlier decades.[36] Although an analysis of past trends suggests that in future decades total employment in the service industries is likely to increase more slowly than population, it is conceivable

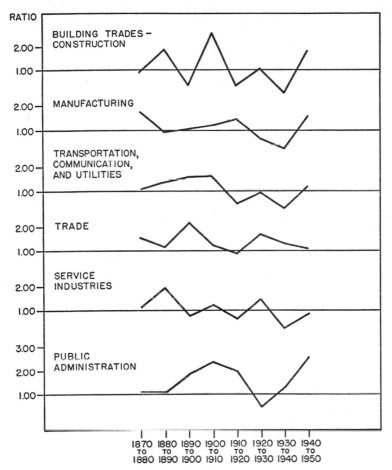

SOURCE: Table A-16, Appendix

Fig. 1. Ratio of percentage increase in number of workers to percentage increase in population per decade, selected major industry groups, California 1870–1950.

---

[36] It should be noticed that certain activities now classified under service industries were included in other industry divisions from 1870 to 1930. This was particularly true of business and repair services. In adjusting our 1930 employment by industry figures, we attempted to transfer these categories, wherever possible, to the service group.

that there may be a rapid growth of services which are relatively unimportant or even completely unknown today.

Public administration appears to be the only industry division in which the ratio of employment expansion to population growth has been increasing, but perhaps here, above all, it is hazardous to draw any inferences as to what is likely to happen in the future. The importance of political developments in relation to the growth of employment in this branch of the economy is apparent.[37]

The ratios in table 8 conceal wide variations in the corresponding ratios for ten-year periods which (except for agriculture and the other extractive industries) are presented in figure 1.[38] Furthermore, the pattern of variation has been different in almost every industry division.

In the building trades-construction group, the ratio of the rate of increase in number of workers to the rate of population growth has tended to fluctuate upward and downward in successive decades. These fluctuations reflect the effects of building cycles, which will be discussed in greater detail in chapter vi. Building cycles in California, which have been very similar in timing and duration to those in the United States, have not lasted precisely twenty years, nor have their peaks and troughs coincided with census dates. Nevertheless, their timing and duration have been such that census data on the number of workers in the building trades (and more recently on construction employment) tend to show a decade of relatively rapid expansion followed by a decade of retarded expansion. The decades of rapid expansion of employment in this industry, moreover, have been been the decades of most rapid population growth. The fact that the ratio of the percentage increase in number of building trades workers to the rate of population growth was considerably lower in 1920–1930 than in 1880–1890 or in 1900–1910 probably reflects the fact that the peak of the building cycle in California in the 'twenties occurred in 1923 and was followed by a substantial decline in building activity between 1923 and 1930. In both 1890 and 1910, on the other hand, the census date was separated only by a few years from the peak in the building cycle.

If we turn from the building industry to *manufacturing*, we find that the ratios presented in figure 1 show quite a different pattern of variation. Except for the first decade for which we have data (1870–1880), the highest ratios of growth in number of workers in manufacturing to population growth were recorded in the two war decades, 1910–1920 and 1940–1950. No further comment on the growth of manufacturing employment is needed

---

[37] For a recent comprehensive analysis of the expanding scope of government activity, see S. Fabricant, *The Trend of Government Activity in the United States since 1900* (New York: National Bureau of Economic Research, 1952).

[38] See, also, Appendix, table A-16.

at this point, in view of the more detailed discussion which will follow in chapter iv.

In the third industry division—transportation, communication, and public utilities—there is still a different pattern of decade-to-decade variation in the ratios. The high ratios which prevailed in the three decades from 1880–1890 to 1900–1910 reflected primarily the rapid growth of railroad employment during this period when the state's railroad system was being expanded. After 1908, expansion of railway mileage fell off substantially, and total mileage began to decline somewhat from 1915 on. Employment on street railway systems also increased rapidly before World War I. Since 1910, the ratios for this industry group have been substantially lower and have fluctuated upward and downward in successive decades, largely in response to war developments, the business cycle, and shifts among competing forms of transportation. The moderate upward trend since 1910–1920 has been discussed earlier.

The *trade* group shows a pattern of variation unlike any of those yet considered. It is interesting to observe that the ratio for this industry group was extraordinarily high for the depressed decade 1890–1900 and that this was the only industry division outside of public administration in which the ratio exceeded 1.00 in 1930–1940, reflecting the relative insensitivity of trade to the business cycle. On the other hand, employment in trade increased comparatively slowly in both war decades, 1910–1920 and 1940–1950. The sharp rise in the ratio in 1920–1930, following World War I, undoubtedly reflects in large part a tendency for employment expansion in the trade industries to "make up for lost time" once the man-power shortages associated with the war began to disappear. A comparable development cannot be expected in the 1950's, since there had already been five years of relatively rapid expansion between V-J Day and 1950. On the basis of annual estimates available for the decade of the 'forties, we find that from 1940 to 1945 the ratio of the rate of employment expansion in "trade" to the rate of population growth was only 0.53, whereas in the second half of the decade it was 2.26.[39]

The behavior of employment in the trade sector of the economy is explained in part by the fact that, particularly in retail trade establishments, labor tends to be a relatively fixed cost, at least as compared with the situation in many other industries. Thus, in wartime, when the labor market is tight and wage rates are rising rapidly, retail sales may expand substan-

---

[39] For annual population estimates, see U.S. Bureau of the Census, *Current Population Reports*, Series P-25, No. 47, March 9, 1951; for employment estimates, see California, Department of Industrial Relations, *Handbook of California Labor Statistics: 1951–1952* (San Francisco, 1953), pp. 18–19. For conformity with the coverage of the ratios in chart 1, finance, insurance, and real estate are included in the trade category in computing these ratios.

tially without requiring an expansion of employment in retail establishments. Conversely, in a depression, as sales contract, employment cannot be reduced beyond a minimum point needed to keep an establishment in operation.

In the service industries, the ratios have tended to fluctuate upward and downward in successive decades, following the pattern of variation which was found in the building trades-construction group, though with somewhat less marked fluctuations. Apparently the decades of most rapid population growth have also been most favorable for expansion of employment in the service industries. On the other hand, periods of economic depression have been particularly unfavorable, for the ratios fell off sharply in both 1890–1900 and 1930–1940.

The pattern of variation in the ratios for public administration does not resemble that for any other industry division. For the most part, the ratios have tended to be high. The sharp drop between 1910–1920 and 1920–1930 reflects the fact that the abnormally rapid expansion of federal government activities in World War I was followed by a period of much more modest expansion in the 1920's. The developments since 1930 in this employment category are so familiar as to require little comment.

Conclusions

An analysis of historical changes in the distribution of employment suggests that further changes will occur in future decades, along the lines of those which have taken place in the past, but probably at a somewhat diminishing rate. Employment in agriculture and the other extractive industries is likely to continue to represent a declining proportion of total employment. The percentage of workers employed in the construction industry will probably fluctuate irregularly from decade to decade and, in the long run, decline somewhat if the rate of population growth declines and if, as seems likely, there is a trend toward more efficient utilization of labor in the industry. No conclusions about manufacturing will be attempted until its development has been discussed in greater detail in chapter iv.

The distributive and service industries (including public administration) are likely to continue to represent an increasing share of total employment, but the data suggest that changes in this direction will probably take place somewhat more slowly in the future than in the past. Among the various sectors of employment in the distributive and service industries, public administration seems most likely to increase in relative importance.

No simple generalization will suffice to describe the relationship between the rate of employment expansion in the various sectors of California's

economy and the rate of population growth. Outside of the extractive industries, in which a declining rate of employment expansion has been apparent for many decades, a long-run decline in the ratio of employment
expansion to population growth seems to be most clearly discernible in
the service industries, attributable primarily to the behavior of employment
in personal services. Some evidence of a declining ratio of employment
expansion to population growth also appears in the trade sectors of the
economy. In other industry groups, no clear-cut trend, either upward or
downward, is discernible.

The fact that employment in certain sectors of the California economy
may not be expanding as rapidly in relation to population growth as in
earlier decades does not, of course, imply a downward trend in the rate of
expansion of *total* employment to population growth. Disregarding short-
run fluctuations, total employment may be expected to expand secularly
at approximately the same rate as population, except so far as changes in
the age distribution of the population or in labor force participation rates
may affect the proportion of the population in the labor force.

Thus, if the ratio of employment expansion to population growth is tending to decline in one sector of the economy, it must be tending to expand
elsewhere, though the industry groups analyzed in the present chapter may
be too broad to permit positive identification of the categories in which
such expansion is occurring.

To put the same point in a somewhat different way, although the analysis in the present chapter sheds light on the relationship between employment expansion in *particular* sectors of the economy and population growth,
it sheds very little light on the relationship between total employment expansion and population growth. It is anticipated that, in the next several
decades, employment expansion and population growth will occur at approximately the same rates, but very little has been said thus far as to how
this adjustment is likely to be brought about. The analysis in subsequent
chapters will shed further light on this point.

Probably the most interesting and significant conclusion which may be
drawn from the analysis in the present chapter is that the ratios of employment expansion in the various sectors of the economy to population growth
have shown marked instability from decade to decade. A different pattern
of variation was discernible, moreover, in nearly every industry division.
If we were to analyze the course of employment expansion in each of the
eight decades since 1870, we should find that each decade was characterized by a somewhat distinctive pattern of expansion. Only a detailed analy-
of the economic development of the state in each of these decades would
serve to explain all the differences.

Thus, although population growth *per se* may have accounted, from a long-run point of view, for some substantial fraction of the employment expansion that has occurred, it is clear that the addition of a given number of persons to the state's population does not automatically lead to a given amount of employment expansion, in accordance with a predictable pattern. Even the trade and service sectors of the economy, which largely cater to the local market and might be expected to expand in *response* to changes in the rate of population growth, have shown distinctive patterns of response from decade to decade, which can be explained only in terms of the impact of economic developments, cyclical and otherwise, on these industry groups.

In the light of these findings, it is clear that any attempt to predict the rate of employment expansion in the various sectors of the economy on the basis of trends in the preceding decade—or even in the two most recent decades—is almost certain to lead to erroneous results. This is unfortunate, in view of the inadequacy of employment data for years before 1940, but it is a fact that must be faced by all those who are interested in studies relating to the future development of California's economy. The analysis in the remaining chapters will shed further light on some of the reasons for the instability of the pattern of employment expansion from decade to decade.

IV. TRENDS IN MANUFACTURING EMPLOYMENT

IN RELATION to the broad objectives of this study, a detailed analysis of trends in employment in California manufacturing is of fundamental importance. When fluctuations in the expansion of employment are analyzed in chapter vi, much evidence will be found that the rapid development of manufacturing in the state has provided the chief impetus to employment expansion in the last two decades and played a relatively important, though somewhat less dominant, role in the first three decades of the century. In the absence of unexpected developments, moreover, it is likely that the rate of increase in manufacturing employment will be of fundamental importance in relation to the rate of expansion of total employment in California during the next several decades.

In analyzing long-run trends in manufacturing employment it is possible to rely primarily on Census of Population data, collected on a household basis, or on Census of Manufactures data, collected on an establishment basis.[1] For a number of reasons, the Census of Manufactures data are more satisfactory for historical analysis and will be chiefly utilized in the present chapter. One of their major advantages is that they have related throughout to the average number of production workers[2] actually employed in a census year, whereas, until 1940, the Census of Population data, as has been seen, related to the number of gainful workers who "usually" worked at a given occupation.

It was not until 1939, however, that the Census Bureau classified production workers by major industry groups within manufacturing in its published Census of Manufactures statistics. The data for earlier years are presented in the form of a long and detailed alphabetical list of industries. In preparing the tables which are analyzed in the present chapter, therefore, it was necessary to classify the data for the years 1899 to 1929, draw-

---

[1] Detailed monthly data on employment in manufacturing are also published by the Division of Labor Statistics and Research of the California State Department of Industrial Relations, but they are not available for years before 1925 and have been subjected to a number of changes in form of presentation, which impair their usefulness for purposes of a historical study.

[2] In recent years, the Census of Manufactures has included data on the total number of employed workers, as well as the number of production workers, in each industry, but these data are not available in detail for the early years of our period. The term production workers, as used by the *Census of Manufactures*, includes those workers who are engaged in the physical processes of production and in maintenance and repair work; it is essentially similar to the term wage earners which was used in *Census of Manufactures* reports up to 1939. Proprietors, managerial personnel, and clerical and office workers are included in total employment but not in the data on production workers.

ing to some extent on earlier work by other investigators.[3] Since it was impossible to achieve perfect comparability with the statistics for 1939 and later years, the data must be interpreted with a considerable degree of caution.

TABLE 9

PERCENTAGE DISTRIBUTION OF EMPLOYED WORKERS IN MANUFACTURING BY MAJOR INDUSTRY GROUP, CALIFORNIA AND UNITED STATES, 1947

Industry group	California (1)	United States (2)	Ratio of (1) to (2)	California's share of U.S. manufacturing employees (in per cent)
Total manufacturing employees.....	100.0	100.0	1.00	4.6
Nondurable goods.................	43.8	44.8	0.98	4.5
Food and kindred products.......	18.2	10.1	1.80	8.4
Canning, preserving, and freezing	6.2	1.4	4.43	20.5
Other......................	11.9	8.7	1.37	6.4
Textile mill products............	0.8	8.6	0.09	0.4
Apparel and related products.....	6.5	7.6	0.86	4.0
Paper and allied products........	1.8	3.1	0.58	2.7
Printing and publishing industries..	6.3	5.0	1.26	5.9
Chemicals and allied products.....	4.1	4.4	0.93	4.3
Petroleum and coal products......	3.2	1.5	2.13	10.1
Rubber products...............	2.0[a]	1.8	1.11	5.0[a]
Leather and leather products.....	0.9	2.7	0.33	1.5
Durable goods...................	54.0	51.1	1.06	4.9
Lumber and lumber products, excluding furniture.............	5.8	4.4	1.32	6.1
Furniture and fixtures...........	2.8	2.3	1.22	5.7
Stone, clay, and glass products....	4.1	3.2	1.28	5.9
Primary metal industries........	4.7	8.1	0.58	2.7
Fabricated metal products........	8.2	6.8	1.21	5.6
Machinery (except electrical).....	7.9	10.8	0.73	3.4
Electrical machinery.............	2.7	5.6	0.48	2.2
Transportation equipment........	16.9	8.3	2.04	9.5
Motor vehicles and parts.......	2.5	4.9	0.51	2.3
Aircraft and parts.............	10.8[a]	1.5	7.20	32.7[a]
Ships and boats...............	2.8	1.0	2.80	12.2
Instruments and related products..	1.0	1.6	0.62	2.9
Miscellaneous manufactures (including tobacco and products)........	2.2	4.0	0.55	2.6

SOURCE: U.S. Bureau of the Census, *Census of Manufactures: 1947*, Vol. III, pp. 22, 28, 92, 93, and 96.
[a]Employment in this industry group was not disclosed by the census; it has been estimated on the basis of data published by the California State Department of Industrial Relations.

INDUSTRIAL DISTRIBUTION OF FACTORY EMPLOYMENT

Manufacturing in California is widely diversified but, nevertheless, there are important differences between the state and the nation as a whole in the industrial distribution of factory workers. If comparison is based on the situation in 1947, the latest year for which complete Census of Manufac-

[3] See Appendix B for further discussion of these problems.

tures data are available, these differences show up primarily *within* the nondurable and durable goods sectors of manufacturing (see table 9). The distribution of workers *between* nondurable and durable goods industries is quite similar in state and nation.

In the nondurable goods sector, California's outstanding specialties are food and petroleum refining. Printing and publishing industries, as well as rubber products, also account for relatively more workers in the state than in the nation. The heavy concentration of California workers in the food industry is primarily attributable, of course, to the predominant importance of the canning industry (especially fruit and vegetable canning) in the state, but other branches of the food-processing industries are also comparatively heavily represented.

California's leading deficiency, in the nondurable goods sector of manufacturing, is the almost complete absence of a textile mill industry. Less than 1 per cent of all workers in the state were employed in this industry in 1947, as compared with nearly 9 per cent of the nation's workers. On the other hand, the apparel industry is well developed in California and accounted for almost as large a percentage of the state's workers in 1947 as was true in the country as a whole. The leather industry is relatively underrepresented, though it once played a leading role, and the paper industry, which has been growing rapidly in recent decades, still employed relatively fewer workers than in the nation in 1947.

In the durable goods sector, California's workers, of course, are quite heavily concentrated in the manufacture of transportation equipment, chiefly aircraft and parts. More than a tenth of all factory workers in the state and nearly a third of the nation's aircraft workers in 1947 were employed in the California aircraft industry. The state also plays a fairly important role in the shipbuilding industry, accounting for 12 per cent of the nation's shipyard workers in 1947. On the other hand, most branches of the metal and metal products industries, except for fabricated metal products, represented considerably smaller percentages of total factory employment in California than in the nation, in spite of rapid growth in recent decades. The lumber industry, which played a dominant role in the early history of manufacturing in the state, still employed a somewhat larger percentage of California's workers than was true in the nation, as did stone, clay, and glass products.

To what extent are the special characteristics of California's manufacturing employment structure a product of recent developments and to what extent do they reflect long-run historical trends? Appendix tables A-18 to A-20 show that, although some of the distinguishing characteristics of California's factory employment structure were already present in 1899—the

first year for which true factory employment statistics are available[4]—
many of the industries which are dominant today were either nonexistent
or in an "infant" stage of development at the turn of the century.

The food-processing industry was already established as an industry of
dominant importance in the state in 1899, accounting for nearly a quarter
of total factory workers. In fact, on the basis of employment data, the "location quotient" (or ratio of the percentage of the state's workers to the
percentage of the nation's workers employed in the industry) for the food-
processing industry was substantially higher in 1899 than it was fifty years
later. The fruit- and vegetable-canning industry had begun to develop
rapidly in the 1880's, together with the shift to irrigated crops and away
from wheat production, and, by 1899, accounted for more than 10 per cent
of all factory workers in the state.

Other nondurable goods industries which were relatively important in
the state in 1899 were chemicals and printing and publishing. The latter
industry, at least in its newspaper publishing and job-printing sectors, is
one that tends to be predominantly market-oriented.

It is interesting to notice that the leather and leather products industry
was, relatively, considerably more important in the state at the turn of the
century than it has been in recent decades, accounting for about the same
percentage of California's factory workers in 1899 as was true in the nation
as a whole. In fact, during the first few decades of California's history as
a state, when cattle-raising was the leading branch of California agriculture, the leather industry acquired a position of considerable significance.
In 1869, more than 10 per cent of all workers then classified as manufacturing wage earners (including those in hand and neighborhood establishments) were producing leather and leather products. As the cattle ranches
gave way to large wheat ranches, the leather industry began to diminish in
relative importance, and during much of the present century the number
of factory workers employed in this industry in the state has actually declined, though there was something of an upward spurt in the 1940's. In
the nation as a whole, the industry has been characterized by comparatively slow growth in the present century.

The almost complete absence of a textile mill industry was as conspic-
uous a feature of California's factory employment structure in 1899 as it
was in 1947. On the other hand, the apparel industry employed approximately the same percentage of the state's workers in 1899 as was true in the

---

[4] Data on employment in manufacturing were collected in conjunction with the decennial population censuses from 1850 on, but they included "hand and neighborhood
trades" and are not, therefore, comparable with present-day *Census of Manufactures* data.
The reader should note that tables A-18 to A-20 relate to *production workers* in manufacturing, rather than to *all employed* workers.

nation. Paper, petroleum refining, and rubber industries had scarcely begun to develop in the state in 1899 and employed negligible numbers of workers.

Among the durable goods industries, the lumber and wood-products industry was the leading employer of labor in 1899, occupying a position of considerably greater relative importance in California than in the nation as a whole. In fact, the lumber industry had risen to a position of dominant importance in the early decades of the state's history, and by 1869 lumber and wood products accounted for nearly a quarter of all workers then classified as manufacturing workers. During the latter part of the nineteenth century, the lumber industry alone employed by far the larger proportion of all workers in the various branches of the forest-products industry. It was not until after the turn of the century that the furniture industry began to develop to any considerable extent.

Among other durable goods industries, none accounted for as large a percentage of workers in California as in the nation in 1899. The growth of the transportation-equipment industry to a position of dominant importance in the state was yet to come, and other branches of the metal and metal-products industry employed a substantially smaller percentage of all factory workers in the state than in the nation. Yet it would be a mistake to maintain that the metal and metal-products industry was almost completely undeveloped in the state at the beginning of the century. More than 5,000 workers were employed in foundry and machine shops, and more than 3,000 were producing nonferrous metal products of various kinds.[5] But relatively little development had occurred in the iron and steel industry proper (excluding foundry and machine shops), which employed only 773 workers in the state in 1899 out of a total of 369,000 in the nation.

To a considerable extent, the manufacturing industries which had acquired a position of leading importance in California in 1899 and which, at least as measured in terms of employment, were demonstrating their ability to grow rapidly and withstand competition, were those which were either based on flourishing extractive industries or which catered to a local market. There were a few exceptions to this rule, which are not apparent in the data on broad industry groups that we have been examining. In response to the needs of the gold-mining period—and later, of the Nevada silver-mining boom—specialized types of mining equipment were developed and produced, which acquired something of a market in other states and in foreign countries. At a later stage, other specialties were developed to serve peculiar local needs—notably pumps and other types of irrigation equipment; these also began to develop markets outside the state. But these

---

[5] See Appendix, table A-17.

industries did not constitute very important factors in employment.[6]

On the whole, the changes which have occurred since 1899 in the composition of factory employment in California have resulted in (1) greater diversity, and (2) greater relative importance of the durable goods industries. But these changes have not come about as the result of a completely consistent and steady development in one direction. The growth of the durable good industries, in particular, has taken place in an irregular manner. In fact, since each of the decades from the beginning of the century on has been characterized by a somewhat distinctive pattern of development, it will be worth while to trace briefly the developments decade by decade.

DECADE TO DECADE CHANGES IN MANUFACTURING EMPLOYMENT

1899–1909.—The first decade for which there are true factory employment statistics was characterized by a very rapid rate of population growth, but not by a commensurately rapid rate of increase in manufacturing employment. While population increased 58.5 per cent between 1899 and 1909, the number of production workers in manufacturing rose only 42.1 per cent.[7]

In part, the fact that manufacturing employment did not show a more marked increase between 1899 and 1909 must be blamed on the San Francisco earthquake of 1906. San Francisco was far and away the leading manufacturing center of the state in the first decade of the century, and employment in her factories increased rapidly from 1899 to 1904. But between 1904 and 1909, the number of factory wage earners in San Francisco declined 26.5 per cent, in contrast to a substantial increase elsewhere in the state.[8] This suggests that the decline was primarily attributable to the interruption of production, and resulting loss of markets, occasioned by the earthquake, though other factors may also have played a role.[9] In this connection, it is interesting that employment in the apparel industry in the

---

[6] As F. L. Kidner has pointed out, manufacturing activity in California did not enter its most important and rapid development until after the turn of the century. (Cf. *California Business Cycles*, Berkeley: University of California Press, 1946, pp. 26–29.)

[7] See Appendix, table A-21. *Census of Population* data give a somewhat different picture of developments from 1900 to 1910 (see table A-15), indicating that the number of manufacturing and mechanical workers increased more rapidly than population during the first decade of the century. But, in addition to the year's difference in the dates for which comparison is made, there are other important differences between the two sets of data. Manufacturing and mechanical workers, as classified by the *Census of Population*, include tailors, dressmakers, and other similar occupation groups, as well as factory workers, and also refer to "gainful workers" rather than to persons actually employed.

[8] See *Thirteenth Census of the United States: 1910*, Vol. IX, *Manufactures*, pp. 92–97.

[9] After the earthquake, although some manufacturers built new factories in San Francisco to replace those destroyed by the fire, a good many of them decided to locate in other parts of the Bay Area. The number of factory wage earners in Oakland, for example, more than doubled between 1904 and 1909 (*ibid.*)

state, which in this period was largely centered in San Francisco, fell off substantially in the first decade of the century.

More than three-fourths of the gain in factory employment from 1899 to 1909 occurred in the durable goods industries and more than half of the total gain occurred in the lumber and stone, clay, and glass industries, that is, in the two industries most closely dependent on the level of building activity. This was not surprising in a decade of rapid population growth and rapid expansion in construction. Though the value of building permits had declined somewhat from the peak reached in 1907 (following the San Francisco earthquake), construction activity was still at a relatively high level in 1909 (see figure 11). The metal and metal-products industries also accounted for a substantial proportion of the increase in employment in this decade, with most of the gain occurring in foundry and machine-shop employment.

In the nondurable goods sector of the economy, most of the increase occurred in the food industry. Spectacular percentage increases also took place in employment in the paper, petroleum, and rubber-products industries, but the level of employment in these industries was still so low that these increases did not contribute substantially to the total gain in employment.

On the whole, it is clear that the chief stimulus to expansion in manufacturing employment in the first decade of the century came from the expansion in building activity. Other substantial gains in employment occurred chiefly in industrial groups which were already well established by 1899, such as the food industry, printing and publishing, and foundry and machine shops. Three infant industries—paper, petroleum, and rubber products—had begun to grow but had not yet reached a point of contributing materially to employment expansion.

1909–1919.—The following decade presented quite a different pattern of development, dominated, as it was, by the manufacturing boom of World War I. It is clear that both the level and structure of factory employment in 1919 reflected, to some extent, the effects of temporary, war-induced expansion, but it is also clear that the decade was one of rapid development in many fields of manufacturing activity in California, the benefits of which did not by any means disappear after the war.

The over-all percentage increase in factory employment from 1909 to 1919 was more than double the rate of increase in population (see table A-21). Although the rate of growth of employment in the durable goods industries was somewhat higher than that in the nondurable goods industries, the increase in both of these broad sectors of manufacturing exceeded 100 per cent. It was the World War I boom in shipyard activity that accounted for the spectacular advance in employment in the transportation-

equipment industry and for most of the increase in durable goods employment. The number of wage earners in the shipbuilding and repair industry
rose from 1,800 in 1909 to 47,500 in 1919.[10] Undoubtedly, as in World War
II, this boom in shipyard activity was directly responsible for at least part
of the increase in employment in the metal and metal-products industries.
The pattern of development in these industries, moreover, was quite different from that which had occurred in the preceding decade. Employment
in foundry and machine shops increased relatively little, and employment
in the the nonferrous metal industry actually declined somewhat.[11] On the
other hand, spectacular advances occurred in employment in the iron and
steel industry and in the machinery industry (outside of foundry and machine-shop products). In fact, it may fairly be said that the modern development of California's iron and steel and machinery industries began in
the World War I period.[12]

Employment in the lumber and wood-products industry, which had risen
so markedly in the first decade of the century, increased relatively little
from 1909 to 1919, and employment in stone, clay, and glass products declined. Again, the behavior of employment in these industries had responded to the level of building activity, which had declined from 1912–
1913 on and had barely begun to recover by 1919.

In the nondurable goods sector, the major part of the expansion of employment between 1909 and 1919 occurred in the food industry, with most
of the increase taking place after 1914. Employment of wage earners in
fruit and vegetable canning and preserving alone increased from 7,500 to
21,000 between 1909 and 1919, and employment in other branches of the
food industry also increased spectacularly in the same period.

Although other nondurable goods industries accounted for relatively
small proportions of the over-all increase in manufacturing employment
from 1909 to 1919, most of them experienced substantial percentage gains
in this period. This was the decade in which petroleum refining became
established as an industry of importance in the state. It was also a decade
of significance for the apparel industry, in which employment increased
from 3,500 in 1909 to 7,700 in 1919, accounting for most of the gain in employment in the textile industry during the decade. Again, as in other industries, most of the increase occurred after 1914.

Thus the World War I period was one of notable, all-round advance in
manufacturing employment. Although the enormous increase in shipyard

---

[10] See Appendix, table A-17.

[11] The nonferrous metals group includes sheet metal and fixtures, largely used as
building materials.

[12] Detailed figures from the 1914 *Census of Manufactures* have not been presented, but
most of the gains in these industries occurred after 1914, rather than from 1909 to 1914.

employment was the most spectacular development of the period, the gains in other industries were of greater significance from the point of view of the long-run development of manufacturing in California. As in World War II, and, for that matter, the Civil War, conditions were favorable for an all-round advance in manufacturing in the state, in part because Eastern manufacturers were frequently not in a position to supply California markets, and in part because rapidly rising prices made it relatively easy for new and expanding firms in California to finance the expansion of plant and equipment.

1919–1929.—At first glance, it would appear that the decade of the 'twenties was not especially favorable to the development of manufacturing in California. Employment of production workers in manufacturing increased only 22.0 per cent in a period in which population rose by 65.6 per cent. Furthermore, almost the entire gain occurred in the nondurable goods sector of manufacturing, whereas total employment in durable goods industries scarcely increased at all. Failure of total employment of production workers in durable goods industries to expand appreciably was largely attributable to the fact that shipyard employment fell from 47,500 in 1919 to 4,200 in 1929. In all other major durable goods industries, the percentage increase in employment in the 'twenties was substantial. If shipyard employment is eliminated, it is found that total employment of production workers in manufacturing increased 54.1 per cent from 1919 to 1929, and employment of production workers in durable goods industries increased 61.3 per cent, or more than the rate of increase in nondurable goods industries.

Among nondurable goods industries, gains in employment were widely distributed in the 'twenties. The largest percentage increases in employment occurred in the less mature industries, such as rubber, paper, and the various branches of the textile industry. Not only did employment in the apparel industry nearly double from 1919 to 1929, but an even larger percentage increase occurred in employment in the nonapparel branch of the textile industry, chiefly in the manufacture of fabricated textile products. Although the rise in employment in the food industry was smaller, percentagewise, than in most other nondurable goods industries, it was large enough to account for more than 30 per cent of the over-all gain in manufacturing employment.

In the durable goods sector of the economy, the largest share of the increase in the 1920's occurred in the metal and metal-products industries. The gains were widely distributed, moreover, throughout the various subdivisions of this group of industries. A study of the detailed data in table A-17 indicates that the subdivisions which had experienced rapid growth during World War I—iron and steel products and machinery—were able to maintain a substantial rate of growth during the following decade, and those whose growth had been held back during the war—nonferrous metal products and foundry and machine-shop products—made up for lost time in the 'twenties.

Employment in the construction-oriented industries—lumber and stone, clay, and glass products—also increased substantially during the 'twenties, though a study of the more detailed data in figure 3 indicates that peak employment in these industries was reached early in the decade. It will be recalled that the level of building activity in the state declined somewhat after 1923.[13] It was during the 'twenties that the furniture industry made its most spectacular gains in employment, and the rapid rate of growth in the industry helped to maintain employment in the lumber and wood-products industry group, even after lumber production had declined.

Although the rate of increase in factory employment in the state in the 'twenties, even after eliminating shipyard employment, was not as rapid as the rate of population growth, it must be kept in mind that total factory employment in the nation as a whole actually declined somewhat in the 1920's.[14] The big gains in employment throughout the nation during this decade occurred, not in manufacturing, but in the trade and service industries. In part, this reflected a very considerable rise in productivity in manufacturing, and in part, changing patterns of consumption. Viewed in the light of the failure of manufacturing employment in the nation to rise during the 'twenties, the rate of growth of factory employment in California appears quite substantial.

One additional comment needs to be made about the manufacturing developments of the 1920's. It was in this decade that the impact of the growth of the automobile industry on the American economy was especially important, and this was true to a very considerable extent in California, as well as in the nation. The effects were evident, of course, not only in the development of manufacturing, but in other branches of the economy—highway construction, the spread of a network of gasoline-filling stations, the acceleration of the movement to the suburbs, and so on. But the effects on manufacturing employment in California were clearly evident as well. If only those industry groups are considered which were most directly affected by the expanding use of the automobile—motor vehicles and parts, rubber products, and petroleum and coal products—they account for 15 per cent of the total rise in factory employment in the 'twenties

---

[13] See figure 11.

[14] See S. Fabricant, *Employment in Manufacturing: 1899–1939* (New York: National Bureau of Economic Research, 1942), p. 212. If shipyard employment is eliminated, the total number of factory production workers in the nation showed a very slight increase between 1919 and 1929.

(eliminating shipbuilding). The indirect effects on other industry groups, particularly the various branches of the machinery industry, must have been substantial, though difficult to measure.

1929–1939.—During the 'thirties, the growth of manufacturing employment in California was slow and spotty. Between 1929 and 1939, although the state's population increased 22.7 per cent, the employment of production workers in manufacturing rose only 3.1 per cent. During the same period, however, employment of factory production workers in the nation fell off by 6.6 per cent.

It was the durable goods sector of manufacturing in California, as in the nation, which suffered most from the depressed conditions of the 'thirties. Employment of production workers in durable goods industries in the state declined slightly in the ten-year period from 1929 to 1939, whereas the number of production workers in factories producing nondurable goods rose 14.3 per cent. But the importance of this contrasting experience of the two broad sectors of manufacturing should not be overstressed, since there were substantial declines in employment in some of the industry groups within the nondurable sector, whereas the most significant single development in California manufacturing in the 'thirties occurred in the durable goods sector, with the growth of the aircraft industry.

If the changes occurring in the nondurable goods industries in the 'thirties are examined more closely, some interesting and significant developments may be observed. Undoubtedly the most important of these was the substantial growth of the apparel industry, in which employment of production workers rose 40.5 per cent in this period. Actually, California's experience was not unique in this respect, since the rate of growth in this industry in the state was approximately equal to that in the nation, and California's share of total production workers in the apparel industry did not rise between 1929 and 1939. Other nondurable goods industries which showed substantial growth in the state during the 'thirties were the paper and chemical industries. Elsewhere in the nondurable sector, only slight gains or actual declines in employment occurred.

The percentage changes in employment in the durable goods industries also varied widely during this period. Substantial declines occurred in both lumber and stone, clay, and glass products, as might have been expected in view of the sharp decline in construction activity in the depression and the relatively modest recovery thereafter.[15] A considerably more moderate decline was experienced in the metal and metal-products industries, though what was happening in the various branches of the industry group cannot be determined because of the far-reaching changes in the classification system between 1937 and 1939.

---

[15] See figure 11.

The substantial rise (92.7 per cent) in employment in the transportation-equipment industry in the state during the 'thirties was entirely attributable to the rapid growth of the aircraft industry, whereas employment in the automobile industry and in the shipyards declined. Aircraft employment increased substantially elsewhere in the nation, also, but California's share of the total rose from 9 per cent in 1929 to about 35 per cent in 1939. From a relatively insignificant factor in total employment of production workers in the transportation-equipment industry in the state in 1929, aircraft employment had come to represent 64 per cent of the total by 1939.

There is little doubt that the growth of the aircraft industry must have had some impact on employment in the metal and metal-products industry group in the 'thirties—and perhaps to some extent on other industry groups as well—but it is impossible to measure the extent of the impact. The fact that total employment in metal and metal products declined somewhat between 1929 and 1939 does not prove anything one way or another in this connection, since whatever expansion may have occurred in response to the growth of the aircraft industry was clearly offset by the influence of other powerful forces making for contraction.

Thus, although the decade from 1929 to 1939 was one of slow and spotty growth in manufacturing employment in California, it was notable for the development of an industry that was to play a decisive role in the manufacturing booms of World War II and of the Korean War period.

1939–1949.—Although California's population increased spectacularly (54.7 per cent) between 1939 and 1949, the percentage rise in employment of production workers in manufacturing was even more spectacular (87.0 per cent). Nearly every industry group experienced a substantial rise in employment, including even the leather industry, which had previously displayed a decided tendency toward secular decline. Much of the expansion, of course, was stimulated directly or indirectly by the military production program of World War II, but, in addition, the rising income and employment levels which prevailed during most of the decade created conditions which were highly favorable for an all-round development of manufacturing activity.

In contrast to the situation in the immediately preceding period, about 60 per cent of the increase in employment of factory production workers between 1939 and 1949 took place in the durable goods industries, with the metal and transportation-equipment industries contributing most of the increase.

As previously indicated, the most significant single factor in manufacturing development during this period was the rise of the aircraft industry to a position in which it not only far outranked all other manufacturing industries in terms of direct employment but was also indirectly responsible for a substantial volume of employment in industries producing materials used in the production of airplanes and their parts, especially metal and metal-products industries. During the war period itself, the shipbuilding industry played as important a role as the aircraft industry in the manufacturing boom, but the cutbacks in employment in the shipyards after the war were more severe than in the aircraft industry, and, by 1949, employment of production workers in private shipyards was down to about 6,100, or not very much above the level of 1939. From the point of view of developments over the decade as a whole, the growth of the aircraft industry was far more significant. Also of considerable importance in the growth of the transportation-equipment industry group during the decade was the fact that employment of production workers in factories producing motor vehicles and parts more than doubled between 1939 and 1949.

The contribution of the growth of employment in the metal and metal-products industries to the over-all gain in factory employment in the 'forties was about as important as the increase in the transportation-equipment group. Although, even in 1949, a relatively smaller proportion (about 21 per cent) of California's production workers were engaged in the metal and metal-products industries than was true in the country as a whole (about 28 per cent), it is interesting to observe that the metal and transportation-equipment groups combined accounted for about the same proportion of all manufacturing production workers in state and nation. The gain in employment in California in the ten-year period was marked in all branches of the metals group—in primary metal products (partly reflecting, of course, the growth attributable to the construction during the war of the Kaiser steel plant at Fontana), in fabricated-metal products, and in the various branches of the machinery industry.

Although employment in the lumber and wood-products industry and in stone, clay, and glass products increased substantially during this period of marked expansion in construction activity, employment in the lumber industry continued to lose ground as a percentage of total employment of manufacturing production workers.

Among the nondurable goods industries, the dominant food-processing group accounted for the largest share of the increase in employment during the decade, but percentage gains in a number of other industry groups were substantially higher. The relatively slow *rate* of growth in food processing reflected primarily the fact that only a very slight gain in employment occurred in fruit and vegetable canning, an industry which had clearly reached a mature stage of growth. If we eliminate fruit and vegetable canning, we find that employment in other food-processing industries increased about 60 per cent, or somewhat more rapidly than population.

Besides food processing, the highest rates of growth (in employment terms) in the nondurable sector were found in the rubber, paper, leather, apparel, and chemical industries.

On the whole, it was the oldest and best established industries in the state which showed the lowest percentage gains in employment during the 'forties, whereas many of the "younger" industries leaped ahead. By the end of the decade, the role played by the branches of manufacturing which were closely related to extractive industries—fruit and vegetable canning, lumber, and petroleum refining—was comparatively less important than it had been ten years earlier, and the "heavy industry" sector—metal and metal products and transportation equipment—had gained in relative importance. These changes represented, for the most part, a continuation of long-run trends toward greater industrial maturity. Yet this process had occurred in a halting and irregular manner throughout the decades, partly because of cyclical disturbances and partly because of the distortions introduced by major wars. There was no reason to assume that changes in the structure of manufacturing employment in the 'fifties or 'sixties would necessarily represent a smooth continuation of the changes that had occurred in the 'forties.

TRENDS IN RATES OF GROWTH IN MANUFACTURING EMPLOYMENT

In the previous chapter, in analyzing trends in rates of growth in the various major industry groups, reliance was placed primarily on an analysis of decade-to-decade ratios of percentage changes in employment to percentage changes in population. This method is somewhat less appropriate as a method of analyzing rates of growth in manufacturing subdivisions, many of which sell their products in regional or nation-wide markets. Yet, because the growth of manufacturing employment has fluctuated with population growth to some extent, there are certain advantages to be gained through computing such ratios, even for purposes of analyzing trends in rates of growth in manufacturing (see table A-22 and fig. 2). The subsequent discussion will be based, however, not only on these ratios, but on the employment data in figure 3.

Since the beginning of the century, the ratio of the rate of growth of manufacturing employment to the rate of population growth has undergone marked fluctuations from decade to decade. The results obtained— for the first five decades of the century—by computing such ratios from Census of Manufactures data vary somewhat from those that we get by basing our computations on Census of Population data, but the differences are not sufficiently pronounced to lead to substantially different conclusions. Both sets of ratios indicate that by far the most rapid rates of growth, in relation to population growth, occurred in the two war decades. If shipyard employment is eliminated from the Census of Manufactures data, the fluctuations between the first and third decades of the century are modified substantially, yielding a much lower ratio for 1909–1919 and a considerably higher ratio for 1919–1929. The justification for this procedure is that, for purposes of analyzing long-run trends, the inclusion of shipyard employment, which dropped off sharply after 1919, gives a distorted impression of the rate of growth in both the second and third decades of the century.[16]

Even after making this adjustment, the ratios for both war decades were substantially higher than those for the remaining decades, whereas the ratio for the depressed decade of the 'thirties was abnormally low. There is no discernible indication either of an upward or a downward long-run trend in the ratio of employment expansion in manufacturing to population growth. It is interesting to find that during the fifty-year period from 1899 to 1949, the percentage increase in factory employment was almost equal to the percentage increase in population; the ratio was 0.96 for the period as a whole. During the same period, however the corresponding ratio for the nation as a whole was 1.46, that is, factory employment was increasing considerably more rapidly than population. Another way of expressing the same set of relationships is to point out that California's share of the nation's factory workers was not increasing as rapidly as her share of the population during the first half of the century. Yet, as Hoover has shown in his study of locational trends, there has been a broad tendency in the direction of equalization of the interregional distributions of population and industry in the United States.[17] It is conceivable that, now that the Western market is large enough to support industries which could not profitably be located here in the past, the rate of growth of factory employment in California might exceed the rate of growth of population in the second half of the century.

Turning from total employment of production workers to employment in the two broad sectors of manufacturing, I find that the ratios for durable goods manufacturing fluctuated more widely, on the whole, than those for nondurable goods. Particularly in the last three decades, the ratios for nondurable goods have been relatively more stable.

Ratios for individual industry groups have shown a wide variety of patterns of decade-to-decade variation. I shall not attempt to analyze all these variations in detail, but shall attempt, rather, to make whatever comments

---

[16] Actually shipyard employment fell from 62,138 in May, 1919, to 24,010 in December, but the average figure for the year was far above the level that prevailed during most of the 1920's.

[17] See E. M. Hoover, *The Location of Economic Activity* (New York: McGraw-Hill, 1948), especially chapter ix.

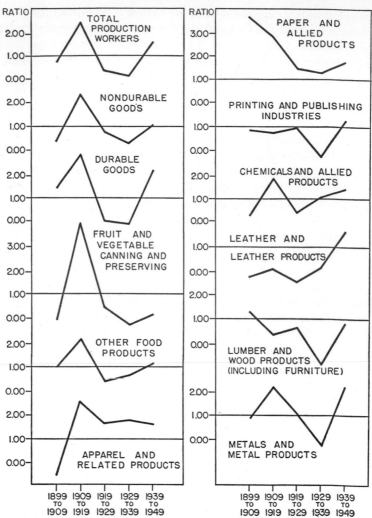

SOURCE: Table A-22, Appendix

Fig. 2A. Ratio of percentage increase in number of production workers in manufacturing to percentage increase in population per decade, selected industry groups, California, 1899–1949. (Because of the wider variability of employment in the industry divisions represented on the second page of the chart, a reduced vertical scale has been used.)

seem justified about long-run trends and about patterns of variations that are common to more than one industrial subdivision.

There are few industry groups in which there is clear evidence of a long-run downward trend in the ratio of the rate of employment expansion to

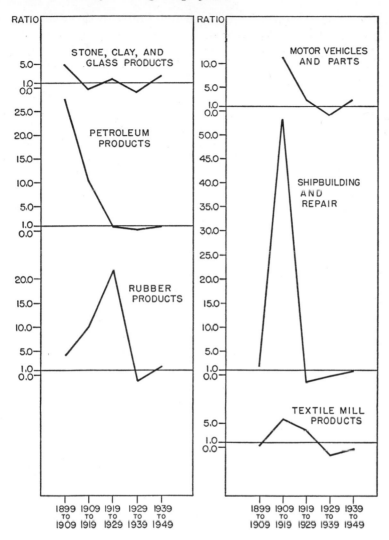

SOURCE: Table A-22, Appendix.

FIG. 2B. Ratio of percentage increase in number of production workers in manufacturing to percentage increase in population per decade, selected industry groups, California, 1899–1949. (Because of the wider variability of employment in the industry divisions represented on the second page of the chart, a reduced vertical scale has been used.)

the rate of population growth. Employment in fruit and vegetable canning and preserving, however, scarcely showed any net gain whatever in the two most recent decades in our period, though there have been some year-to-year fluctuations in the interim, and, of course, marked seasonal variations in employment. This industry appears to have reached a mature stage of very slow growth, and because of its dominant importance among food-processing industries, the rate of growth of employment in the food group as a whole has been somewhat depressed as a result. But if we eliminate fruit and vegetable canning from the food group, we find that the ratio of employment expansion to population growth has tended to increase since 1919–1929 and exceeded 1.00 by a slight margin in the decade from 1939 to 1949. During the entire period from 1899 to 1949 the rate of increase in employment of production workers in the food group (other than fruit and vegetable canning and preserving) was approximately equal to the rate of increase in manufacturing employment as a whole and in total population.

Analysis of the variations in the ratios for this "other food products" group gives the impression that the expansion which occurred in World War I, even in these consumers' goods industries, was more rapid than was justified in the light of long-run trends, and that expansion in the next decade or two was held back as a result. It may well be that the steady rise of the commercial and industrial failure rate in California in the 1920's referred to in another connection in chapter vi, was attributable in part to the excesses of the wartime expansion.[18]

Four of the industry groups for which ratios are computed, experienced much less rapid employment expansion in relation to population growth in the last few decades than in earlier decades of the century—paper, petroleum, rubber, and motor vehicles and parts—but the very high ratios which characterized the growth of these industries in earlier decades were associated with their "infant" stages of growth, and the downward trend does not necessarily indicate that they have now reached a stage in which their "growth ratios" are likely to display a tendency toward secular decline. There is reason to believe, however, that employment in the petroleum-refining industry from now on is likely to increase less rapidly than population. In this industry, production can be expanded substantially without additional man power.

The sensitivity of the lumber and wood products, as well as of the stone, clay, and glass products to the gyrations of the building cycle shows up clearly in the behavior of their ratios, as well as in the more detailed em-

---

[18] It is interesting to notice, in this connection, that after World War II, also, the commercial and industrial failure rate rose more markedly in California than in the nation, though it remained quite low in both areas.

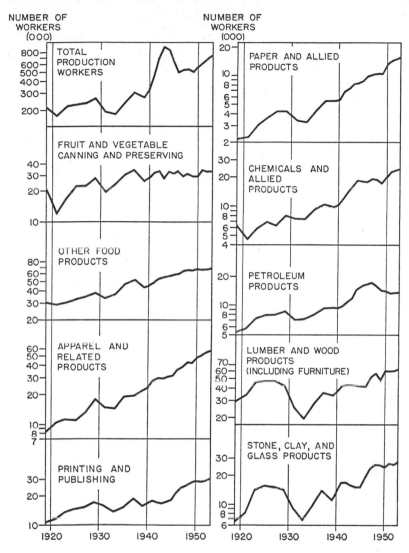

NUMBER OF
WORKERS
(OOO)

NUMBER OF
WORKERS
(OOO)

TOTAL PRODUCTION WORKERS

FRUIT AND VEGETABLE CANNING AND PRESERVING

OTHER FOOD PRODUCTS

APPAREL AND RELATED PRODUCTS

PRINTING AND PUBLISHING

PAPER AND ALLIED PRODUCTS

CHEMICALS AND ALLIED PRODUCTS

PETROLEUM PRODUCTS

LUMBER AND WOOD PRODUCTS (INCLUDING FURNITURE)

STONE, CLAY, AND GLASS PRODUCTS

SOURCES: See Appendix B.

Fig. 3A. Production workers in manufacturing, selected industry groups, California: biennial, 1919–1939, and annual, 1939–1953.
Continuous data for the aircraft industry are not available for years before 1935.

ployment series in figure 3. The similarity between the fluctuations in the growth ratios for these manufacturing industries and for the building trades-construction group (see chart 1) is striking. In view of the fact that the ratios for these industries were abnormally high in the first decade of the

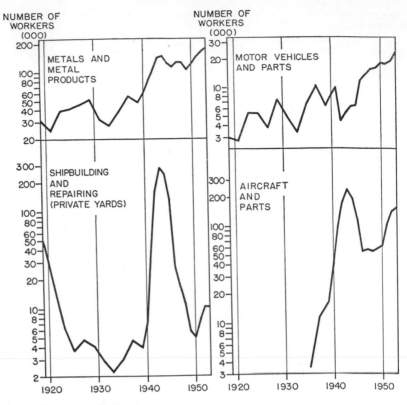

SOURCES: See Appendix B.

FIG. 3B. Production workers in manufacturing, selected industry groups, California: biennial, 1919–1939, and annual, 1939–1953.

Continuous data for the aircraft industry are not available for years before 1935.

century, the conclusion that they display something of a secular downward trend over the fifty-year period as a whole is not necessarily justified.

With a few exceptions (apparel, aircraft, and the transportation-equipment group as a whole) all the ratios which we have computed were higher for the 1939–1949 period than for the preceding decade. For many of the groups, moreover, the ratios for the 1939–1949 decade were higher than for the decade of the 'twenties.

Irrespective of decade-to-decade fluctuations, which manufacturing industries are likely to experience the most rapid secular expansion of employment during the next twenty or thirty years? On the basis of a study of historical data and all the additional information that bears on the situation, the following tentative classification of manufacturing industries according to their probable secular rates of employment expansion in the next several decades may be attempted:

Group I. **Relatively slow employment expansion** (probably considerably less rapid than population growth)—fruit and vegetable canning and preserving; textile mill products; lumber and wood products.

Group II. **Employment expansion probably somewhat less rapid than population growth**—food products other than fruit and vegetable canning and preserving; printing and publishing industries; petroleum products.

Group III. **Employment expansion probably somewhat more rapid than population growth**—apparel and related products; paper and allied products; metal and metal products.

Group IV. **No prediction possible** (because the variability of past behavior makes prediction difficult or because the employment level, for example, in the aircraft industry, is likely to depend heavily on the level of military spending)—leather and leather products; chemicals and allied products; rubber products; stone, clay, and glass products; motor vehicles and parts; aircraft and parts; shipbuilding and repairs.

In interpreting this classification, it should be kept in mind that future changes in productivity, as well as a number of other more or less unpredictable factors, may affect rates of growth.

In the various sectors of manufacturing, as in the broader industry groups analyzed in chapter iii, the ratios of employment expansion to population growth have varied widely from decade to decade. Such variations are to be expected in the industries serving a nation-wide market (for example, fruit and vegetable canning and aircraft), in which there is no reason to assume that the growth of employment is closely related to the growth of the California or Western market. But in industries serving primarily a local market (for example, printing and publishing or "other food products"), a much more stable relationship between employment expansion and population growth might be expected. The fact that the ratios vary considerably, even in such industries, indicates that, in the short run, the rate of growth of employment tends to be strongly influenced by cyclical and other disturbances. One apparent exception to this rule, at least during the period since 1919, is the decade-to-decade behavior of employment in the apparel industry.[19]

Conclusions

What can be said about the outlook for the growth of manufacturing

---

[19] Actually, the apparel industry, which is chiefly centered in Los Angeles County, serves the Western regional market, as do a number of other California industries. Thus, it might be more appropriate to compute ratios of employment expansion to Western population growth rather than to California's population growth. On this basis, the ratios for the apparel industry from 1919 on (3.19, 2.43, and 2.17) turn out to be somewhat higher, but also show a downward trend. For a classification of Los Angeles County industries according to the markets which they serve, see G. H. Hildebrand and A. Mace, Jr., "The Employment Multiplier in an Expanding Industrial Market: Los Angeles County, 1940–47," *Review of Economics and Statistics*, XXXII (1950), pp. 241–249.

employment in California over the course of the next several decades, on the basis of the analysis in this and the preceding chapter? There are a number of considerations which suggest that, although employment in manufacturing will continue to increase rapidly (disregarding cyclical fluctuations), it is not likely to come to represent a materially larger proportion of total employment in California than in 1950. Among these considerations are the following:

1. Manufacturing employment increased at approximately the same rate as population and only a little more rapidly than total employment during the first half of the present century. It would have to increase substantially more rapidly than total employment in the coming decades in order to account for a materially larger percentage of total employment than in 1950. Yet there is no clear evidence of a long-run upward trend in the ratio of employment expansion in manufacturing to population growth.

2. Since 1900, the only two decades in which factory employment has increased much more rapidly than population or total employment have been the two war decades. This has been attributable, not only to expansion of war industries during these two decades, but also to the fact that expansion of civilian goods industries in California was encouraged in periods of nation-wide inflation and tight man power, when Eastern manufacturers were not in a position to supply the California market adequately. It seems reasonable to expect that, just as World War I was followed by several decades of less rapid expansion of factory employment (in relation to population growth), so the unusually marked expansion of the 1940's may not be matched in the 'fifties and 'sixties (unless we should become involved in a full-scale war).

3. Although population on the Pacific Coast continues to grow rapidly, the intermountain West will probably continue to be sparsely settled. It has been suggested that developments in the field of atomic energy may stimulate industrialization in the intermountain West, but the impact of such developments on population growth in that area is likely to be felt only gradually.

On the other hand, there is the possibility that the Western market is now large enough to encourage the growth of industries whose location on the Pacific Coast has previously been impeded by the small size of the market. Those who have a detailed knowledge of industrial developments on the Pacific Coast in the last decade or so can point to many illustrations of expansion attributable to this factor. The development of manufacturing on the Pacific Coast would undoubtedly be stimulated, moreover, by expansion of foreign trade in the Pacific basin, but, in the light of the current political situation in the Far East, the outlook for such expansion in the next decade or two does not appear to be very promising.

Nevertheless, these considerations serve to call attention to the fact that the long-run trends of the last fifty or eighty years do not necessarily provide a reliable guide to future developments. It is conceivable that, twenty or thirty years from now, the proportion of California workers who are employed in manufacturing may be substantially higher than it was in 1950.

V. INCOME AND WAGE DIFFERENTIALS

THERE is little doubt that the relatively high income and wage levels which have prevailed in California throughout the decades have tended to encourage migration to the state. It is likely, moreover, that the decline of California wage rates and family incomes to the national level, or even below it, would be accompanied by a substantial decline in the state's rate of population growth through migration, although some people would probably continue to move to California because of its climate. Although an individual worker who migrates to California at a given time may be influenced more by the prospect of relatively favorable job opportunities in the state than by the comparatively high wage levels, a rising or declining trend in income and wage differentials would be likely to reflect the influence of a similar trend in the rate of expansion of employment opportunities in the state relative to the nation.[1]

Pursuing this line of reasoning a bit further, it might be argued that one way of gaining insight into employment trends in the state, relative to those in the nation, would be to analyze trends in income and wage differentials between state and nation. Such an analysis must take account of changes in industrial structure and other factors which affect the comparisons, particularly of per capita income levels. Because of these complications, it is difficult to arrive at clear-cut conclusions on the basis of a study of readily available data. Even so, it will be useful to consider what has been happening to income and wage differentials.

Incomes and wages have been relatively high in California ever since the Gold Rush era—most conspicuously so during the Gold Rush itself. As the population of the state has grown and labor has become a less scarce factor of production, in relation to capital and natural resources, there has been a tendency for income and wage differences between California and the nation to decline. This much is generally known. But has this narrowing of income and wage differences continued in recent decades, and, if so, what are the implications in relation to population and employment trends?

INCOME DIFFERENTIALS

Unfortunately, no reliable estimates of total income by states are available for years before 1919. Thus discussion of income trends must be largely confined to the period since the end of World War I.

A glance at figure 4 and Appendix table A-24 indicates that the ratio of

---

[1] Here, as elsewhere, we use the term employment opportunities to mean job openings *in relation* to the available labor supply.

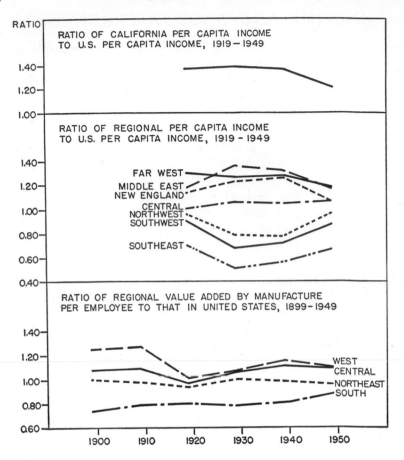

SOURCES: See Appendix B.

Fig. 4. Trends in regional per capita income differentials.

per capita income in California to that in the nation declined from 1.37 in 1919 to 1.24 in 1952, but that the decline apparently occurred entirely in the decade from 1939 to 1949, with some increase in the ratio taking place between 1949 and 1952. Chapter vi takes up short-run fluctuations in economic conditions in the state, and points out that there were some rather marked year-to-year fluctuations in this ratio *within* each of the three complete decades covered by the data, but for the time being attention will be directed to longer-run trends.

It requires only a brief study of Appendix table A-23 to observe that the decline in the per capita income differential between California and the nation from 1939 to 1949 cannot be explained solely or even primarily, in terms of what was happening in California. The higher percentage increase in per capita income in the country as a whole reflected the fact that per capita income in certain other parts of the country rose, percentagewise, much more than it did in California. The rise in California was a little lower, in percentage terms, than that in the Far West as a whole, whereas it was approximately equal to that in the Middle East and slightly higher than that in New England. It was much lower, however, than the rise in the Southeast, Southwest, or Northwest regions, and substantially lower than that in the Central states.

By and large, the most pronounced percentage increases in per capita income took place in those regions whose per capita incomes were relatively low in 1939, and the least marked increases occurred in the regions with comparatively high incomes in 1939. The result was a substantial narrowing of regional income differentials in the decade. This narrowing of regional income differentials had its counterpart in a narrowing of occupational wage and income differentials during the 'forties. Both developments reflected, at least to some extent, the effects of labor mobility—there were substantial movements of workers from low wage to higher wage occupations[2] and from low income to higher income regions during the decade.[3]

But the narrowing of regional income differentials during the 'forties cannot be explained solely as a reflection of the effects of interregional migration, without taking into account regional differences in industrial structure, or indeed, the changes that occurred in industrial structure during the 'forties. The states in which agriculture is a relatively important source of income experienced the most marked increases in per capita income during the 'forties, largely because per capita income in agriculture rose much more sharply than in other industry groups.[4] In part this development, *too*, reflected the effects of labor mobility—there was a substantial net movement of workers out of agriculture during the 'forties. But in large part it reflected the influence of the various factors which tend to make agriculture prices more variable than the prices of nonagricultural goods and services.

Looking at the entire period from 1919 to 1949 (see fig. 4), it is clear that regional per capita income differences tended, on the whole, to widen in

---

[2] For a discussion of the narrowing of occupational wage differences in California from 1940 to 1947, and some of the factors which were responsible, see the introduction by Arthur M. Ross to Nedra B. Belloc's monograph on *Wages in California* (Berkeley: University of California Press, 1948).

[3] On regional income changes and their relation to inter-regional migration from 1929 to 1949, see "Regional Differences in Jobs, Income, and Migration, 1929–49," *Monthly Labor Review*, LXXI (1950), 433–437.

[4] On the relevance of this factor in explaining changes in regional income differences from 1929 to 1949, see U.S. Department of Commerce, *Regional Trends in the United States Economy* (Washington, 1951), pp. 5–6 and 106.

the first decade of the period and later to narrow, particularly after 1939. The long-run trend toward a narrowing of these differences, which seems to show up clearly if only the period since 1929 is considered (as is usual), seems somewhat less clearly established if comparisons are dated from 1919.[5] Although other factors played a role, the chief explanation of the widening of differences in the 'twenties, as of the narrowing in the 'forties, is apparently to be found in the extreme variability of agricultural income. The states which are heavily dependent on agricultural income were the ones that suffered most from the downward trend in prices of major agricultural products during the 'twenties.

There is some evidence, also, that regional differentials in incomes per worker in at least some nonagricultural industries may also have widened somewhat after World War I and narrowed again in the 'forties. Thus, though the long-run trend may be in the direction of a narrowing of regional income differentials through interregional migration, the process has not been occurring smoothly.

Furthermore, when the changes taking place in a particular state or region, in relation to the nation as a whole, are considered, it is found that these changes cannot all be explained purely and simply as a reflection of the effects of interregional migration. This is the case with the decline in the income differential between California and the nation in the 'forties.

Relative scarcity of labor in relation to other factors of production—or high marginal productivity of labor—has not been the only factor responsible for California's high *per capita* income in the past. Other factors which have contributed have been (1) the relatively small percentage of children in the population, (2) the high degree of urban concentration, (3) the relatively large percentage of people engaged in nonagricultural pursuits,[6] and (4) the extraordinarily high incomes earned in agriculture and the extractive industries in California.[7]

---

[5] The tendency to begin with the year 1929 in comparisons of this sort is natural, in view of the fact that Department of Commerce income data are available only from that year on. Yet the National Industrial Conference Board estimates, which we have used for the year 1919, are probably sufficiently reliable to permit the type of comparison made here.

[6] This, of course, is closely related to the degree of urban concentration.

[7] For a discussion of these factors and their relationship to wartime and postwar changes in income in California, see V. B. Stanbery, "New Changes in California's Postwar Economy Revealed," *Western Industry* (December, 1948), pp. 50–51. A more detailed analysis (also prepared by Mr. Stanbery) may be found in California, Reconstruction and Reemployment Commission, *Purchasing Power of Wartime and Postwar Income Payments, the Nation and California* (Sacramento, 1944). For a more general discussion of factors influencing per capita income differentials between states, see J. L. Fulmer, "Factors Influencing Per Capita Income Differentials," *Southern Economic Journal*, XVI (1950), 259–278; and H. F. Breimyer, "Some Comments on Factors Influencing Differences between State Per Capita Incomes," *ibid.*, XVII (1950), 140–147.

The marked increase in the number of children in the state during the 'forties brought the proportion of children in the population much closer to that in the nation and helped to explain the decline in the per capita income differential between the state and the nation during the decade.[8] If total income in the state and nation is divided by the estimated number of persons fourteen years old and older, rather than by the total population, it is found that the ratio of per capita income in the state to that in the nation was 1.29 in 1939 and 1.18 ten years later. In other words, the *differential* declined only about 8 per cent during the decade on this basis, as compared with about 12 per cent if per capita income is computed on the basis of the total population. Thus, whereas the rise in the proportion of children in the population accounted for *some* of the drop in the differential during the 'forties, there still is a good deal left to explain on other grounds.

If comparison is made between 1919 and 1949, however, there are somewhat different results. In 1919, the ratio of income *per person of working age* (fourteen years and older) in California to that in the nation was only 1.24. Computed on this basis, the differential rose between 1919 and 1939, and fell off again during the 'forties to a level not greatly lower than that of 1919. What happened was that the proportion of children in the state's population did not decline as sharply in the 'twenties and 'thirties as it did in the nation and then rose more markedly in the 'forties. If this had not been occurring, per capita income for California's total population would have risen, relative to that in the nation, from 1919 to 1939, and fallen less sharply from 1939 to 1949. Throughout the thirty-year period as a whole, the fact that California's age distribution was moving closer to that in the nation apparently accounted for a substantial part of the narrowing of the per capita income differential between state and nation. The proportion of children in the state was still slightly below that in the nation in 1950, but the difference was much less pronounced than it had been thirty years earlier.

Chapter ii calls attention to the high degree of urban concentration of California's population and points out that in 1950 more than three-fifths of the total population of the state lived in either the Los Angeles or San Francisco–Oakland metropolitan areas. Since income levels not only tend to be relatively high in urban areas but tend, also, to vary with the size of the community,[9] this high degree of concentration in large metropolitan areas, which, of course, is in turn associated with the state's industrial structure, helps to explain the high level of per capita income.

---

[8] For changes in the age distribution of the population during the 'forties, see table A-11, Appendix.

[9] Cf., for example, H. E. Klarman, "A Statistical Study of Income Differences among Communities," *Studies in Income and Wealth*, Vol. VI (New York: National Bureau of Economic Research, 1943), pp. 206–226.

Urban incomes in California do not tend to exceed those in the nation as a whole by a very wide margin. The median income for urban families and unrelated individuals in California in 1949 was only 5 per cent higher than the corresponding median for the nation as a whole (see table 10).[10]

TABLE 10

MEDIAN INCOME OF FAMILIES AND UNRELATED INDIVIDUALS, URBAN AND
RURAL, CALIFORNIA AND UNITED STATES, 1949

Residence	Families and unrelated individuals	Families	Unrelated individuals
California			
Total..............................	3,021	3,585	1,279
Urban...........................	3,123	3,705	1,341
Rural nonfarm....................	2,480	3,125	1,095
Rural farm.......................	2,323	2,767	952
United States			
Total..............................	2,619	3,073	997
Urban...........................	2,970	3,431	1,150
Rural nonfarm....................	2,186	2,560	780
Rural farm.......................	1,567	1,729	591
Ratio of California to United States			
Total..............................	1.15	1.17	1.28
Urban...........................	1.05	1.08	1.17
Rural nonfarm....................	1.13	1.22	1.40
Rural farm.......................	1.48	1.60	1.61

SOURCE: *United States Census of Population: 1950*, Vol. II, Part 1, p. 104, and Part 5, p. 71.

The widest contrasts between state and nation are to be found in rural farm income. This is consistent with Johnson's findings with respect to regional income differences.[11] He has shown that, whereas there are wide regional differences in incomes of farm operators and farm laborers, the incomes of *white urban* families do not differ very much from region to region for *communities of comparable size.* Nonfarm Negro families in the South have rela-

[10] The fact that median income for families and unrelated individuals exceeded the corresponding national median by a smaller margin than that for either families or unrelated individuals alone is apparently explained by the higher proportion of unrelated individuals in California. (Incomes of unrelated individuals, though substantially higher in California than in the nation, were much lower in both state and nation than those of families.)

[11] Cf. D. Gale Johnson, "Some Effects of Region, Community, Size, Color, and Occupation on Family and Individual Income," *Studies in Income and Wealth*, Vol. XV (New York: National Bureau of Economic Research, 1952), pp. 51–66.

tively low incomes, by comparison with nonfarm white families in the South or with nonfarm Negro families elsewhere, and, of course, farm incomes in the South tend to be comparatively low.

Since urban family incomes tend to vary with the size of the community, it is interesting to inquire how incomes in California urban communities compare with those in communities of comparable size elsewhere. The only data which permit such a comparison are those based on the 1950 Census.[12] If we consider urban family incomes in Standard Metropolitan Areas grouped by size, we find that the San Francisco–Oakland metropolitan area ranked third and the Los Angeles area sixth in median 1949 family income among thirteen metropolitan areas with populations exceeding 1,000,000. Median family income in the Los Angeles area ($3,650) was only 1 per cent above the unweighted average ($3,613) of the medians for all thirteen areas, whereas that in the San Francisco–Oakland area ($3,935) was 9 per cent above the average.[13] San Diego ranked ninth in median family incomes among nineteen metropolitan areas with populations between 500,000 and 1,000,000, with median family income 3 per cent above the average of the medians for the nineteen areas. In the 250,000-500,000 size group, Sacramento, San Jose, Fresno, and San Bernardino ranked third, sixth, twenty-ninth, and thirty-first, respectively, with medians averaging 6 per cent higher than the unweighted average of the medians for the forty-four areas of this size. These comparisons indicate that urban family incomes in large California communities tend, for the most part, to be only slightly above average for metropolitan areas of comparable size, even when the comparison includes southern metropolitan areas, with their substantial proportions of low income nonwhite families. The San Francisco, Sacramento, and San Jose areas (all in the northern part of the state) stand out with relatively higher incomes than the Los Angeles, San Diego, Fresno, or San Bernardino areas, which are farther south.[14]

The contrasts in income differentials for urban and rural families between California and the nation are likewise reflected in similar contrasts between income differentials for workers in industry and agriculture. The 1950 Census data make possible, for the first time, a detailed comparison

---

[12] The 1940 Census provided data only on wage and salary income, whereas the 1935–1936 Consumer Purchases Survey included only a few California urban communities, mostly small.

[13] See *United States Census of Population: 1950*, Vol. II, Part 1, pp. 156–157.

[14] See the discussion on p. 79, below, in which reference is made to the greater proximity of Los Angeles to the South and to Mexico. This would be relevant for the other cities in the southern part of the state as well. Also worth mentioning is the fact that the metropolitan areas in the northern part of the state are more completely urbanized (include relatively less rural territory within their boundaries) than those in the southern part.

of incomes of persons in the experienced civilian labor force by occupation and industry.

They show that median incomes of both farmers and farm laborers in California exceeded those in the nation as a whole in 1949 by a very much higher percentage than did median incomes of other occupation groups (see table 11).[15] They show, also, that there was a broad tendency, par-

TABLE 11

MEDIAN INCOME IN 1949 OF THE EXPERIENCED CIVILIAN LABOR FORCE, BY MAJOR
OCCUPATION GROUP AND SEX, CALIFORNIA AND UNITED STATES

Major occupation group	Men			Women		
	California	United States	Ratio of California to U.S.	California	United States	Ratio of California to U.S.
Total......................	3,170	2,668	1.19	1,883	1,575	1.20
Professional, technical, and kindred workers..............	4,255	3,958	1.08	2,691	2,262	1.19
Farmers and farm managers.....	2,409	1,455	1.66	1,309	759	1.72
Managers, officials, and proprietors, exc. farm..............	4,237	3,944	1.07	2,243	2,122	1.06
Clerical and kindred workers....	3,202	3,010	1.06	2,286	2,042	1.12
Sales workers................	3,347	3,028	1.11	1,587	1,244	1.28
Craftsmen, foremen, and kindred workers.....................	3,455	3,125	1.11	2,205	1,999	1.10
Operatives and kindred workers..	3,060	2,607	1.17	1,505	1,541	0.98
Private household workers......	1,499	1,176	1.27	787	652	1.21
Service workers, exc. private household.................	2,506	2,195	1.14	1,362	1,054	1.29
Farm laborers and foremen.....	1,388	863	1.61	672	576	1.17
Laborers, except farm and mine..	2,369	1,961	1.21	1,568	1,425	1.10
Occupation not reported.......	1,683	1,572	1.07	978	853	1.15

SOURCE: *United States Census of Population: 1950,* Vol. II, Part 1, pp. 279–282, and Part 5, pp. 362–364. (Data based on 20 per cent sample.)

ticularly in the case of men, for income differentials between California and the nation in urban occupations to vary inversely with levels of occupational skill. Median incomes of male professional, managerial, and clerical workers, at the top of the occupational ladder, were only 6 to 8 per cent higher in state than in nation, whereas those of laborers and private household workers, at the bottom of the ladder, deviated by much wider margins from nation-wide medians. Even in numerical terms, incomes of relatively unskilled workers in California tended to exceed those in the nation by wider margins than incomes of the more highly trained and skilled workers. This is consistent with the general tendency for re-

---

[15] The ratio for farm laborers is somewhat reduced (to 1.49) if unpaid family workers (of which there are relatively few in California), are eliminated from the comparison. See the more detailed data in *ibid.*, Part 5, p. 363. The reader will observe, also, that the ratio for female farm laborers and foremen in table 11 is only 1.17.

gional income and wage differentials to vary most widely for the least skilled workers.[16] In a very broad sense, it can be said that migration has done more to equalize income differentials for workers at higher levels of skill or training than for the unskilled,[17] but this is far from a complete explanation of all the forces at work. Given the complex combination of factors tending to depress the incomes of unskilled workers in the southeastern part of the United States, it would probably require a considerably higher "propensity" to migrate on the part of unskilled workers than of other occupation groups to bring about the same degree of regional equalization of their incomes and wages.

It is interesting to observe that skill differentials are wider, at least for men, in the Los Angeles metropolitan area than in the San Francisco–Oakland area.[18] No attempt is made in this study to determine whether Los Angeles' greater proximity to the South and to Mexico, or its comparatively late unionization, or both, are responsible for this relationship.[19] In all probability, the late growth of unionization and the labor supply situation were interrelated.

On an industrial basis, California incomes in 1949 tended to be particularly high not only in agriculture,[20] but also in the other extractive industries and in entertainment and recreation services (see table 12). The comparatively high median income in mining reflects the dominant importance in the state of crude petroleum production, with its relatively high income level, whereas in the nation as a whole coal mining accounts for a large percentage of all workers employed in mining. The high median income in entertainment and recreation services in California, of course, reflects the high income level in motion-picture production.

In other industry groups, median-income differentials between California and the nation ranged from 1.06 to 1.25 for men and from 1.04 to

[16] Cf. W. S. Woytinsky and associates, *Employment and Wages in the United States* (New York: Twentieth Century Fund, 1953), p. 475; C. Glasser, *Wage Differentials: The Case of the Unskilled* (New York: Columbia University Press, 1940); and H. Ober and C. Glasser, "Regional Wage Differentials," *Monthly Labor Review*, LXIII (1946), 509–523.

[17] Cf. Woytinsky and associates, *loc. cit.*

[18] See *United States Census of Population: 1950*, Vol. II, Part 1, pp. 451–452 and 459–460.

[19] Also relevant is the inclusion within the Los Angeles metropolitan area of a substantially larger proportion of rural territory. (See footnote 14.) For a more complete analysis of wages in the Los Angeles area, but with particular reference to industrial differentials, rather than skill differentials, see F. C. Pierson, *Community Wage Patterns* (Berkeley: University of California Press, 1953).

[20] In agriculture alone, the median income of male workers in the state was 38.5 per cent above the national level. This was a considerably smaller differential than prevailed for either farmers or farm laborers, when classified occupationally. The explanation of this apparently inconsistent relationship lies in the fact that farm laborers, with their lower incomes, represent a substantially larger percentage of all agricultural workers in California than in the nation.

1.37 for women. There appeared to be some tendency for income differentials to be relatively high in those industry groups which served the local market (for example, construction and trade) and lower in industry groups whose products or services were partly sold on a regional or national market (for example, manufacturing, transportation, communication, insurance).[21] Other factors, such as, for example, the relative strength of unionism in wholesale and retail trade in the state, probably played a role in explaining the variations.

TABLE 12

MEDIAN INCOME IN 1949 OF THE EXPERIENCED CIVILIAN LABOR FORCE, BY MAJOR INDUSTRY GROUP AND SEX, CALIFORNIA AND UNITED STATES

Major industry group	Men			Women		
	California	United States	Ratio of California to U.S.	California	United States	Ratio of California to U.S.
Total......................	3,170	2,668	1.19	1,883	1,575	1.20
Agriculture, forestry, and fisheries	1,783	1,260	1.42	770	430	1.79
Mining.....................	3,812	2,691	1.42	2,919	2,357	1.24
Construction................	3,125	2,510	1.25	2,382	2,037	1.17
Manufacturing...............	3,338	3,108	1.07	1,928	1,784	1.08
Durable goods............	3,279	2,978	1.10	2,198	2,026	1.08
Nondurable goods..........	3,464	2,949	1.17	1,738	1,676	1.04
Transportation, communication, and other public utilities......	3,405	3,108	1.10	2,526	2,222	1.14
Wholesale and retail trade......	3,212	2,752	1.17	1,653	1,378	1.20
Finance, insurance, and real estate......................	3,585	3,371	1.06	2,144	1,901	1.13
Business and repair services.....	3,130	2,662	1.18	2,060	1,912	1.08
Personal services.............	2,293	2,055	1.12	1,078	786	1.37
Entertainment and recreation services...................	3,387	2,338	1.45	1,739	1,279	1.36
Professional and related services.	3,400	3,009	1.13	2,299	1,892	1.22
Public administration..........	3,509	3,221	1.09	2,592	2,425	1.07
Industry not reported.........	1,686	1,456	1.16	1,022	897	1.14

SOURCE: *United States Census of Population: 1950*, Vol. II, Part 1, pp. 294–296, and Part 5, pp. 447–448.

It would be extremely interesting to determine to what extent these variations in income differentials between state and nation in 1949 prevailed in earlier decades, but historical data on income by industry or occupation are extremely scanty. There are some estimates of total annual income by industry division for states, but it is not easy to relate such estimates to the appropriate number of income receivers, particularly in agri-

[21] Pierson reached a somewhat analogous conclusion in his study of wage rates in Los Angeles manufacturing industries. He found that there was some tendency for wage differentials between Los Angeles and the nation to be comparatively high in industries serving the local market and low in industries serving regional or national markets, with industries serving both types of markets occupying an intermediate position. (*Ibid.*, pp. 91–92 and 161.)

culture, where seasonal variations in employment play such an important role.

In table 13 we have brought together some scattered historical data on per capita gross or net income differentials between California and the nation in selected industry groups. In spite of the weaknesses of the data, the general picture that emerges is consistent and fairly clear. The wider income

TABLE 13

RATIOS OF ANNUAL GROSS OR NET INCOME PER WORKER IN CALIFORNIA TO THAT IN THE UNITED STATES, SELECTED INDUSTRY GROUPS, 1899–1950

Major industry group and description of series	1899 or 1902	1909 or 1910	1919 or 1920	1929 or 1930	1939 or 1940	1949 or 1950
Farm and nonfarm population[a]						
Per capita income						
Farm population	.....	.....	3.57	4.56	.....	.....
Nonfarm population	.....	.....	1.20	1.17	.....	.....
Agriculture						
Value of farm products[b] per worker[c]	2.17	2.46	2.43	2.37	2.35	1.92
Agricultural income[d] per worker[c]	.....	.....	.....	2.57	2.10	1.83
Mining						
Value of mineral products per worker[e]	1.51	2.08	2.53	.....	2.55	.....
Production income[f] per worker[c]	.....	.....	.....	1.31	.....	.....
Construction						
Production income[f] per worker[c]	.....	.....	.....	1.24	.....	.....
Manufacturing						
Value added by manufacture per worker[g]	1.14	1.32	1.06	1.21	1.22	1.14
Transportation, communication, and other public utilities						
Production income[f] per worker[c]	.....	.....	.....	1.11	.....	.....
Trade and service						
Income[d] per worker[c]	.....	.....	.....	1.19	1.23	1.14

SOURCES: [a]M. Leven, *Income in the Various States* (New York: National Bureau of Economic Research, 1925), pp. 262–263 (for 1920 data), and M. Leven and others, *America's Capacity to Consume* (Washington: The Brookings Institution, 1934), p. 173 (for 1929 data);[b] U. S. Bureau of Agricultural Economics, *The Farm Income Situation* (monthly) and California State Chamber of Commerce; [c]Tables A-13 and A-14; [d]J. A. Slaughter, *Income Received in the Various States: 1929–1935* (New York: National Industrial Conference Board, 1937), p. 43 (for 1930 data) and U.S. Department of Commerce, *Survey of Current Business*, August issues (for 1940 and 1950 data); [e]U. S. Bureau of the Census, *Special Reports, Mines and Quarries: 1902* (Washington, 1905), pp. 36 and 177, and *Sixteenth Census of the United States: 1940, Mineral Industries: 1939*, Vol. I, p. 28, and Vol. II, p. 25; Slaughter, *op. cit.*; and U. S. Bureau of the Census, *Census of Manufactures* (for 1899 to 1939 data) and *Annual Survey of Manufactures: 1949 and 1950* (for 1949 data).

differentials in agriculture have apparently prevailed throughout the present century, and probably earlier. Per capita income differences between California and the nation have been considerably lower in manufacturing and, so far as we can judge from scanty data, in other broad industry groups as well.

In all the industry groups for which we have data, the per capita income differential between California and the nation narrowed during the decade of the 'forties. Caution must be exercised, however, in inferring that this development is indicative of a long-run trend toward a decline in the income-producing capacity per worker in California industry in *relation* to that of the nation. In agriculture, the increase in income per worker during the 'forties was most pronounced in the cattle-raising states and in the grain belt, reflecting the sharp rise in demand for agricultural staples. A movement in the reverse direction is not unlikely in the 'fifties, even if price supports are quite extensively used to prevent a serious decline in the prices of these staples.

Except for agriculture, increases in income per worker in the various industry groups tended to be most pronounced in the regions which had the lowest per capita incomes in 1940. Here again is a development that may conceivably be partly reversed in the 'fifties or 'sixties. In manufacturing, the only industry for which there are data going back before World War I, a similar narrowing of regional differentials in value added by manufacturing occurred in the World War I decade, only to be partly reversed in the 'twenties (see fig. 4). There appears to be little doubt, however, that the long-run trend is in the direction of a decline in regional differences in value added per worker.

Since regional differences in per capita income are so much wider in agriculture than in other industry groups, the long-run decline in the relative importance of agriculture as a source of income and employment has undoubtedly been an important factor in such narrowing of regional income differentials as has occurred, and will continue to exert its influence in this direction in the future. As agriculture declines in relative importance, moreover, the variability of agricultural income should tend to give rise to fewer fluctuations in the pattern of regional income differentials. So far as income differences between California and the nation are concerned, moreover, employment in such comparatively high income industries as mining and entertainment and recreation services is also losing ground as a percentage of total employment.

On the whole, then, it would appear that the long-run trend is probably n the direction of a narrowing of regional income differentials, and, as part of this pattern, toward a narrowing of the differential between California and the nation. But this does not mean that the ratio of California per capita income to that in the nation will necessarily decline as much in the 'fifties as it did in the 'forties. In fact, it is quite possible that a temporary reversal of the downward trend might occur.

WAGE DIFFERENTIALS

The conclusions which may be drawn from an analysis of long-run trends in wage differentials between California and the nation are, in many respects, similar to those bearing on income differentials; they will be discussed only very briefly. The story can be carried back a good deal further in the case of wages, even though the data are somewhat spotty.

The pattern of wage differentials by industry division between California and the nation is, on the whole, very similar to the pattern of income differentials (see table 14). Wage differentials in 1950 were highest in agriculture and tended to vary from 1.10 to 1.20 in most other industries, with the variations showing at least rough resemblances to the variations in income differentials. The fact that the wage data apply, in some instances, to more refined classifications accounts for some apparent differences in pattern. Wage differentials in mining, for example, appear much smaller than would have been anticipated on the basis of the 1.42 income differential for men engaged in mining (see table 12), but it will be recalled that it was primarily the difference in "industry-mix" (as between petroleum and coal production) that accounted for the unusually high income level in California mining.

The historical data in table 14, spotty as they are, indicate that very much the same patterns of wage differentials have prevailed since 1870 but that wage differentials between state and nation in all industries and occupations have tended to narrow substantially in the eighty-year period. Most of the narrowing appears to have occurred, however, before the end of World War I.[22] Since then, changes have been much more moderate and do not necessarily appear to be indicative of a decisive long-run trend.

There was apparently some slight tendency for wage differentials between California and the nation in agriculture and manufacturing to widen between 1919 and 1939 and to narrow again in the 1940's.[23] On the other hand, union hourly wage rates in the building trades in the two leading California cities actually fell substantially below an average of corresponding rates in selected cities in other parts of the nation in the 'twenties, rising somewhat thereafter.

[22] Cf. J. W. Block, "Regional Wage Differentials: 1907–46," *Monthly Labor Review*, LXVI (1948), p. 371.

[23] The data in table 14 on annual average earnings in manufacturing (computed from Census of Manufactures data on average annual employment and total annual wages) are not entirely satisfactory as a basis for measuring wage differentials, since they may reflect differences between state and nation in the amount of time the average worker was employed in a census year, as well as differences in wage rates. Ratios computed from these data, however, agree very closely with ratios computed from average hourly earnings data for those years for which both sets of data are available.

The rather close correspondence between decade-to-decade changes in ratios computed from value added per manufacturing employee (table 13)

TABLE 14

RATIOS OF AVERAGE EARNINGS OR WAGE RATES IN CALIFORNIA TO THOSE IN
UNITED STATES, SELECTED OCCUPATIONS AND INDUSTRIES, 1869 TO 1950

Description of series	1869 or 1870	1898 or 1899	1909 or 1910	1919 or 1920	1929 or 1930	1939 or 1940	1949 or 1950
Agriculture							
Monthly farm wage rate[a]							
With board	2.88	1.84	1.54	1.67	1.55	1.69	1.43*
Without board	2.99	1.85	1.68	1.70	1.76	1.94	.....
Mining							
Average hourly earnings[b]							
Metal mining	.....	.....	.....	.....	.....	0.98	0.97
Crude petroleum and natural gas production	.....	.....	.....	.....	.....	1.14	1.04
Nonmetallic mining and quarrying	.....	.....	.....	.....	.....	1.24	1.30
Building trades or construction							
Average daily wage rate[c]							
4 skilled building trades	1.35	1.21	.....	.....	.....	.....	.....
Hod carriers	1.67	1.60	.....	.....	.....	.....	.....
Union hourly wage rates in large cities							
5 skilled building trades	.....	.....	1.17	1.07	0.87	0.94	1.03
Average hourly earnings[b]							
Contract construction	.....	.....	.....	.....	.....	.....	1.12
Manufacturing							
Annual earnings per production worker[d]	1.71	1.23	1.43	1.09	1.12	1.15	1.09
Average hourly earnings[b]	.....	.....	.....	.....	.....	1.13	1.12
Transportation							
Average hourly earnings[b]							
Local railways and buses	.....	.....	.....	.....	.....	0.97	1.07
Trade							
Average hourly earnings[b]							
Wholesale trade	.....	.....	.....	.....	.....	1.12	1.11
Retail trade	.....	.....	.....	.....	.....	1.14	1.20
Service							
Average hourly earnings[b]							
Hotels and other lodging places	.....	.....	.....	.....	.....	1.26	1.27

SOURCES: [a]U.S. Bureau of Agricultural Economics, *Crops and Markets* (May, 1942), *Farm Wage Rates by States, Revised: 1910–1948* (1951), and *Farm Labor* (monthly); [b]California, Department of Industrial Relations, *Handbook of California Labor Statistics: 1951–1952* (San Francisco, 1953) and earlier publications, and, for U.S. figures, U.S. Bureau of Labor Statistics, *Handbook of Labor Statistics: 1950 Edition* (Washington, 1951) and earlier editions; [c]U.S. Bureau of Labor Statistics, *History of Wages in the United States from Colonial Times to 1928* (Washington, 1934); and [d]Computed from data on annual wage payments and average annual employment of production workers in U.S. Bureau of the Census, *Census of Manufactures* (selected years) and *Annual Survey of Manufactures: 1949 and 1950* (Washington, 1952).
*With board *and room.*

and average annual earnings per manufacturing production worker (table 14) is significant. In his study of wages in manufacturing in the Los Angeles area, Pierson found that variations in wage rates by industry division appeared to be more closely associated with differences in value added per worker than with any other variable.[24] A detailed analysis of historical changes would probably show that the long-run decline from 1869 to 1919 in the differential between state and nation in both value added per worker and average annual earnings in manufacturing reflected at least to some extent changes in "industry-mix," particularly the decline in the relative importance of the lumber industry, in which California earnings and value added per worker have been particularly high, and the rise in relative importance of, for example, metal and metal products industries, in which differentials in earnings and in value added per worker between state and nation have been much less marked.

If changes in wage differentials between California and the nation from 1940 to 1950 are considered for all industry groups for which there are any data, it is found that the changes were almost evenly distributed between upward and downward movements in the ratios. In the industry groups for which information begins only with 1940, there is no way of knowing whether or not these changes reflected longer-run trends.

CONCLUSIONS

The decline in the per capita income differential between California and the nation in the three decades from the end of World War I to 1949 did not appear to reflect, to any appreciable extent if at all, a decline in the ratio of average income per worker, industry group for industry group, in California relative to that in the nation. Rather, it reflected chiefly (1) the virtual disappearance during this period of the pronounced relative underrepresentation of children in the state's population compared with that of the nation, and (2) the decline in the relative importance of the extractive industries in the economies of both state and nation.

During the same period, there was very little change in wage differentials, so far as can be judged from spotty data, between state and nation, except in agriculture, in which the wage differential was relatively high at the end of World War I. The long-run decline in wage differentials which characterized the decades before the 1920's does not show up clearly in the data for the last three decades. There were divergent movements in individual industry groups in the intervening decades, but it is not clear that there was an appreciable net change between 1919 and 1949, although a more detailed study might lead to a different conclusion.

This is somewhat surprising, in view of the widely held theory that interregional migration is likely to be accompanied by a steady decline in

---

[24] *Op. cit.*, p. 162.

interregional income and wage differences. But, as the data examined in
the present chapter indicates, this process does not necessarily take place
steadily and smoothly. The equalization of income and wage differences,
both occupational and regional, tends to be accelerated in periods of tight
labor markets, such as World War I and World War II, to be slowed down
in periods of moderate labor surplus, and perhaps to be reversed in an acute
depression. Pronounced fluctuations in farm income also may complicate
the picture.

In addition, though relative income and wage levels in a given region
are likely to be affected by a change in its ratio of population to resources,
relative to those of other regions, it must be recognized that new and un-
foreseen events may modify the potential value of the resources of a given
region relative to those of other regions. Technological developments or
new discoveries, for example, of mineral deposits, may require a reappraisal
of the region's resources. In subsequent chapters, there will be occasion to
refer to the key roles played by oil discoveries and by the growth of aircraft production in the industrial development of California. In both these
cases, a reëvaluation of the state's potential resources was in order—in the
petroleum case, for obvious reasons, and, in the aircraft case, because it
was found that California's climate had specific industrial advantages
which could not have been recognized earlier. Similarly, of course, the location of defense industries in areas regarded as comparatively "safe" from
the point of view of potential bombing raids by an enemy may, if carried
far enough, result in the need for a complete reappraisal of the regional
distribution of resources. "Safety of location" will become a valuable re-
source and will have to be recognized as such.

In the light of these considerations, it is clear that no one can foresee what
is likely to happen to income and wage differences between California
and the nation over the course of the next several decades. The trend
toward equalization of income and wage differentials might well be affected
by unpredictable developments which would favor industrial location in
other areas or encourage the location of industry in California. In the
absence of decisive new developments of this character, long-run tendencies
may result in some decline in income and wage differentials in the next
several decades—interrupted, probably, by short-run fluctuations.

VI. MIGRATION WAVES AND ECONOMIC FLUCTUATIONS

THUS FAR attention has been concentrated on long-run trends in California's population growth and employment expansion, but the most striking fact about the state's population growth is that it has not taken place at an even rate but in a series of long and very pronounced waves (see fig. 5). In view of the fact that migration has been the major component of California's population growth, it seems reasonable to suppose that fluctuations in the volume of net in-migration have been primarily responsible for these variations in the rate of growth. This was clearly true from 1920 to 1940, a period for which reasonably satisfactory estimates of annual net in-migration can be arrived at by deducting the excess of births over deaths (natural increase) in the state from the estimated annual change in population (see fig. 6). For years before 1920, vital statistics were not sufficiently complete to permit this type of estimate, and for the years from 1940 on, movements into and out of the Armed Forces complicate the picture and make it difficult to arrive at annual estimates of net civilian in-migration. According to estimates prepared by the Census Bureau, net civilian in-migration during the 'forties was as follows:[1]

Time Period		Net civilian in-migration	
		Total	Average annual
April 1, 1940 to July 1, 1942		554,000	246,000
July 1, 1942 to July 1, 1945		1,468,000	489,000
July 1, 1945 to April 1, 1950		567,000	119,000

Thus, net civilian in-migration evidently reached a peak annual rate during the war years and dropped off substantially during the postwar period.

Population growth through natural increase has also fluctuated widely since 1920, but throughout most of the period for which there are data, natural increase was so much smaller than net in-migration that it did not contribute to any great extent to the fluctuations in total population growth. Even in more recent years, when natural increase has tended to be much closer to net in-migration than formerly, the annual *fluctuations* in total population growth have been largely attributable to variations in net in-migration. Thus, in determining what factors have been responsible for the variations in the rate of growth of population and the labor force, attention must be directed chiefly to changes in the rate of net in-migration.

---

[1] U.S. Bureau of the Census, *Current Population Reports* Series P-25 No. 72 (May, 1953).

At first glance, there is a temptation to conclude that these changes have corresponded with cyclical fluctuations in economic activity,[2] but a careful

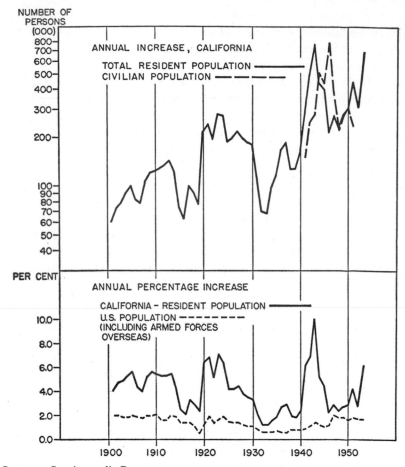

SOURCES: See Appendix B.

Fig. 5. Estimated annual population growth of California and annual percentage growth of California and the United States, 1901–1953.

All estimates are as of July first of each year; the estimates for 1953 are provisional.

[2] Since numerous indices of business activity are readily available, a chart showing cyclical fluctuations in business activity has not been included. The Cleveland Trust Company publishes a monthly index which has been widely reproduced. For detailed information on turning points in business activity through 1938, see G. H. Moore, *Statistical Indicators of Cyclical Revivals and Recessions*, National Bureau of Economic Research, Occasional Paper 31 (New York, 1950), p. 6. A table indicating the turning points as established by the National Bureau of Economic Research through 1949, as well as other useful information on indices of various types, may be found in R. A. Gordon, *Business Fluctuations* (New York: Harper, 1952), chapters viii and ix.

study of the data in figures 5 and 6 suggests that this generalization is not altogether accurate. Although there has apparently been some tendency

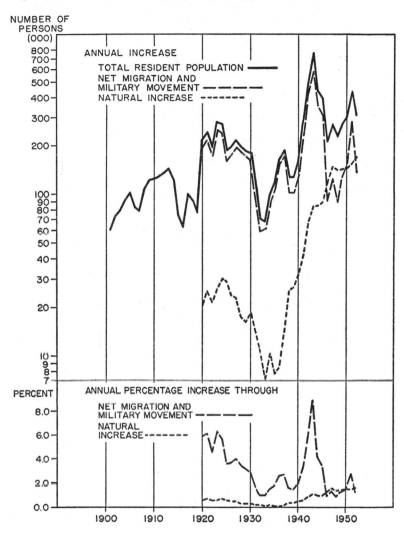

SOURCES: See Appendix B.

Fig. 6. Estimated annual increase in population of California, 1901–1952, and com ponents of growth, 1920–1952.

for net in-migration to rise in periods of cyclical upswing and to decline in periods of cyclical downswing, the major variations have been of con- siderably longer duration than the ordinary business cycle (some fifteen to twenty years in length), and in certain periods (for example, the late 'twenties and late 'forties) the direction of change has not precisely corresponded with cyclical movements. In fact, the interesting aspect of developments in the late 'twenties and late 'forties is that net in-migration tended to decline while a period of economic expansion was still under way.[3]

Three major waves in population growth are discernible in figure 5, but the upswing of the first wave probably began before 1900, and it is not clear as yet whether the upswing from 1948 to 1953 represents the beginning of a new wave or merely a temporary spurt in in-migration associated with the Korean War.[4] There is evidence that somewhat similar long waves in migration characterized the latter part of the nineteenth century, with peaks occurring at the time of the Gold Rush, in the early 'seventies, and in the late 'eighties. The school enrollment data which are available from the late 'fifties on probably give some rough indication of the contours of these waves (see fig. 13).[5]

For convenience, those long and pronounced waves in net migration to California may be termed "migration waves." The remainder of the present

---

[3] V. B. Stanbery has pointed out that a similar tendency prevailed with respect to migration into Oregon in the late 'twenties. See his *A Study of Migration into Oregon, 1930–1937* (mimeographed report, Oregon State Planning Board, Salem, 1938). See, also, further comments by the same author in "Population Trends and Outlook for the West," *Proceedings*, Western Farm Economics Association (1944), pp. 17–18.

[4] The annual population estimates for California presented in figures 5 and 6 are the revised census estimates as published in U.S. Bureau of the Census, *Current Population Reports*, Series P-25, No. 72 (May, 1953). The earlier provisional estimates, published in Report No. 47 of the same series, had indicated somewhat larger population growth in 1944 to 1946, followed by a marked decline to a trough in 1948–1949, with net out-migration implicit in the estimate for the latter year. (Since all estimates are as of July 1, the difference between the annual estimates for 1949 and 1950, for example, represents population growth between July 1, 1949 and July 1, 1950.) Provisional estimates prepared by Dr. Carl Frisen of the California Department of Finance also showed somewhat larger population growth in 1945–1946, followed by a decline to a trough of 204,-000 (net annual increment) in 1949–1950, which would have implied net in-migration of about 60,000 in the latter year. See California Department of Finance, *Provisional Annual Estimates of the Population of the State of California, 1940–1953* (Sacramento, 1951), and *Estimated Population of California: 1950–1953* (Sacramento, 1953). The revised census estimate for 1949 represents an average of estimates obtained by the "migration-and-natural-increase method II" (as normally employed by the Census Bureau) and a method employing age-specific death rates (employed by the California Department of Finance).

[5] School enrollment data provide one of the most valuable basic sources of information utilized by the Bureau of the Census and other agencies in preparing current population estimates. Their usefulness depends in large part, however, on the fact that a very high percentage of children between the ages of six and seventeen are enrolled in school. The proportion of children attending school in the nineteenth century was much lower and was subject to a pronounced upward trend during the course of the century, with the result that the methods currently being used in estimating total population from school enrollment data are much more difficult to apply for this earlier period. Furthermore, there is a serious question as to how accurate these data are.

chapter will be devoted to an attempt to determine the nature of the relationship, if any, between these migration waves and fluctuations in economic and labor market conditions in the state. As a preliminary step, to help focus the analysis, a hypothesis will be stated which might reasonably be expected to offer an explanation of the relationships between fluctuations in population growth and in economic activity.

Although migration to California has tended to increase after every depression the most marked spurts in in-migration cannot be interpreted merely as a response to improving economic conditions. The periods of heaviest in-migration have been associated with periods of unusually rapid economic development, when the rate of economic expansion of the state has exceeded that of the nation. Such periods have tended to coincide, moreover, with periods of rapid expansion of economic activity in the nation as a whole. The more pronounced rate of expansion in California has been in large part explained by the relatively favorable investment opportunities which might be expected to exist in an area in a *comparatively* immature stage of economic development. As job opportunities expanded in such periods, the rate of in-migration sharply increased. The influx of migrants accelerated the increase in demand for consumers' goods and services. A pent-up demand for housing and nonresidential construction, as well as the influx of newcomers, stimulated a building boom, which contributed to the upswing in business activity.

After a time, which has varied in length according to the special circumstances prevailing in each period, the increase in the rate of in-migration has begun to outrun the rate of expansion of employment opportunities. As this occurred, job opportunities became somewhat less favorable, and the rate of net in-migration slowed down. Some of the in-migrants became discouraged and left the state, and those who remained found increasing difficulty in obtaining jobs. Meanwhile the improvement in employment opportunities which was occurring elsewhere in the nation tended to make it more attractive for potential migrants to remain where they were. (This may well account for the fact that, at least in the late 'twenties and late 'forties, the flow of net migration to California tended to decline while a nation-wide upswing in business activity was still under way.) If these developments were eventually followed by a sharp nation-wide downturn in business activity (as in 1929), the flow of migration to California fell off sharply and did not recover until there were clear signs of improvement in economic conditions in the state.

By implication, this hypothesis expresses a causal sequence, running from: (1) an initial improvement in economic conditions, to (2) the exploitation of unusually favorable investment opportunities in California, to (3) a relatively rapid increase in employment opportunities in the state, to (4) an acceleration in the rate of net in-migration, to (5) increased demand for consumers' goods and services, particularly housing, to (6) a turning point when the increase in the rate of net in-migration begins to outrun the expansion of employment opportunities. The remainder of this chapter will be devoted to an attempt to determine to what extent such a hypothesis is supported by the available statistical data.

WAVES IN THE EXPANSION OF ECONOMIC ACTIVITY

In order to identify the periods in which economic activity in California has expanded (or contracted) more (or less) rapidly than in the nation as a whole, we shall turn first, for recent decades, to the income estimates available for both California and the country as a whole. Changes in California's *share* of total income in the nation may be interpreted as providing some indication as to relative rates of change in economic activity in the two areas.[6] For the period before 1919, the share of the two leading California cities in bank clearings in principal cities "outside New York" has been computed as a rough measure of the rate of change in economic activity in California as compared with the nation.[7] If the conclusions drawn from a study of these general economic series prove to be consistent with other evidence based on an analysis of more specialized series, it may be inferred that identification of periods of relatively rapid (or slow) economic expansion or contraction is reasonably accurate.

A study of the income and clearings data (see figs. 7 and 8) suggests that there have been, since 1888, four periods when economic activity was rising more rapidly in California than in the nation. The first three of these periods may be dated as lasting (approximately) from 1899 to 1913, from 1918 to 1930, and from 1935 to 1944. The fourth lasted from 1948 to at least 1952, and perhaps to 1953 or even later, but there is no reliable basis, as yet, for identifying its peak. Both the clearings data for the first period and the income data for the second period suggest a decided tapering off in the rate of relative expansion from 1907 to 1913 and from 1923 to 1930.

The reader will recognize that these periods of relatively rapid economic expansion tended, on the whole, to coincide with periods of upswing in the rate of population growth. It may be argued, of course, that California's share of clearings or income would have been *expected* to rise in periods when her share of the nation's population was rising rapidly, merely as a reflection of the fact that her share of the nation's income-earners was rising during such periods. The important point, however, is that in these periods of relatively rapid economic growth, the state's share of clearings or income was rising *more* rapidly than her share of the population, whereas in other periods California's share of clearings or income was either declining or remaining constant even though her share of the population was slowly ris-

---

[6] By computing California's *share* of total national income, an implicit adjustment is made for the effects of price changes, and a measure (albeit somewhat crude) of California's share in terms of *constant* dollars is achieved. This follows from the fact that both the California and the national income estimates are affected in *approximately* the same way by price changes.

[7] Again, the computation of California's *share* has the effect of adjusting (roughly) for the effects of price changes.

ing.[8] This is equivalent to saying that the ratio of per capita income in California to that in the nation rose in the periods of comparatively rapid

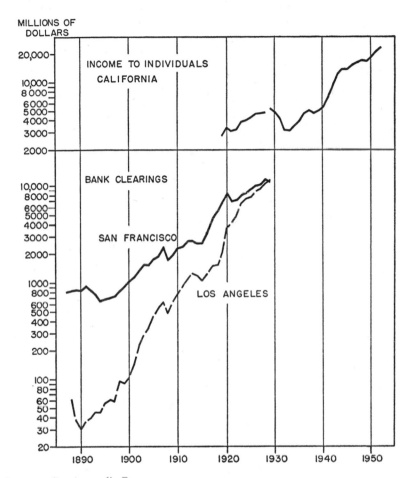

SOURCES: See Appendix B.

Fig. 7. Growth of the California economy: selected series. I.

growth and declined or remained constant in other periods. Actually, as figure 8 indicates, although there was an increase in this ratio between the beginning and end of each of the two long periods of comparative expan-

---

[8] California's share of the total population rose in every year from 1900–1901 on, that is, over the entire period for which there are annual estimates. In certain years, however, the increase was so small that it becomes apparent only if the computations are carried to hundredths of a per cent.

sion from 1919 on,[9] the moderate increase during the period as a whole reflected the net result of a rapid rise in the early part of each period (1919–
1922 and 1935–1938), followed by a declining tendency in the remainder

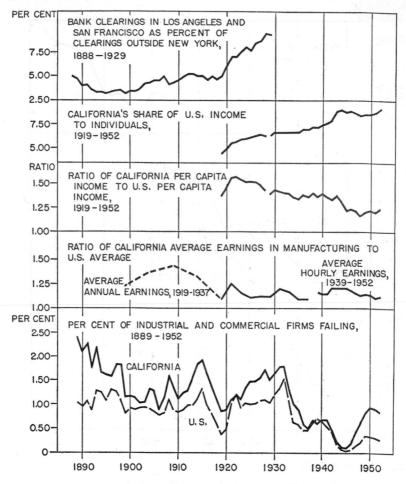

SOURCES: See Appendix B.

Fig. 8. Growth of the California economy: selected series. II.

of the expansion period (1922–1930 and 1938–1944). This suggests that
the stimulus to rapid growth may be traced to developments in the early
part of each of these periods. Similarly, although there was an increase in
the per capita clearings ratio between 1901 and 1919, this reflected the net

[9] Although there is evidence that the period of relatively rapid expansion should be
dated from 1918 on, no income estimates are available before 1919.

result of a rapid rise in the ratio from 1901 to 1907, followed by a declining tendency from 1907 to 1919.[10]

In interpreting these findings, the long-run downward tendency in the ratio of California per capita income to national per capita income, analyzed in chapter v, must be remembered. Apparently in the periods when this ratio was rising, the influence of the forces contributing to a long-run decline was offset by more powerful forces contributing to an increase.

Clearly, the evidence provided by income and clearings data needs to be supplemented by other types of evidence if definite conclusions are to be drawn about the relationship between migration waves and fluctuations in economic activity. One statistical indicator which is useful for this purpose, since it is available over a long period, is the industrial and commercial failure rate (see fig. 8).

It is interesting that, throughout most of the period covered by the chart, the percentage of industrial and commercial firms failing tended to be higher in California than in the nation, as is doubtless to be expected in the case of a comparatively immature and rapidly growing area.[11] The difference was particularly marked in 1889, the first year for which we present data, and tended, on the whole, to narrow throughout the ensuing decade. In all probability, this is to be explained largely by the fact that in 1889 California business was suffering from the shock of the crisis of 1888, which resulted largely from overspeculation in real estate in southern California.[12]

By 1899, the failure rate was down to a relatively low point in both state and nation, and for the next twenty years, fluctuations in the two series were similar. It is interesting that in neither state nor nation did the failure rate rise to as high a point following the crisis of 1907 as it did in 1915, although other measures of nation-wide business activity suggest that the recession of 1907–1908 was at least as severe as that of 1913–1915. Further-

---

[10] No attempt has been made to show the per capita clearings ratio in figure 8, partly because it is impossible to compute it precisely. Clearings data for California relate to the cities of San Francisco and Los Angeles, but, since these two cities are the leading financial centers of the state, it can be argued that fluctuations in their bank clearings tend to reflect changes in economic activity in the state as a whole. For this reason, the statement in the text is based on a study of changes in the ratio of "San Francisco plus Los Angeles clearings per California resident" to "clearings in principal cities outside New York per resident of the United States."

[11] Between 1889 and 1951, the total number of business concerns (as compiled by Dun and Bradstreet's) in California increased from 29,531 to 189,322, or 541 per cent, whereas the total number in the nation increased from 1,051,000 (in round numbers) to 2,608,000, or approximately 148 per cent.

[12] For an interesting account of this episode, which was associated with a heavy influx of migrants to the Los Angeles area during the period of cutthroat competition in transcontinental railway passenger rates, see G. S. Dumke, *The Boom of the Eighties in Southern California* (San Marino: Huntington Library, 1944).

more, the failure rate data seem to describe a long cycle from the late 'eighties to 1915 for California and from 1896 to 1915 for the United States.

The fluctuations in the series for state and nation show some interesting contrasts during the 1920's. The United States failure rate rose more sharply than did the California rate in the depression of 1921–1922 but then dropped back and showed only a very moderate and gradual rise between 1923 and 1929. The California rate seems to have been less markedly affected by the 1921–1922 recession, but to have displayed a distinctly rising tendency throughout the entire period from 1919 to 1932. Indeed, on the basis of this particular California series, the Great Depression appears less as a sudden, disastrous collapse than as a culmination of an unstable business situation which was developing in the state throughout the 'twenties.

From 1932 to 1943, the California failure rate deviated very little from the national failure rate and showed quite similar fluctuations. The California rate did not decline quite as sharply in 1944 and 1945, however, and rose to a considerably higher point between 1945 and 1950, continuing to rise in the latter year after the nation-wide rate had turned downward again (though, of course, failure rates were very low in both areas throughout the 'forties). In these developments there is evidence, as in certain of the other statistical series which will be examined, of somewhat more serious stresses and strains concealed beneath the broad picture of postwar prosperity in California than were to be found in the nation as a whole.

In the entire period covered by the data, there is shown somewhat more clearly in the California series than in that for the United States, evidence of three long and rather pronounced cycles in failure rates. For California, these long cycles would be dated from about 1889 to 1915, from 1915 to 1932, and from 1932 to 1950. With minor variations these cycles appear to represent inverted models of the migration cycles which show up in our population data. It is not known, of course, how annual population data would look for the 'eighties and 'nineties, but a guess may be hazarded that a low point in net in-migration was reached sometime during the early 'nineties.

The behavior of wage differentials between California and the nation is also of great interest for this study. There is some evidence that these wage differentials have tended to widen during the relatively early stages of periods of rapidly rising in-migration and to level off or decline in the later stages of such periods. Although this evidence will not be examined in detail in the present study,[13] it may be found in the behavior of other

---

[13] It would require a great deal of statistical work, not directly related to the main purpose of this study, to convert the available historical wage data into usable form.

wage and earnings series, as well as in the data on average earnings in manufacturing which are presented in figure 8.[14] The rise in the differential in manufacturing earnings in 1929–1931, which reflected a less sharp decline in California than in the nation in the early stages of the depression, occurred, of course, in a period of declining net in-migration and appears to be inconsistent with the main hypothesis. The rise in 1919–1921 likewise may have been attributable chiefly to a tendency for factory earnings in California to drop less sharply in a recession. But the increase in earnings differentials in manufacturing between 1899 and 1909 and from the late 'thirties to 1942 appears to be consistent with the general hypothesis.

A tendency for wage differentials to rise in the *relatively* early stages of an upswing in in-migration would suggest that in such periods employment opportunities were rising more rapidly in California than in the country as a whole and that the rise in net in-migration had failed to keep pace with the expansion of job opportunities. A reverse movement of wage differentials in the later stages of a period of upswing in in-migration would suggest an easing of labor market conditions in California, *relative* to those in the nation. Much more direct evidence on this point would be provided, of course, by continuous data on unemployment, if they were available. The next chapter will analyze such sporadic unemployment data as can be assembled. The remainder of the present chapter will be devoted to an attempt to identify the industrial developments which accounted for the acceleration or retardation of California's rate of economic expansion, relative to that in the nation, in particular periods.

CHANGES IN THE RATE OF GROWTH IN PARTICULAR INDUSTRIES

In attempting to indentify the particular economic developments which appeared to account for alternating periods of acceleration or retardation in the expansion of economic activity in California, relative to that in the nation, attention is directed first to the period from the late 'nineties to 1913.

---

[14] It should be stated that the data on average annual earnings in manufacturing, which are based on *Census of Manufactures* data, are not very satisfactory as a measure of changes in wage rates, since they reflect fluctuations from year to year in the length of time the average worker is employed as well as other types of variations (for example, changes in the relative importance of the various industrial subdivisions within manufacturing). For purposes of comparisons between California and the United States, however, these objections are relatively less important than they otherwise would be, since both the California and U.S. data would be likely to be affected in much the same way by, for example, variations in the total time employed per worker.

For a detailed and interesting analysis of wage changes in California during World War II and immediately thereafter, see N. B. Belloc, *Wages in California* (Berkeley: University of California Press, 1948).

It will be recalled that the bank clearings data examined earlier in the chapter suggested that California's rate of growth, compared with that in the country as a whole, began to rise in 1899 and increased quite sharply from 1901 to 1907. As nearly as can be determined, on the basis of an examination of a substantial number of statistical series, this spurt in California's rate of economic growth was attributable chiefly to the following developments:

TABLE 15

GROWTH OF CALIFORNIA CRUDE PETROLEUM PRODUCTION,
SELECTED YEARS, 1880–1950

Year	Production			Year	Production		
	Thousands of barrels	Percentage of U.S. physical output	Thousands of dollars		Thousands of barrels	Percentage of U.S. physical output	Thousands of dollars
1880	40.6	0.15	60.8	1922	138,468.2	24.84	173,381.3
1890	307.4	0.67	384.2	1923	262,875.7	34.89	242,731.3
1895	1,245.3	2.35	1,000.2	1924	228,933.5	32.07	274,652.9
1900	4,330.0	6.81	4,152.9	1925	232,491.1	30.44	330,610.0
1905	34,275.7	25.44	9,007.8	1930	227,329.0	25.31	271,699.0
1910	77,697.6	37.08	37,689.5	1935	205,980.0	20.67	179,335.3
1915	91,146.6	32.42	43,503.8	1940	223,294.8	16.50	207,479.8
1920	103,377.4	23.34	178,394.9	1945	328,262.4	19.16	342,756.8
1921	112,600.0	23.85	203,138.2	1950	327,607[a]	16.60	707,630[a]

SOURCE: California data from California, Division of Mines, Bulletin 139 (April, 1948), pp. 10 and 18, and Bulletin 156 (August, 1950), p. 27. U.S. data from U.S. Bureau of the Census, *Historical Statistics of the United States: 1789–1945* (Washington, 1949), p. 146, and *Statistical Abstract of the United States: 1952*, p. 688.
[a]Preliminary.

1. *A series of important oil discoveries between 1896 and 1902.*[15]—One of the new fields (Brea-Olinda, 1897) was in the Los Angeles area, but the chief discoveries were in the San Joaquin Valley. Table 15 shows the rapid acceleration in the growth of California production, both in absolute terms and as a percentage of nation-wide production, between 1900 and 1905. Development on this scale obviously involved substantial investment in the industry[16] and called for the use of considerable man power in the exploration and drilling operations. As production increased, the price fell precipitately, and in value terms the rise in production between 1900 and 1905 was not nearly so spectacular. From a level of about $0.96 per barrel of crude oil in 1900, the price fell to $0.20 a barrel toward the close of 1903.[17] In the later years of the decade, with some recovery in price, the dollar value of production rose to $37,700,000 in 1910 and reached a prewar peak of $48,600,000 in 1913. It was during this latter period that Cali-

[15] For a discussion of the significance of these discoveries, see J. S. Bain, *The Pacific Coast Petroleum Industry: Part II* (Berkeley: University of California Press, 1945), p. 4. See, also, J. Ise, *The United States Oil Policy* (New Haven: Yale University Press, 1926), pp. 87–91.
[16] In 1905, it was reported that the petroleum industry in California was "attracting the attention of capitalists throughout the country." Cf., California State Agricultural Society, *Annual Report*, 1905, p. 130.
[17] Cf. Ise, *op. cit.*, p. 89.

fornia's percentage of the nation's mineral production (in value terms) rose appreciably (see fig. 10).

2. *The rapid development of California's electric power industry.*—At the time of the first census of electrical industries, in 1902, total electrical generating capacity in California amounted only to 84,000 kilowatts, or 6.9 per cent of that in the nation. By 1907, California's installed capacity had increased to 238,000 kilowatts, or 8.8 per cent of national capacity, and, when the electrical census of 1912 was taken, California, with 588,000 kilowatts, had 11.4 per cent of the generating capacity of the nation (see fig. 10).

3. *A widespread shift to oil and to electricity as sources of industrial power.*—Commenting on the industrial position of San Francisco in 1901, two contemporary observers reported with great satisfaction that the fuel question had been "solved for good" and that "all the leading industries of the city and the State had started in to use oil instead of coal," thus placing "us at once on an equal footing with the manufacturers of the East."[18] By 1909, California manufacturers, who employed only 1.8 per cent of the manufacturing wage earners of the nation, were using, as a source of power, 23.0 per cent of the fuel oil used by manufacturers in the nation but less than 0.1 per cent of the coal.[19] In the same period, California manufacturers were also turning to electricity on a considerable scale. As table 16 indicates, electricity was rapidly growing in relative importance as a source of manufacturing power in the nation in the first decade of the century. In California, where a considerable start in the use of electricity had been made during the 'nineties, electrical power represented 35.4 per cent of all horsepower used in manufacturing by 1909.

TABLE 16

ELECTRIC HORSEPOWER AS A PERCENTAGE OF TOTAL
HORSEPOWER USED IN MANUFACTURING,
CALIFORNIA AND UNITED STATES, 1899–1919

Year	California	United States
1899.	7.6	1.8
1904.	18.7	3.3
1909.	35.4	9.4
1919.	68.0	31.7

SOURCES: *Thirteenth Census of the United States: 1910*, Vol. VIII, *Manufactures*, p. 348; and *Fourteenth Census of the United States: 1920*, Vol. IX, *Manufactures*, p. 98.

Though probably not an initiating factor, as will be seen in the latter part of this chapter, the building boom that accompanied the inrush of population during the early 1900's certainly played an important role in contributing to the upswing in economic activity. In this connection, moreover, what was said in chapter iv about the expansion of manufacturing employment between 1899 and 1909 should be recalled. There it was found that far more than half of the increase in the total number of production

---

[18] *Statistics of California Production, Commerce, and Finance for the Years 1900–1* (San Francisco: M. Barnet and J. O'Leary, 1901), p. 83.

[19] *Thirteenth Census of the United States: 1910*, Vol. IX, *Manufactures*, p. 85.

workers in manufacturing occurred in the lumber and stone, clay, and glass industry groups—that is, in those most directly dependent on building activity.

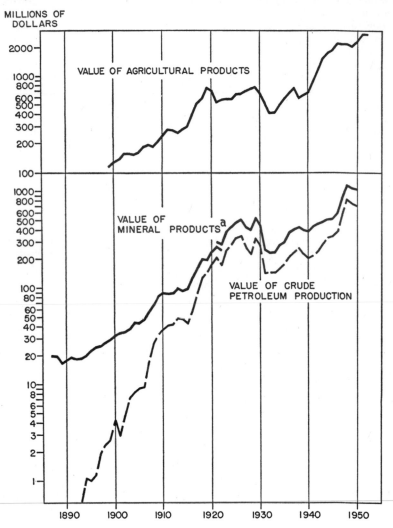

SOURCES: See Appendix B.

FIG. 9A. Growth of the California economy: selected series. III.

The break in the mineral products series represents minor changes in the inclusiveness of the data.

By 1913, the rate of expansion in many sectors of California's economy had slowed down, particularly if considered in relation to the rate of ex-

pansion in the nation. The period from 1913–1914 was one of business recession, and the four years that followed were apparently years of less rapid
expansion in California than in the country as a whole, in *spite* of the boom

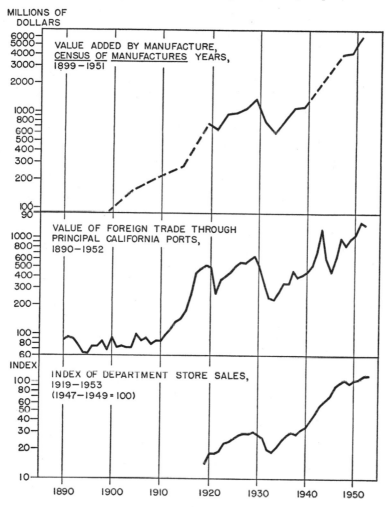

SOURCES: See Appendix B.

FIG. 9B. Growth of the California economy: selected series. III.
The break in the mineral products series represents minor changes in the inclusiveness of the data.

that occurred in World War I.

The absence of a sharp rise in net in-migration and the failure of California's economy to expand as rapidly as the nation's economy during

World War I call for explanation, in the light of what happened during
World War II. It is true that the proportion of the nation's foreign trade
going through California ports rose sharply and the state's share of "value
added by manufacture" increased moderately during World War I, but
the more general measures of economic activity indicate that California's
rate of expansion was less spectacular than that of the country as a whole.

The fact that California's aircraft industry had not yet been developed
in the World War I period appears to be the chief factor in explaining the
contrasts between her experiences in the two war periods.[20] In fact, there
was relatively little expansion in war-related industries in the Los Angeles
Area during World War I, though there was, as discussed in chapter iv,
rapid and diversified manufacturing growth, stimulated largely by the in-
ability of Eastern manufacturers to supply the Western market.[21] Furthermore, the increase in employment in California shipyards (chiefly in the
Bay area) during World War I, though spectacular, was not nearly as sharp
as in World War II. Employment of production workers in private shipyards in California rose from an average level of 3,457 in 1914 to 62,138
in May, 1919 (an increase of 1,697 per cent).[22] During World War II, on
the other hand, the number of production workers in private shipyards
rose from an average level of 7,300 in 1940 to 282,500 in September, 1943
(or 3,769 per cent).[23] Factory earnings data for the World War I period,
moreover, suggest that the effects of the war production boom on labor
market conditions were more pronounced in such centers as Detroit and
Seattle than in the major California cities.[24]

It was in the years immediately after World War I that California experienced once more both a spectacular rise in in-migration and a more
rapid expansion of economic activity than the nation as a whole. Again, an

[20] Airplane production in World War I was centered chiefly in the Buffalo, Dayton,
and Detroit areas. A few planes were manufactured in Sacramento and in San Francisco, but none in Los Angeles. See W. G. Cunningham, *The Aircraft Industry* (Los Angeles: L. L. Morrison, 1951), p. 202. (World War I production data there cited are from
U.S. House of Representatives, *Report on Aircraft Surveys*, Doc. No. 621, 66th Cong., 2d
Sess., Jan. 19, 1920, pp. 4–10.)

[21] On the industrial development of the entire Pacific Southwest area during World
War I, see U.S. Bureau of Foreign and Domestic Commerce, *Commercial Survey of the
Pacific Southwest* (Washington, 1930), p. 399.

[22] *Fourteenth Census of the United States: 1920*, Vol. IX, *Manufactures*, pp. 85 and 87.

[23] California, Department of Industrial Relations, *Labor in California: 1943–1944* (San
Francisco, 1945), p. 28.

[24] The increase in average annual earnings per wage earner in manufacturing between 1914 and 1919 amounted to 110.9 per cent in Detroit, 94.2 per cent in Seattle,
74.8 per cent in Oakland, 54.5 per cent in San Francisco, and 51.9 per cent in Los
Angeles. *Fourteenth Census of the United States: 1920, Earnings of Factory Workers: 1899 to
1927*, Census Monograph X (Washington, 1929), pp. 392–93.

attempt has been made to identify the leading factors that were responsible:

1. During the years immediately following the war, the conditions which had contributed to the rapid wartime growth of civilian-goods manufacturing industries, particularly in the Los Angeles area, were still apparently present to a considerable degree. As a result, total manufacturing employment fell off much less in California between 1919 and 1921 than in the country as a whole. If shipyard employment is eliminated, it is found that factory employment in California declined only 5.3 per cent between 1919 and 1921, as compared with a 20.6 per cent drop in the nation.[25] Furthermore, the number of workers employed in many branches of manufacturing in California actually increased substantially between 1919 and 1921, whereas in the country as a whole the decline in manufacturing employment in this period affected every major industry division. Advances in California were recorded in the following industry divisions (in order of percentage rates of increase): rubber products, textile products (chiefly apparel), stone, clay, and glass products, forest products, printing and publishing, petroleum products, paper and paper products, and miscellaneous. For the most part, these were the industry divisions in which the largest percentage increases in employment were to occur during the 'twenties.

2. Between 1920 and 1923, there was another series of important petroleum discoveries, this time in the Los Angeles area. California petroleum production shot up from 103.4 million barrels in 1920 to a peak of 262.9 million in 1923, with most of the increase occurring in Los Angeles County. Although the 1923 peak was not surpassed until a second set of discoveries brought a new spurt in 1929, production from 1922 to 1930 was at a substantially higher level than before, exceeding 200 million barrels annually throughout the period. The nature of the boom which accompanied these discoveries is lucidly described by J. S. Bain in his three-volume work on the Pacific Coast petroleum industry.[26]

"The boom arose from the discovery in rapid succession of a number of unusually rich oil fields and from the fact that both the drilling of wells and the production of drilled wells was conducted (in an atmosphere of fevered speculation and without restraint) on numerous small land holdings. The great surpluses accumulating from the earlier discoveries at Signal Hill and Santa Fe Springs and the consequent weakening of the crude market do not seem to have deterred frenzied drilling activity in other parts of these fields and in new fields as they were brought in. Even with 'low' crude prices, the difference between the expected return from a successful well and the cost of drilling and operating it was so substantial that any discovered field was likely to be mercilessly exploited by small operators unless some type of collective action was adopted."

3. The growth of the electric power industry was also of considerable importance in California during the 'twenties, as it had been in the first decade of the century.

[25] In computing these percentages, *Census of Manufactures* data as adjusted by the National Resources Planning Board and F. L. Kidner for California and by Fabricant for the United States were used. See F. L. Kidner, *California Business Cycles* (Berkeley: University of California Press, 1946), p. 27, and S. Fabricant, *Employment in Manufacturing: 1899–1939* (New York: National Bureau of Economic Research, 1942), pp. 207 and 214.
[26] Bain, *op. cit.*, pp. 14–16. For a more detailed description of the boom, see Ise, *op. cit.*, chapter xii. Ise comments on the fact that in Long Beach in 1922, there were "1600 real estate agents, an unnumbered horde of 'unit' oil promoters, sharks, lawyers, and the necessary complement of dupes and suckers."

Total installed capacity increased 95 per cent in the first half of the decade and 49 per cent between 1925 and 1930, though in numerical terms the actual growth in capacity was about equal in the two halves of the decade. California's share of total installed capacity in the nation rose from 7.2 per cent in 1920 to 8.9 per cent in 1928, after which it declined somewhat.[27]

4. Developments in California agriculture likewise helped to explain the favorable economic environment of the 'twenties. The value of farm production fell off much less sharply in the state than in the nation from 1919 to 1921 and rose more rapidly during the period from 1924 to 1929, with the result that by 1929 California's share of the total value of agricultural production in the nation amounted to 6.8 per cent, as compared with 4.3 per cent in 1918 (see figs. 9 and 10). The period from 1918 to 1932 was distinguished from the periods that preceded and followed it in that nation-wide production of important agricultural staples, such as corn, wheat, and cattle, either declined or failed to rise. Meanwhile, the production of many California specialty crops showed rapid growth. Furthermore, California farm prices fell much less sharply from 1919 to 1921 than did those in the nation, though a subsequent rise in United States farm prices (from 1922 to 1924) tended to restore the previous relationship.[28]

5. Finally, among the factors making for relatively rapid economic growth in the 'twenties was the sharp rise in the value of exports and imports moving through California ports after the 1920-1921 decline. During the period from 1921 to 1929, in fact, the share of total United States exports and imports moving through California ports rose substantially (see fig. 10). On the export side, this was attributable primarily to the rapid growth in exports of petroleum through the Los Angeles–Long Beach port area, and on the import side to the marked growth in imports of raw silk from Japan during the 'twenties.

The fact that net in-migration reached a peak in 1923 and declined somewhat thereafter was apparently explained chiefly by developments associated with the oil boom and the real estate boom that accompanied it in the Los Angeles area. As will be seen in a later section, the peak of the building cycle was reached in the state and in Los Angeles in 1923, whereas in San Francisco and in the nation as a whole, it was not reached until several years later.

The third period of accelerated growth appears to have got under way in 1935 and to have lasted until about 1944. Although migration to California began to increase slowly from 1932–1933 on, there is little evidence that recovery was proceeding more rapidly in the state than in the nation. It was not until 1935–1936 that California's share of total individual income began to rise or that the state's share of total bank debits exceeded its 1933 level.[29]

[27] See U.S. Federal Power Commission, *Electric Power Statistics* (Washington, 1941).
[28] An index of California farm prices (1910–1914 = 100) prepared by the Giannini Foundation of Agricultural Economics (University of California, Berkeley) rose from 211 in 1919 to 223 in 1920 and then fell to 155 in 1921. In the same years, the index of prices received by farmers prepared by the U.S. Bureau of Agricultural Economics (on the same base) fell from 215 in 1919 to 211 in 1920 and to 124 in 1921.
[29] The bank debits data are not shown in the charts.

An analysis of the available statistical data for the period strongly suggests that the growth of manufacturing in general, and of the aircraft industry, in particular, was the major factor in explaining the relatively

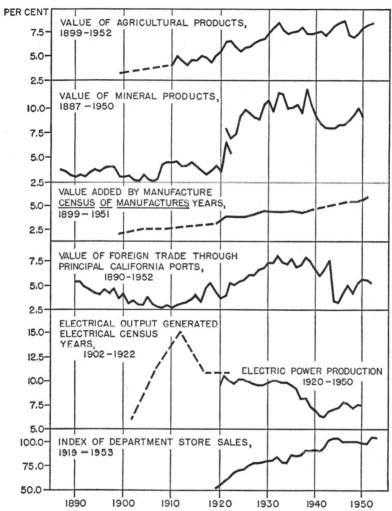

Sources: See Appendix B.

Fig. 10. Growth of the California economy: selected series. IV. (All series are expressed as percentages of the corresponding U.S. series.)

rapid increase in economic activity in California from 1935 to Pearl Harbor. Even by 1935, factory employment in California had increased slightly more than in the nation, but it was from 1935 to 1937 and again, from 1939 to 1941, that factory employment in the state made especially rapid gains.[30]

By 1937, the transportation equipment industry had achieved by far the largest percentage gain over 1929 factory employment of any of the major manufacturing groups. Most of this increase was attributable to the growth of the aircraft industry, although a substantial gain in employment in the automobile and parts industry over the 1929 level also played a role. Although development of the southern California aircraft industry had begun during the 1920's, only 1,277 production workers were employed in the aircraft and parts industry in California in 1929. By 1935, this number had risen to 3,482[31] and by 1937 to 11,526. In numerical terms, these gains were small in relation to those which were to come a few years later as the defense production program began to get under way. But it was during this period that southern California became established as a major aircraft production center,[32] and it is particularly in this sense that the growth of the aircraft industry was the most significant development of the 1933–1937 upswing in business in the state. The fact must be remembered, also, that before production in the industry could be increased substantially, engineers and designers had to be hired, plants had to be built, and equipment purchased.[33] The precise impact of the growth of the industry on employment expansion in the state from 1933 to 1937 cannot, of course, be measured, but it is clear that it went considerably beyond the increase in production workers directly employed in plants producing aircraft and parts.

From 1939 on, the role of aircraft production and, also, of shipbuilding, in stimulating the relatively rapid expansion of economic activity in California became increasingly clear. The spectacular expansion of these industries had direct repercussions on the growth of the metal and metal-products industries, and indirectly, of course, helped to generate enor-

---

[30] As figure 10 indicates, however, California's share of total value added by manufacture did not rise until after 1937. Although the "value added" data have not been subjected to all the adjustments which have been undertaken in the case of the production worker data, this is apparently not the explanation of their differing behavior. It would be impossible to determine, without a much more detailed analysis, precisely why factory employment increased considerably more rapidly in California than in the nation from 1935 to 1937, but "value added" did not. Given the differing "industry-mixes" of the two areas, price increases may have had a more pronounced impact over the country as a whole and/or there may have been greater gains in productivity in the nation as a whole.

[31] *Census of Manufactures* data. Aircraft employment in the state was not disclosed in 1931 or 1933.

[32] California's share of total aircraft production workers in the nation rose from 9 per cent in 1929 to 31 per cent in 1935 and to 48 per cent in 1937.

For a brief survey of the early history of the industry in the state, see S. O. Blythe, "Flight Builders," in *California: Magazine of Pacific Business* (October, 1936).

[33] In this connection, it is interesting that the aircraft industry employs a relatively high proportion of people in the salaried brackets. Cf. Federal Reserve Bank of San Francisco, *Monthly Review*, October, 1952, p. 91.

mously increased demands for consumers' goods and services in the large metropolitan areas of the state—demands which could be met only in part during the war period itself, owing to wartime shortages and restrictions.

Certain other factors played a part in the boom after Pearl Harbor. Expansion of port activity, as movements of men and equipment to the Pacific theater of war got under way, played an important role. There were many large military and naval installations in the state, ranging all the way from Mare Island Navy Yard to training camps for desert warfare in the Mojave.[34] Another important stimulus to economic expansion during the war was the rise in farm production. As figure 10 indicates, California's share of the total value of farm production in the nation rose somewhat between 1942 and 1944, and again very slightly between 1945 and 1946. The value of petroleum production also increased somewhat during the war, though California's share of the total value of mineral production in the nation declined considerably.

For the years from 1939 on, it is possible to compare the industrial pattern of employment expansion in California and the United States on the basis of annual data, and this comparison will be worth while, because it will bring out some of the reasons for the decline in the relative rate of expansion toward the end of the war. For this purpose, the statistics on wage and salary workers in nonagricultural establishments are the most satisfactory (see table 17).[35] Percentagewise, the increase in total employment of wage and salary workers in nonagricultural pursuits was considerably more marked in California than in the United States from 1939 to 1943, largely because of the very much higher rate of expansion of manufacturing employment in California. But percentage gains in employment in California were considerably greater than in the nation in most other industry divisions, also, particularly in contract construction and government, in both of which much of the gain was directly attributable to the war effort.[36]

---

[34] There was, of course, some increase in the activities of military and naval installations even before Pearl Harbor.

[35] These data are available, also in monthly form. In addition, estimates of total employment by major industry group, prepared by the California State Departments of Employment and Industrial Relations, are available for the years from 1943 on for California and from 1937 on for the United States. Reliance will be primarily on annual data in the ensuing discussion, with references to monthly data occasionally. Monthly data must be used with caution in making comparisons between the state and the nation, because of differences in patterns of seasonal variation of total employment and of employment in some of the major industry groups.

[36] It should be remembered that government employment, as here classified, includes all civilian government employees, regardless of the activity in which the worker is engaged. This means that wartime expansion of civilian employment at such government installations as Mare Island and Hunters Point Navy Yard is reflected in the government category. Census statistics, on the other hand, exclude such workers from public administration, classifying them under the major industry group which includes the activity in which they are engaged.

TABLE 17

Estimated Number of Wage and Salary Workers in Nonagricultural Establishments, By Major Industry Division, and Percentage Changes, California and United States, Selected Years, 1939–1953

Major industry division	Number of workers (in thousands)[a]						Percentage change[b]				
	1939	1943	1945	1948	1949	1953	1939–1943	1943–1945	1945–1948	1948–1949	1949–1953
California											
Total wage and salary workers	1,812	3,084	2,961	3,163	3,088	3,895	70.2	−4.0	6.8	−2.4	26.1
Mineral extraction	40	29	31	36	34	37	−26.5	4.1	16.3	−3.4	6.4
Contract construction[c]	76	138	137	225	198	257	80.5	−0.9	64.9	−12.3	29.9
Manufacturing	384	1,166	861	734	702	1,064	203.2	−26.1	−14.7	−4.5	51.6
Transportation, communication, and utilities	183	248	276	313	301	341	35.4	11.3	13.5	−4.0	13.4
Trade	505	596	654	791	767	886	18.1	9.7	20.8	−3.0	15.5
Finance, insurance, and real estate	96	97	100	140	141	172	0.9	3.0	39.5	1.0	21.5
Service[d]	277	344	369	424	421	496	24.5	7.2	14.7	−0.6	17.8
Government[d]	250	465	534	501	525	644	85.8	14.8	−6.1	4.7	22.7
United States											
Total wage and salary workers	30,287	42,042	40,069	44,382	43,295	49,138	38.8	−4.7	10.8	−2.4	13.5
Mineral extraction	845	917	826	982	918	832	8.5	−9.9	18.9	−6.5	−9.4
Contract construction[c]	1,150	1,567	1,132	2,169	2,165	2,538	36.3	−27.8	91.6	−0.2	17.2
Manufacturing	10,078	17,381	15,302	15,321	14,178	17,002	72.5	−12.0	0.1	−7.5	19.9
Transportation, communication, and utilities	2,912	3,619	3,872	4,141	3,949	4,275	24.3	7.0	6.9	−4.6	8.3
Trade	6,612	7,189	7,522	9,519	9,513	10,475	8.7	4.6	26.5	−0.1	10.1
Finance, insurance, and real estate	1,382	1,401	1,394	1,711	1,736	3,032	1.4	−0.5	22.7	1.5	17.0
Service[d]	3,321	3,919	4,055	4,925	5,000	5,315	18.0	3.5	21.5	1.5	6.3
Government[d]	3,987	6,049	5,967	5,614	5,827	6,669	51.7	−1.4	−5.9	4.0	14.3

Sources: California, Department of Industrial Relations, *Handbook of California Labor Statistics: 1951–1952* (San Francisco, 1953), pp. 21–32. 1953 data for California were supplied by the Department and, for the United States, are from U.S. Bureau of Labor Statistics, *Monthly Labor Review*, LXXVII (1954), 205–208.
aDoes not include employers, own account workers, unpaid family workers, domestic servants, and agricultural workers.
bCalifornia percentages are computed from data which were carried to the nearest hundred.
cDoes not include force account and governmental construction workers

Employment of production workers in the aircraft plants reached a peak in April, 1943, and in the shipyards in September, 1943,[37] but the decline in employment was moderate until after V-J Day. Total nonagricultural employment declined by about the same percentage in California and the nation from 1943 to 1945, but there were interesting differences in the industrial pattern of changes that took place. The decrease in manufacturing employment was considerably more marked in California than in the nation, but in every other industry division, employment in the state showed somewhat larger increases or less marked declines than in the nation. What was happening, apparently, was that the decline in aircraft and shipyard employment was considerably more marked than in other branches of manufacturing employment throughout the nation in these years. This meant that California, with its heavy concentration in these two industries, experienced a sharper drop in manufacturing employment than was occurring in the nation as a whole. The workers released from these two industries, in this period of high and only very slightly declining employment, apparently shifted into other industries in California to a considerable extent, whereas fewer shifts of this kind, relatively, could take place in the nation as a whole in view of the less marked decline in manufacturing employment.

The months from August to November, 1945, were characterized by a sharp and rapid decline in employment, as plants throughout the nation curtailed military production and, in most cases, undertook the changes needed for reconversion to peacetime production programs. From about February, 1946, until the latter part of 1948, employment levels expanded in both California and the nation but by a smaller percentage in the state than in the country as a whole. Estimated employment of wage and salary workers in nonagricultural establishments increased only 6.8 per cent in California, as compared with 10.8 per cent in the nation, from 1945 to 1948. The industrial pattern of employment changes, moreover, differed in a number of significant respects from that in the nation during this period. In only three out of the eight major industry divisions represented in table 17—(1) mineral extraction, (2) transportation, communication, and utilities, and (3) finance, insurance, and real estate—was the rate of employment expansion more marked than in the nation, and these three accounted for only 15 per cent of total employment of wage and salary workers in the state in 1948. In the other five industry divisions, the increase was less marked than in the nation or the decline more pronounced. The differences were sharpest in contract construction and in manufacturing; in fact, in manufacturing, California experienced a substantial decline

---

[37] *Labor in California: 1943–1944, op. cit.*, p. 31.

in employment between 1945 and 1948, whereas manufacturing employment in the nation showed almost no change.

If the annual estimates of manufacturing employment are considered, it is found that the 1945-1946 decline was more pronounced in California than in the nation, and the recovery in 1946–1947 was less pronounced. Measuring the decline from 1943 on, we find that the level of employment of wage and salary workers in manufacturing in the state fell 39 per cent from 1943 to 1946, whereas the decline in the nation during the same period amounted to only 17 per cent. Thus, not only had the wartime expansion of manufacturing been considerably more pronounced in California than in the nation, but the contraction from the wartime peak was also much sharper. In the aircraft plants and shipyards, postwar readjustment took the form of sharp cutbacks in production and employment, whereas many of the other wartime industries, which played a relatively more important role in the country as a whole, went through a process of reconversion to peacetime production.

Actually, nearly all major branches of manufacturing in California experienced substantial gains in employment from 1945 to 1948 (see fig. 3). The exceptions were those industry divisions which had grown at an extraordinary rate during the war—shipbuilding, aircraft production, metals and metal products (though certain subdivisions of this group showed postwar gains), chemicals and allied products, and petroleum products. Cutbacks in shipyard employment, though sharpest in 1945–1946, continued throughout the postwar expansion period, and it was not until 1950 that employment of wage and salary workers in private shipyards reached its postwar low point of 6,200 workers (on an annual average basis). Reductions in aircraft employment were less severe but continued, nevertheless, until 1948, when the number of wage and salary workers in the industry reached an annual average level of 75,000.

Although employment in contract construction failed to expand as rapidly in the state as in the nation from 1945 to 1948, it had contracted much less sharply from its wartime peak (reached in 1942) than had construction employment in the country as a whole, and the over-all gain from 1939 to 1948 was considerably more pronounced (196 per cent) than that in the nation (89 per cent).

On the whole, there seems to be little question that the failure of income and employment levels to advance as substantially in California as in the nation from 1945 to 1948 was attributable chiefly to the severity of the cutbacks in the two industries which had led the wartime expansion, although there were other factors at work. The decline in the volume of exports from California ports to a point well below the prewar level was an important element in the situation. Another factor which has largely been overlooked in discussions of California's postwar problem is that the postwar readjust-ment process actually got under way relatively early in California, as was apparent in the discussion of developments in the 1943–1945 period.

The Korean War period was marked by a more pronounced expansion of economic activity in California than in the nation. Once again, as in World War II, expansion of aircraft employment played a large part in ex-plaining the more rapid rise in nonagricultural employment in California, though this time it was accompanied by only a moderate expansion of ship-yard employment, chiefly in government yards. Of the total rise in manu-facturing employment in the state from 1949 to 1953, the expansion of aircraft employment accounted for nearly two-fifths. Much of the remain-ing expansion occurred in the metal and metal-products industries, par-ticularly in the production of machinery, both electrical and nonelectrical. If the increase in employment in all metal and metal-products industries is added to that in aircraft, more than two-thirds of the rise in manufacturing employment in the state from 1949 to 1953 is accounted for. Increases oc-curred in most other branches of manufacturing as well, but for the most part at moderate rates.

Outside of manufacturing, the percentage rise in nonagricultural em-ployment in California from 1949 to 1953 was somewhat higher than in the nation in all major industry divisions, with especially wide differences in mineral extraction, construction, and service. Furthermore, although average annual employment in agriculture is estimated to have increased about 9 per cent in the state between 1949 and 1953, it declined 18 per cent in the nation in the same period,[38] reflecting a substantial farm-to-city movement.

During the latter part of 1953 and the early months of 1954, employ-ment both in California and in the nation was showing a tendency to de-cline. As this is being written (April, 1954), it is not yet clear whether the decline has come to a halt. The only thing that is certain is that the ex-pansion directly associated with the Korean War has ended.

BUILDING CYCLES IN CALIFORNIA

Discussion of the relation of migration waves to changes in economic activ-ity in the state needs, at this point, to be rounded out by an analysis of the role of the building cycle.

[38] See California, Department of Employment, *Employment and Unemployment in Cali-fornia* (February, 1954); and Department of Industrial Relations, *Handbook of California Labor Statistics: 1951–1952*, p. 19. (The published estimates of employment in "agricul-ture, forestry, and fisheries" must be adjusted to exclude forestry and fisheries.) U.S. data are from U.S. Bureau of the Census, *Current Population Reports*, Series P-50, No. 19, March 2, 1950, and Series P-57, No. 140, March 26, 1954.

I shall not dwell at length here on the nature of the building cycle, which shows up in American data relating to building activity—and in data for other countries as well—going back into the nineteenth century. A number of investigators have shown that there have tended to be pronounced cycles in building activity which have been somewhat longer in duration and wider in amplitude than the ordinary business cycle, lasting from fifteen to twenty years if measured from peak to peak or from trough to trough.[39] These cycles have been most pronounced in residential construction (the most important component of construction activity), but have been apparent, also, in certain other branches of the construction industry. Their actual timing and duration have been influenced by wars and by changes in the rate of population growth, as well as by factors inherent in the character of the building industry.

As figure 11 indicates, building cycles in California since the turn of the century have tended to be quite similar, on the whole, to those in the United States.[40] According to Burns and Mitchell, the first two building cycles in our period for the country as a whole should be dated from 1900 to 1918 and from 1918 to 1933 (on a trough-to-trough basis).[41] After 1933, there was an upswing in building activity which reached a peak in 1941–1942, but the subsequent contraction was clearly attributable to wartime restrictions on building, and an upward movement got under way again

[39] See, in particular, C. D. Long, Jr., *Building Cycles and the Theory of Investment* (Princeton: Princeton University Press, 1940); N. J. Silberling, *The Dynamics of Business* (New York: McGraw-Hill, 1943); and J. R. Riggleman, "Building Cycles in the United States, 1875–1932," *Journal of the American Statistical Association*, XXVIII (1933), 174–183. Two recent investigators are not convinced that the existence of a building cycle has been clearly demonstrated. See M. L. Colean and R. Newcomb, *Stabilizing Construction: The Record and Potential* (New York: McGraw-Hill, 1952).

[40] Data relating to the value of building permits issued in leading cities (for years before 1939) have been relied upon in constructing the index used for California in figure 11. For the earlier years, only a few cities are included in the index—for the years, 1902 to 1906, only Los Angeles and San Francisco—owing to the fact that more complete data are not readily available. The coverage for these early years, however, compares favorably with the coverage of Long's index for the United States, which is used for this period. (For further discussion of the two indices, see Appendix B.)

For most purposes, data relating to the value of building permits issued are more useful than those relating to the number of permits, since they provide a better index of construction expenditures. Data on the number of building permits issued, however, probably provide a better measure of fluctuations in residential construction. Both types of data for California have been collected. The series relating to number of building permits (not presented here, because data are lacking for a few years) fluctuates in much the same manner as the value series, except for the first building cycle represented in the period. Although our index of value of permits issued reached a peak in 1907 (probably reflecting post-earthquake construction in San Francisco), a similar index based on number of permits reaches a peak in 1913 and then falls off sharply.

[41] Cf. A. F. Burns and W. C. Mitchell, *Measuring Business Cycles* (New York: National Bureau of Economic Research, 1946), p. 422. These authors, of course, used monthly, rather than annual, data in determining turning points.

immediately after the war. Although some authorities regard the low point reached in 1944 as a trough in the building cycle, a strong case could be made for treating it as a temporary interruption of the upswing, brought on by exogenous factors (in this case, wartime restrictions).

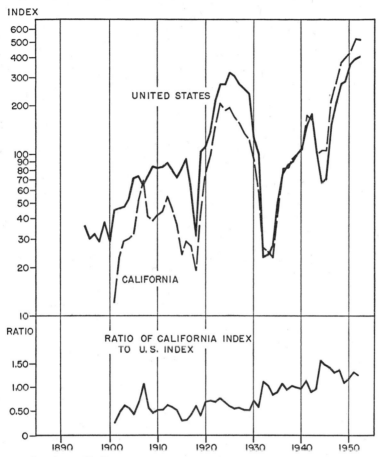

SOURCES: See Appendix B.

Fig. 11. Indexes of annual fluctuations in value of building permits, California and U.S. cities, 1895–1939, and in construction expenditures, California and United States, 1939 1952 (1939=100).

It is interesting that the first two of the building cycles represented in figure 11 agree fairly closely in timing and duration with the waves in migration to California which were discussed earlier in the chapter.[42] The minor differences in timing will be discussed at a later stage.

---

[42] The agreement in the case of the first cycle is even closer on the basis of *number* of permits.

If building cycles in California and the nation are compared, it is found that there have been some differences in timing and amplitude. As figure 11 indicates, the ratio of the California index to the United States index has not maintained a constant level. To begin with, of course, there has been a marked upward trend in the ratios, which reflects the more rapid secular rate of increase in the value of building activity in California. Secondly, the ratios have shown, in the period for which we have data, some major fluctuations which conform (almost, but not quite) to the building cycle itself. These fluctuations in the ratios reflect the wider amplitude of at least the first two cycles of the century in California, as well as certain differences in development and timing. These differences may be summarized as follows, bearing in mind the fact that our data do not justify refined comparisons and that small differences may not be significant:

1. There has been some tendency for peaks in building activity in California to precede those in the country as a whole, but by a diminishing time period with each successive cycle.[43] It is too early to date the peak of the current upswing.

2. There has been no observable tendency for recovery from the trough of a building cycle in California to precede that in the United States, so far as we can judge from these annual data. In fact, the recovery in California after the Great Depression seems to have got under way somewhat later than in the country as a whole.

3. The upswing in California in the first two building cycles in our period was somewhat more pronounced than in the country as a whole, but the height of the California peak in the first cycle was at least partly explained by the San Francisco earthquake of 1906. The upswing from the trough in building activity in the Great Depression to the wartime peak was somewhat less marked in California than in the United States, though there was a tendency toward a sharper upswing in California from 1934 to 1936.

4. The downswing in California during the entire period from peak to trough was also somewhat more pronounced in each of the first two building cycles of the period. The decline in the later stages of the downswing, however, was not as pronounced in California as in the nation, as indicated by the fact that the ratio of the California index to the United States index moved sharply upward from 1915 to 1918 and again from 1929 to 1932. This undoubtedly reflects the influence of the sharper upward trend in California, which is associated with the more rapid rate of population growth.

On the whole, the differences in timing and amplitude between California and the nation appear to have become less marked as time has gone on.[44]

There is a good deal of evidence to suggest that speculative forces tend

[43] On the basis of number of permits issued, rather than value of permits, the peak of the first cycle in California occurred in 1913, or three years earlier than the peak (on the same basis) in the country as a whole.

[44] This statement is based, not only on collected data, but also on the conclusions drawn by Maverick on the basis of his study of real estate cycles in San Francisco, Alameda, and Los Angeles Counties. See the reference cited in footnote 48, below.

to be more rampant in the early stages of growth of a community or area than is true later on. In interpreting the differences in timing and amplitude of the building cycle in California and the United States, it must also be recognized that residential construction constitutes a substantially larger percentage of total construction activity in California than in the country as a whole. Department of Commerce data on construction expenditures indicate that in recent years expenditures on private residential construction have tended to represent approximately one half of all construction expenditures in California, but not much more than a third of the total in the country as a whole.[45] So far as can be judged from the limited statistical data available, the tendency for residential building to be relatively more important in California has been true at least as far back as the early 'twenties. In view of the fact that, among the various types of construction activity, residential construction is most sensitive to changes in the rate of population growth, it seems reasonable to suppose that the differences between state and nation in this respect may have been most pronounced in the decades in which the ratio of California's rate of population growth to that in the nation has been highest.

The relatively greater importance of residential building in California could have accounted, at least in part, for the wider amplitude of building cycles in California and for some, but not all, of the differences in timing. Building cycle research has shown that the building cycle shows up more clearly in residential construction than in other types of construction, whereas industrial construction shows relatively greater sensitivity to the ordinary business cycle and less to the building cycle.[46] It has been shown, also, that residential building tends to lead other types of construction at both the lower and upper turning points of the building cycle. In the light of these findings, the upswing in building activity in California might be expected to lead that in the nation at the lower turning point, but it may well be that, in that phase of the building cycle, residential construction may not be much more important, relatively, in California than in the nation. It would require a more detailed study of the cyclical behavior of the various components of construction activity in both state and nation to shed light on this point.

For practical purposes, the differences in the behavior of construction activity between California and the nation are less important than their similarities. The building cycle has represented an extremely important aspect of industrial fluctuations in California, as it has in the nation. In

[45] See U.S. Department of Commerce, *Construction and Building Materials*, Statistical Supplement, June, 1953.
[46] See Long, *op. cit.*, pp. 128–149, and Burns and Mitchell, *op. cit.*, pp. 418–427. See also J. M. Clark, *Strategic Factors in Business Cycles* (New York: H. Wolff, 1934), pp. 27–29.

view of the close relationship observed between waves of migration into the state and building cycles, it is interesting to inquire whether population movements induce upswings and downswings in building activity, or whether changes in the level of construction activity tend to precede changes in the volume of in-migration.

On the basis of the limited data available for California, it is not easy to reach a conclusion on this point. The low point in population growth in 1916 preceded the low point in value of building permits by two years, but it is not certain when the low point in net in-migration occurred, and, as stated earlier, normal building activity was interrupted during World War I. The next low point in net in-migration occurred in 1932, two years before the trough in our value of building permits index. These relationships suggest that in all probability an increase in net in-migration tends to precede a revival in building activity. At the upper turning point, no consistent relationship can be observed. The first peak in population growth covered by our data occurred in 1913, a year after a secondary peak in value of building permits, but in the same year as the peak in number of building permits (not charted here). The second peak in population growth and in net in-migration occurred in 1923, as did the peak in both value and number of building permits issued in California cities. During World War II, the peak in construction activity preceded the peak in net in-migration, but, as has been previously observed, this particular downturn in construction activity was brought on by wartime restrictions on nonessential building. The postwar period was unique in that construction activity rose sharply in the face of a decline in net in-migration, but the explanation is fairly obvious. Wartime restrictions had prevented an expansion of residential construction during the period of hostilities and had left a heavy backlog of demand for housing.

Although California data do not provide a basis for positive conclusions as to the relationship between fluctuations in migration and in building activity, other investigators have looked into various aspects of the same problem, with results that are of interest for our purposes. On the basis of a comparison of estimated annual population growth and value of building permits for seventeen cities in the United States from 1875 to 1933, Newman found that there were long cycles in population growth in these cities, similar in timing and duration to building cycles, and concluded that, for the seventeen cities combined, there was a tendency for changes in population growth to anticipate major changes in building activity by a year or two.[47] When he examined data for four of the cities individually, he

---

[47] W. H. Newman, "The Building Industry and Business Cycles," *Journal of Business of the University of Chicago*, VIII (1935), No. 3, Part 2. School enrollment data were used as a basis for estimating annual population growth in each city.

found (1) that changes in population growth had an important influence on changes in building activity in each city, (2) that there were minor differences in timing of the building cycles in each city—often explained by variations in the timing of changes in population growth, and (3) that the correlation between changes in population growth and in building activity was not perfect for any individual city. Other investigators have found similar relationships in various localities.[48]

Although the evidence suggests that building cycles do not play an initiating role in relation to fluctuations in economic activity in rapidly growing areas, such as California, there is reason to believe that their impact on the economy tends to be somewhat more important, relatively, in areas of rapid growth than in more stable areas. In the first place, the amplitude of building cycles may be somewhat wider in such areas, though figure 11 suggests that this is becoming less true in California. In the second place, the construction industry tends to account for a larger share of economic activity and of employment in a rapidly growing area than in a more mature area. As seen in chapter iii, construction workers represented 7.7 per cent of all employed workers in California at the time of the 1950 census, as compared with 6.1 per cent in the country as a whole. Certain states with unusually rapid rates of growth in recent years (for example, Florida and Arizona) had even more workers employed in the construction industry, relatively, than did California, whereas states in a more mature stage of growth (for example, Massachusetts, Pennsylvania, and Ohio) had fewer workers, comparatively, in this industry than did the nation as a whole.[49]

It has been estimated that, for every five workers employed at the site on new construction, another six workers may be employed in activities servicing construction (distribution, transportation, and manufacturing). The corresponding ratio is somewhat lower for maintenance and repair work, but it would appear that the total number of workers whose employment is directly attributable to construction activity is at least double the number of workers actually employed on the site.[50] Although it would be difficult to arrive at equivalent estimates for individual states, it seems

[48] Cf., for example, H. Hoyt, *One Hundred Years of Land Values in Chicago* (Chicago: University of Chicago Press, 1933); L. A. Maverick, two articles on cycles in real estate activity in San Francisco, Alameda, and Los Angeles counties, *Journal of Land and Public Utility Economics*, May, 1932, and February, 1933; and K. A. H. Buckley, "Urban Building and Real Estate Fluctuations in Canada," *The Canadian Journal of Economics and Political Science*, XVIII (1952), 41–62.

[49] See *1950 Census of Population: Advance Reports*, Series PC-14, No. 10, March 13, 1953.

[50] Cf. Colean and Newcomb, *op. cit.*, pp. 10–11. The corresponding ratio was apparently somewhat higher in the late 'twenties and early 'thirties. See U.S. 79th Congress, 1st Sess., *Seventh Report of House Special Committee on Postwar Economic Policy and Planning*, House Report No. 852 (Washington, 1945), p. 16; and Long, *op. cit.*, p. 7.

unlikely that the ratio would be smaller for California, with its substantial production of lumber and other building materials, than for the nation. On the assumption that the California ratio is the same as the nation-wide ratio, approximately 15.4 per cent of California's employed workers, as compared with 12.2 per cent of those in the nation, would have owed their employment to construction activity at the time of the 1950 census. By the same token, a recession in building activity might well entail more unemployment in California than in the nation.

Since major variations in building activity have shown close correspondence in California and the nation, it is necessary to appraise the factors that are likely to determine the level of construction activity in the nation if there is to be much insight into the probable level of building activity in California during the next decade.

If the recession in construction activity in World War II is regarded as an artificial decline attributable to wartime restrictions, it can be said that by 1953 an upswing in building activity, as measured by construction expenditures, had been under way for twenty years. This is a longer span of years than the entire period from trough to trough or from peak to peak in many earlier building cycles. Yet the fact that an upswing has continued for so long a period is not particularly difficult to explain, nor does it necessarily indicate that the building cycle is obsolete. Before World War I, the level of building activity tended, as has been seen, to change in response to changes in the rate of population growth, which reflected primarily the ebb and flow of immigration. Since the beginning of World War I, and particularly since enactment of the Immigration Act of 1924, the volume of immigration has ceased to be the chief determinant of fluctuations in the rate of population growth, which now reflects chiefly changes in the birth rate.

Actually, careful analysts of probable trends in the building industry recognize that it is the rate of family formation, rather than the rate of population growth *per se*, that influences the level of residential construction. The chief factor affecting the formation of households is the marriage rate, which reached a peak of 16.4 (per 1,000 population) in 1946, reflecting both a rush of postwar marriages and a tendency to marry at a somewhat earlier age than formerly. In the next three years, the marriage rate declined to about the 1939 level, of 10.7, around which it has tended to fluctuate in the last few years. In view of the fact that the number of girls reaching the age of marriage will tend to be relatively small throughout most of the remainder of the decade of the 'fifties (reflecting the low birth rates of the 'thirties), it is not anticipated that the marriage rate will rise materially until after 1960, when girls born in the high birth rate period of the 'forties will begin to reach the average age for first marriage (twenty years). In fact, the marriage rate may decline somewhat in the next few years if income and employment fall off from their present high levels.

Total household formation was estimated to have averaged about 1,500,000 annually in the years following the war and to have declined to about 950,000 in the year ending April, 1953.[51] According to the Census Bureau (medium estimate), annual increases are expected to average 700,000 from 1953 to 1955 and 625,000 from 1955 to 1960.[52]

In the light of these estimates, it does not seem likely that the current annual rate of a little more than a million new permanent nonfarm dwelling starts per year can be long maintained. Early in 1952, it was predicted that the backlog of demand, which was estimated at about 500,000 units in early 1952, would continue to sustain a high level of demand for new housing until sometime in 1953, but that after that a decline in new dwelling starts could be anticipated unless a much larger replacement market developed than had existed for two decades.[53] Actually, on the basis of seasonally adjusted monthly data, the number of new dwelling units started in the latter half of 1953 was consistently below the level for the corresponding month of 1952. Whether this tendency will continue into 1954 is not yet clear. On the whole, however, a fairly substantial decline in the volume of residential construction seems probable in the middle and late 'fifties, although the severity of the decline may well depend on what happens to the general level of income and employment. Other branches of the construction industry, commercial construction, in particular, can be expected to be heavily influenced by the same factors that will affect residential construction. The backlog of need for expanded school facilities and other public works may help to sustain a relatively high level of public construction in the late 'fifties, however, particularly in California, although clearly this will depend in part on political developments.

CONCLUSIONS

On the whole, the data examined in the present chapter tend to be consistent with the hypothesis that was set forth at the beginning of the chapter. There is considerable evidence that the pronounced waves in California's rate of population growth have tended to correspond roughly, in timing and duration, with waves in the rate of expansion of economic activity in the state relative to that in the nation. There is also considerable evidence that the timing of the major spurts in the rate of growth has been explained

---

[51] See U.S. Bureau of the Census, *Current Population Reports*, Series P-20, No. 48, October 4, 1953, and No. 53, April 11, 1954.

[52] See "Population Growth and Markets," *Survey of Current Business*, April, 1953, pp. 21–22.

[53] See "New Construction Activity in 1952," *Survey of Current Business*, April, 1952, p. 9.

largely by economic developments associated with the exploitation of unusually favorable investment opportunities.

Further, changes in the rate of expansion (or contraction) of employment opportunities in the state, relative to that in the nation, have *induced* changes in the rate of net migration, rather than the reverse. This conclusion does not rest on a statistical demonstration that a change in the relative rate of expansion of employment has always tended to *precede* a change in the rate of net in-migration. The "lead-lag" type of statistical analysis is virtually ruled out in this case by the necessity of relying on annual population estimates, whereas monthly, or at least quarterly, data would be required for analyzing leads and lags successfully. Rather the conclusion rests (1) on a logical inference drawn from the fact that there is no apparent explanation for the timing of changes in the rate of net in-migration other than the influence of economic developments, and (2) on inferences drawn from the behavior of wage differentials and such series as that relating to commercial and industrial failures. As will be seen in the next chapter, moreover, an analysis of available unemployment data supports this interpretation.

The alternative position is tenable that it was the initial rise in the rate of in-migration in the first few years of each of the periods of rapid growth that set in motion a process in which the resulting increase in demand for consumers' goods and services created employment opportunities which, in turn, attracted additional migrants who added to the increased demand, and so on. In other words, it might be argued that it was the initial increase in population which was responsible for all the subsequent developments. But if this were *all* that was involved, fluctuations in California's rate of population growth would probably have been more moderate and would have conformed to the pattern of the ordinary business cycle. It was in considerable part the exploitation of unusually favorable investment opportunities in new or young industries which explained the unusually rapid spurts of growth in certain periods and helped to account for the fifteen-twenty year migration waves. The timing of the exploitation of these investment opportunities was probably not accidental. Undoubtedly the improvement in economic conditions which preceded each of the periods of rapid growth encouraged the exploitation of investment opportunities. Even the timing of the important series of oil discoveries in 1896–1902 and again in 1920–1923 was probably explained in large part by an intensification of the search for petroleum deposits which came with an improvement in business conditions.

The timing of the fifteen-twenty year migration waves, however, cannot be explained merely in terms of what was happening in California. They are part of a much broader phenomenon, as will be seen in chapter viii.

VII. UNEMPLOYMENT RATES IN STATE AND NATION

ANALYSIS of short-run fluctuations in employment conditions in California would be incomplete without some discussion of variations in unemployment. The fact that unemployment was comparatively severe in California during the period from V-J Day to the beginning of the Korean War has given rise to a good deal of discussion as to whether this was a strictly temporary phenomenon or an indication of chronic susceptibility to relatively severe unemployment in the California economy.

This problem will be considered only very briefly.[1] Although historical data on unemployment in California are extremely limited, they deserve a more thorough analysis than the one attempted here. Such an analysis, however, would require a separate study almost as long as the present one.

In table 18 is assembled, so far as possible, the results of practically every census or sample survey which has provided a basis for comparisons of unemployment rates in the state and the nation. The data should not be regarded as providing even an approximation to variations in unemployment rates from one period to another, since the definition of both the workers or persons to be covered and of unemployment varied substantially from one census or survey to another. But each individual survey probably provides a reasonably reliable indication of the relative severity of unemployment in state and nation, since in every case the coverage and methods used were uniform throughout the country.

It is obvious that differences in unemployment rates between California and the United States might be attributable to any one of a number of factors—differences in industrial structure, differences in the timing and amplitude of seasonal or cyclical variations in employment, and numerous other influences. Furthermore, the relative impact of these various factors might be expected to change substantially from one period to another. Even if there were access to detailed monthly employment and unemployment data for the entire period, it would not be easy to determine the precise reasons for differences in unemployment rates between state and nation at various points in time, and in the absence of such complete data, it is virtually impossible.

---

[1] For further discussion of the problem, see California, Department of Employment, *Economic Factors Affecting the Cost of Unemployment Insurance in California* (Sacramento, 1950) and *A Sourcebook on Unemployment Insurance in California* (Sacramento, 1953); A. P. Allen, *Unemployment Insurance in California* (Los Angeles: The John Randolph Haynes and Dora Haynes Foundation, 1950); and J. W. Garbarino, *The Unemployed Worker During a Period of "Full" Employment*, Reprint No. 50, Institute of Industrial Relations, University of California, Berkeley (1954).

TABLE 18

Unemployment Rates in California and the United States, Selected Dates, 1890–1950

Description and date of census or special survey	Persons included in base from which rate is computed	Definition of unemployment	Unemployment rate			
			California	United States	Specified areas or groups	
					California	United States
Census of 1890[a] (June)	All gainful workers (10 years of age and older)	Unemployed at principal occupation during any part of year ending May 31, 1890	16.6	15.5	Extractive Industries......17.5 Other industries......16.3 Los Angeles......18.9 San Francisco......11.0	Extractive industries........13.6 Other industries....16.7
Census of 1900[a] (June)	Same as in 1890	Unemployed at any occupation during any part of year ending May 31, 1900	19.8	22.2	Nonagricultural workers......20.8 Agricultural workers......16.6 Los Angeles......17.5 San Francisco......16.4	Nonagricultural workers........23.1 Agricultural workers........20.7
U.S. Bureau of Labor Statistics cost-of-living survey, 1901	Sample of family heads	Idle (nonemployed) during any part of year, 1901	29.1	49.8		
Metropolitan Life Insurance Company sample survey,[b] June-July, 1915	All wage earners in families holding industrial insurance policies	Wage earners who were (1) wholly unemployed (2) part-time workers at time of enumeration			5 leading California cities......(1) 13.1 (2) 25.4	12 leading western cities......(1) 12.9 (2) 20.2
Census of 1930[a] (April)	Same as in 1890	Persons out of a job, able to work, and looking for work the day before enumerator's visit	6.5	5.0	Los Angeles...... 7.7 San Francisco..... 6.4 Cities of 50,000 and more............ 7.3 Rural............ 4.4	Cities of 500,000 and more......... 8.0 Cities of 50,000 and more......... 7.2 Rural............ 2.5

Survey	Base	Unemployment measure			3 leading California cities	46 leading U.S. cities
Metropolitan Life Insurance Company sample survey,[b] 1930 (December)	Same as in 1915	Wage earners who were (1) wholly unemployed (2) part-time workers at time of enumeration			(1) 20.9 (2) 15.9	(1) 23.8 (2) 21.3
Census sample survey, 1931[b] (January)	Same as in 1890 (1930 data)	Same as in 1930			Los Angeles.....16.9 San Francisco.....12.3	19 cities in U.S.....15.3
Unemployment relief census, 1933[b] (October)	Total population in 1930	Persons in families on relief	6.6	10.3		
Census of unemployment,[c] 1937 (November)	Estimated number of gainful workers, July, 1937	(1) Wholly unemployed or on public emergency work (2) Partly unemployed at time of registration	12.2 4.7	15.4 6.3		
Census of 1940[e] (March)	Civilian labor force	Unemployed or on public emergency work in census week	14.6	14.5	Los Angeles.....14.5 San Francisco.....14.3 Urban.....13.9 Rural nonfarm.....18.5 Rural farm.....10.0	Cities of 100,000 and over.......16.3 Urban.......15.4 Rural nonfarm.....17.9 Rural farm.......8.3
Census sample survey of selected metropolitan districts,[d] 1947 (April)	Civilian labor force	Unemployed in week preceding interview			Los Angeles*.......6 San Francisco-Oakland*........5	Unweighted average of rates in 34 metropolitan districts.. 4
Census of 1950[e] (April)	Civilian labor force	Unemployed in week preceding interview	7.9	4.8	Los Angeles*..... 7.3 San Francisco-Oakland*....... 7.7 Urban....... 7.9 Rural nonfarm... 9.4 Rural farm....... 4.2	Unweighted average of rates in 34 metropolitan areas........ 5.3 Urban........ 5.3 Rural nonfarm..... 5.1 Rural farm....... 1.7

SOURCES: [a]Eleventh, Twelfth, and Fifteenth Censuses of the United States; [b]U. S. Bureau of Labor Statistics, Bulletin, No. 109, 195, 541, and 616; [c]Census of Partial Employment, Unemployment, and Occupations: 1937, Final Report; [d]U.S. Bureau of the Census, Current Population Reports, Series P-51, No. 35, August 24, 1947; [e]United States Census of Population: 1950, Vol. II, Part 1, p. 100 and Part 5, p. 67.
*Metropolitan District (1947) or Standard Metropolitan Area (1950); all earlier data for Los Angeles and San Francisco in the table apply to the central cities and not to the surrounding metropolitan area.

The analysis will be confined to an attempt to answer two rather simple questions: (1) Has the unemployment rate in California tended to be consistently higher or lower than that in the nation, and (2) if not, have variations in the relationship between the two rates been consistent with the hypothesis posed at the beginning of the previous chapter? According to this hypothesis, the pronounced waves in net migration to California were in large part explained by the relatively more favorable employment opportunities prevailing in the state in periods of rising migration and the relatively less favorable employment opportunities in periods of declining migration. Thus, if there has been a tendency for unemployment rates in California (a) to be relatively low at the lower turning point of a migration wave and during the early stages of an upswing in migration and (b) to be relatively high at the upper turning point and during the early stages of a downswing in migration, the variations would be consistent with the hypothesis.

One additional problem in connection with the interpretation of the data in table 18 needs to be mentioned at this point. Since urban unemployment rates tend to exceed those in rural areas, and since a relatively large proportion of California's population has resided in urban areas throughout the period under survey, comparisons between the state and the nation are likely to be somewhat misleading. Wherever possible, data on unemployment rates in relatively large cities and in urban and rural areas are included, in order to provide more meaningful comparisons.

Fortunately, the dates of a good many of the censuses or surveys which form the basis of table 18 were fairly close to a turning point of a migration wave. A study of the table indicates that (1) the unemployment rate in California has not been consistently higher or lower than that in the nation, and (2) that variations in the relationship have on the whole, been consistent with the hypothesis, though the differences in unemployment rates between state and nation have, more often than not, been relatively narrow.

The Census of 1890 occurred several years after a peak in in-migration and after the collapse in real estate speculation which marked the culmination of the boom of the 'eighties in southern California. It shows unemployment to have been slightly more severe in the state than in the nation during the preceding year. When the figures are broken down, however, the higher rate in California is found to be attributable to the larger percentage of workers in the extractive industries who had experienced some unemployment during the year. It is interesting to observe, also, that the proportion of workers who had experienced some unemployment in Los Angeles was considerably higher than in San Francisco. Parenthetically, it is important to recognize that the unemployment data based on the 1890 and 1900 censuses are not at all comparable with those for later periods, referring as they do to the percentages of gainful workers who had experienced some unemployment during an entire year.[2] It is probably for this reason that the rates for workers in the extractive industries (chiefly agricultural workers) are so much higher, relatively, than in some of the more recent censuses.

By 1900, an upswing in migration had apparently been under way, on a moderate scale, for four or five years and was soon to be accelerated. Unemployment rates for both agricultural and nonagricultural workers during the year 1899–1900 were somewhat lower in California than in the nation. The percentage of family heads who experienced some idleness (voluntarily or involuntarily) during the year 1901 was *substantially* lower in California and the nation, moreover, according to the results of a survey conducted by the Bureau of Labor Statistics.

It is unfortunate that the results of the sample survey of 1915 are not more useful for purposes of this study, in view of the fact that the survey was conducted a few years after the upper turning point of a migration wave. Since Eastern and Midwestern cities were surveyed in March and April, and the enumeration in Western cities did not take place until June and July, the results are not strictly comparable.[3] Yet, in spite of the fact that there was apparently some improvement in employment conditions between the spring and summer of 1915,[4] the percentage of wage earners who were found to be wholly unemployed (12.9 per cent) in Western cities was higher than the corresponding percentage for Eastern and Midwestern cities (11.5 per cent).[5] The slight difference between the rate for the five California cities in the survey and all twelve Western cities is probably not statistically significant, but it is interesting to notice that the percentage of parttime wage earners was somewhat higher in the California cities.

There are no data which permit a comparison of unemployment rates in California and the United States during the 1920's.[6] Not until the Cen-

---

[2] The reader should observe, also, that the definition of unemployment used in 1890 differed from that used in 1900.

[3] See U.S. Bureau of Labor Statistics, *Unemployment in the United States*, Bulletin No. 195 (Washington, 1916), p. 6.

[4] Surveys conducted in New York City on an identical basis in February and again in September showed that the proportion of unemployed wage earners declined from 16.2 per cent to 6.7 per cent between the two dates (*ibid.*, p. 99), and Jerome's index of factory employment showed a moderate rise between March and June (U.S. Bureau of the Census, *Historical Statistics of the United States: 1789–1945*, p. 329).

[5] Because of the differing dates of the surveys, the percentage for Eastern and Midwestern cities is not shown in table 18.

[6] Annual estimates of unemployment by states have been prepared by Herring for the period 1900–1940, but since they are based on the assumptions that (1) the labor force increased at a uniform annual rate in each state and in the nation as a whole between decennial censuses, and (2) that the ratio of employment to the labor force in the United

sus of 1930 is there any useful statistical material. In April, 1930, when the census was conducted, unemployment was apparently slightly more serious in California than in the United States.[7] Here again, however, the comparison is somewhat misleading, since the percentages of gainful workers unemployed in both Los Angeles and San Francisco were lower than the average figure for cities of 500,000 and more in the nation as a whole, whereas, if all cities of 50,000 and more are included, it appears that the

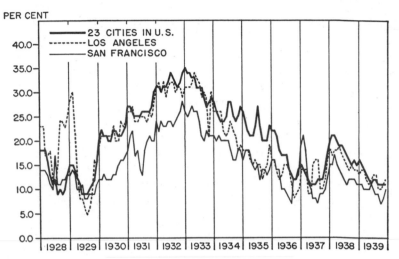

SOURCE: *American Federationist*, monthly issues, 1928–1940.

Fig. 12. Percentage of union members unemployed, American Federation of Labor, California and U.S. cities, monthly, 1928–1939.

California figure was almost identical with that for the nation. On the other hand, unemployment in rural areas was somewhat more severe in California, reflecting at least in part the differences in the pattern of seasonal variation in agricultural employment, to which attention was called in chapter iii.

Surveys conducted at subsequent dates during the depression indicated that unemployment rates in large California cities were somewhat lower than in large cities throughout the nation. The data based on the Unem-

States is a usable approximation to the ratio of employment to the labor force in each state, they are useless for our purposes. See J. P. Herring, *Labor Force, Employment, and Unemployment: Annual Estimates by States: 1900–1940* (Seattle: University of Washington Press, 1951).

[7] In computing the rates shown in table 18, only Class A of the unemployed is included, since Classes B to G of the unemployed would not be classified as unemployed on the basis of the current Bureau of Census definition of unemployment. See Appendix B for further discussion of this problem.

ployment Relief Census of 1933 reflect primarily the situation in large cities, but the results must be interpreted with caution, since they undoubtedly reflect differences in administrative relief standards, as well as genuine differences in the severity of unemployment.

For the late 'twenties and the decade of the 'thirties, monthly data on unemployment of union members, based on reports of local unions belonging to the American Federation of Labor, are also available (see fig. 12). Although they apply only to union members and also reflect differences in the relative strength and industrial composition of union membership in the various cities to which they refer, their movements are interesting. Consistently with other unemployment data for the depression period, they indicate that unemployment was somewhat less severe in San Francisco than in Los Angeles throughout the depression. The greater relative importance of the cyclically less vulnerable trade and service industries, not only in the industrial structure of San Francisco, but also in the distribution of union membership, was probably responsible.

These union unemployment figures constitute the only unemployment data which provide any picture of the course of developments during the early stages of the recovery period. They suggest that the progress of recovery in San Francisco was much like that in the rest of the nation, but that in Los Angeles recovery proceeded at a somewhat accelerated pace for a period extending from the spring of 1934 to the middle of 1936. This is consistent with the interpretation of developments in the middle 'thirties in the preceding chapter.

By November, 1937, when a nation-wide census of unemployment was conducted, an upswing in migration to California had been under way for about four years. Although it is generally considered that the method employed for collecting data in this census was unsatisfactory as a means of arriving at an accurate estimate of unemployment, there is no obvious reason for assuming that there was any systematic source of bias which would invalidate a comparison between the results for California and for the country as a whole. In any event, the results indicated that unemployment was relatively less severe in California.

By the time the enumerators for the 1940 Census were making their rounds, an increase in migration was once again under way, after a brief recession in 1938. Although the unemployment rate for the state of California was almost identical with that for the nation, rates for both Los Angeles and San Francisco were somewhat below that for cities of 100,000 and larger in the country as a whole, and the rate in urban areas generally in California was slightly below that in the nation. On the other hand, unemployment in rural nonfarm and in rural farm areas in California was somewhat more severe than in the United States as a whole, as had been true for rural areas in 1930.

Unemployment fell to extremely low levels in both state and nation as the war boom reached its peak. Unemployment estimates that are available for the period suggest that the unemployment rate was somewhat lower in California than in the nation throughout 1943 and much of 1944.

TABLE 19

ESTIMATED AVERAGE ANNUAL UNEMPLOYMENT RATES,[a]
CALIFORNIA AND UNITED STATES, 1943–1953

Year	California (in per cent)	United States[b] (in per cent)	Year	California (in per cent)	United States[b] (in per cent)
1943	0.7	1.9[c]	1949	9.2	5.9
1944	0.8	1.2[c]	1950	6.6	5.0
1945	3.1	1.9[c]	1951	3.8	3.0
1946	8.8	3.9[c]	1952	3.7	2.7
1947	7.3	4.1	1953	3.4	2.8
1948	6.7	3.9			

SOURCES: Data for 1943 to 1945 are computed from California, Department of Industrial Relations, *Handbook of California Labor Statistics, 1951–1952*, pp. 18 and 75, and from U.S. Bureau of the Census, *Current Population Reports*, Series P-50, No. 2, September 10, 1947, pp. 11–17; data for 1946 to 1952 are from *A Sourcebook on Unemployment Insurance in California*, p. 60; and data for 1953 are computed from California, Department of Employment, *Employment and Unemployment in California*, February, 1954, and from U.S. Bureau of the Census, *Current Population Reports*, Series P-57, Nos. 127–139 (February 13, 1953 to February 8, 1954).
[a]The unemployment rates are expressed as the percentage of the civilian labor force unemployed.
[b]United States data for 1947 to 1953 are adjusted to comparability with California data by including in the number unemployed those not working because of bad weather or because of temporary layoffs.
[c]Data not adjusted to comparability with California.

They also suggest that the unemployment rate in California reached a low point in September-October, 1943, whereas the low point in the nation as a whole was not reached until a year later. Although this is consistent with all the information available on economic developments during this period, it must be recognized that the unemployment estimates for California and the United States are prepared by quite different methods and are not precisely comparable.[8] In addition to differences in sources and method-

[8] The Census Bureau estimates of unemployment in the United States are based on a monthly sample survey of the characteristics of persons residing in about 25,000 households in the United States. One of the purposes of the survey is to provide information for the monthly reports on the labor force, which summarize the survey data relating to the *employment* characteristics of all persons fourteen years of age and older in these households. For a more detailed discussion of Census Bureau methods, see, for example, U.S. Bureau of the Census, *Current Population Reports*, Series P-50, No. 45, July, 1953, pp. 9–12.

The California unemployment estimates are based on unemployment compensation data, supplemented by estimates of unemployment in uncovered industries or types of employment. Estimates of *employment* are based on *establishment* reports made under the social security system and involve some duplicate counting of workers who are employed by more than one employer during the report week. These data must be supplemented by estimates of employment not covered by the social security program. The estimated number of persons in the civilian labor force represents the sum of estimated employ-

ology, there are differences in the definition of unemployment which must be taken into account. All persons who were not at work during the report week because of bad weather, temporary layoffs, or delay in starting a new job, are classified as employed in the United States estimates but as unemployed in the California estimates. In table 19, the data for the United States have been adjusted, for the years from 1947 on, to make them more nearly comparable with the California data. It is impossible, however, to "correct" for all the differences in methods of preparing the estimates.

Throughout the period from 1945 to 1950, the unemployment rate was substantially higher in California than in the country as a whole. Monthly data suggest that the period of materially higher unemployment rates in the state extended approximately from V-J Day to the outbreak of the Korean War. A sample survey conducted in large metropolitan areas in 1947 showed that unemployment rates in both the Los Angeles and San Francisco areas were somewhat above the average rate for all areas in the survey (see table 18). The 1950 Census also showed that the unemployment rate was substantially higher in California than in the nation, and that the difference was wider in rural than in urban areas.

Our analysis of postwar employment changes in the preceding chapter sheds a good deal of light on the reasons for the comparatively high unemployment rate in the state during this period. Furthermore, given the rate of employment expansion in the state, the rate of net in-migration was probably too high in the early postwar years. In this connection, it is interesting that Garbarino's study of a sample of workers who were receiving unemployment compensation in the San Francisco area in late 1947 indicates that migrants were somewhat more heavily represented in the sample of unemployed workers than would have been expected on the basis of their representation in the population as a whole.[9] The author wisely refrains from concluding that the presence of the migrants among the unemployed was necessarily attributable to their migration status, pointing out that the disproportionate representation of migrants was more marked among nonwhite unemployed workers than among the whites and that the racial characteristics of the workers appeared to have a more decisive influence on their presence among the unemployed than did their migration status. All things considered, however, it seems reasonable to

---

ment and estimated unemployment. In addition to these basic differences from Census Bureau methods of compiling the data, there are differences in the definitions of employment and unemployment, as suggested in the text. For further discussion of the methods used in preparing California estimates, see California, Department of Industrial Relations, *Handbook of California Labor Statistics: 1951–1952* (San Francisco, 1953), pp. 16–17 and 74.

[9] The migrants in his sample were defined to include all persons who had moved to the Bay area from January, 1940 on.

infer that, given the relatively adverse employment opportunities for Negroes and their heavy concentration in unskilled and service occupations, the rate of in-migration of Negro workers, in particular, was probably too high in relation to the occupational pattern of expansion of employment opportunities in the postwar period, and that a similar situation prevailed, to a less marked degree, for white workers.

Studies by Arthur D. Allen and by the California State Department of Employment call attention to certain other factors which probably played a role in explaining the relatively high unemployment rates in California in the postwar period.[10] Comparatively high labor turnover in the state, in particular, is emphasized as a contributing factor. In part, this tendency toward high turnover in California is apparently associated with the state's rapid secular rate of growth in economic activity and its accompanying high rate of in-migration.[11] In part, it appears to reflect the influence of other factors, which are not necessarily independent of the rate of growth, such as the size distribution of California firms.[12] This whole question of the relationship between labor mobility and unemployment is one which calls for further exploration and analysis.

During the Korean War period, unemployment fell to low levels in both state and nation. Except during the months of peak seasonal employment in California, the estimated unemployment rate in the state tended to be somewhat higher than that in the nation, and was slightly higher on an average annual basis throughout the period. Of the eight major labor market areas in California, seven were classified by the United States Bureau of Employment Security as having a "moderate labor surplus" throughout most of the Korean War period, although there were shortages of specialized types of professional, technical, and skilled labor needed in defense plants.[13] Only in San Diego did a general shortage of labor constitute a problem during much of the period, gradually easing from the spring of 1952 on. Most of the major labor market areas in the nation were also

---

[10] See the references cited in footnote 1.

[11] The Six-City Occupational Mobility Survey showed that workers in Los Angeles and San Francisco had experienced more job shifts, on the average, in the 1940–1949 period, than the workers in the other four cities in the survey and that these higher mobility rates in the West Coast cities were apparently explained in large part by their higher rates of in-migration. See A. J. Reiss, Jr., and E. Kitigawa, "Demographic Characteristics and Job Mobility of Migrants in Six Cities," *Social Forces*, XXXII (1953), 70–75; M. S. Gordon, "Research Design of the Survey of Patterns and Factors in Mobility in Six Cities," *Journal of the American Statistical Association*, XLVIII (1953), 633; and G. L. Palmer, *Labor Mobility in Six Cities* (New York: Social Science Research Council, 1954), pp. 42–43.

[12] See California, Department of Employment, *Economic Factors Affecting the Cost of Unemployment Insurance in California*, p. 23.

[13] See U.S. Bureau of Employment Security, *Bimonthly Summary of Labor Market Conditions in Major Areas*, seriatim.

classified as having moderate labor surpluses throughout the greater part of the period, but a very substantial minority were classified in the somewhat tighter "balanced labor supply" category.[14]

Both the quantitative and qualitative information for these years suggest that the rate of in-migration into California rose rapidly, as employment in defense plants expanded, to a point at which the supply of inmigrant workers was slightly more than adequate to take care of the increased demand. The reëmployment of previously unemployed workers, as well as the entry of substantial numbers of local workers (chiefly women) into the labor force likewise contributed, of course, to the easing of the labor market situation.

Comparisons between unemployment rates in California and the United States in particular months tend to be affected to a certain extent by differences in the amplitude and timing of seasonal variations. According to the available estimates, it would appear that seasonal variations in both employment and unemployment are somewhat wider in the state than in the nation and follow a somewhat different pattern. The differences are explained chiefly by differences in the timing of seasonal variations in agricultural employment, to which we have already referred. Yet these differences, particularly as they relate to the timing of the seasonal *peak* in farm employment in state and nation, are probably attributable in large part to contrasts in statistical methods. According to Census Bureau estimates, the seasonal peak in farm employment in the nation regularly occurs in June, but the Bureau of Agricultural Economics estimates indicate that the seasonal peak in the nation tends to be reached in September. In California, the peak usually occurs in September, according to estimates prepared by the State Department of Employment, although in certain recent years it has been reached in October. There is reason to believe that the Bureau of Agricultural Economics estimates provide a more accurate indication of *seasonal variations* in farm employment in the nation than the Census Bureau estimates, though they are less satisfactory in certain other respects.[15] If this is true, seasonal variations in total employment and unemployment may differ less in state and nation than the available monthly estimates would suggest, particularly in the early fall months. For this reason, although indices of seasonal variation of employment and unem-

[14] In November, 1951, for example, about a third of the 174 labor market areas covered in the report of the Bureau of Employment Security were classified as areas of "balanced labor supply" conditions and 3 per cent as having a labor shortage. (Cf. *ibid.*, November, 1951.)

[15] For a discussion of the differences between the Census Bureau and BAE estimates, see D. G. Johnson and M. C. Nottenburg, "A Critical Analysis of Farm Employment Estimates," *Journal of the American Statistical Association*, XLVI (1951), 191–205.

ployment for state and nation have been computed for analytical purposes, they are not included among the tables.[16]

So far as nonagricultural employment is concerned, there appear to have been no material differences in either the timing or amplitude of seasonal variations in California and the United States in recent years, at least if comparisons are based on Bureau of Labor Statistics estimates for the nation and California Department of Industrial Relations estimates for the state (which are prepared on a comparable basis).

Whatever the actual situation may be with respect to total employment and unemployment, the apparent differences in seasonal variation must be kept in mind in comparing monthly estimated unemployment rates for state and nation.

CONCLUSIONS

For the most part, the statistical evidence, spotty as it is, indicates that variations in the relationship between unemployment rates in California and the nation have been consistent with our general hypothesis about the relationship between fluctuations in migration and the rate of employment expansion. The unemployment rate in California has tended to be relatively low in the neighborhood of the lower turning point of a migration wave and in the early stages of an upswing in in-migration. It has tended to be relatively high, on the other hand, in the neighborhood of the upper turning point and in the early stages of a downswing. It has not been possible, however, to demonstrate that other factors may not have been at least partly responsible for the variations which we have observed. It is doubtful if the various factors at work in the early decades of the century could be fully disentangled even on the basis of a much more thorough analysis than the one attempted here, in view of the spottiness of the statistical data, although a careful study of the qualitative historical evidence might permit us to reach somewhat more positive conclusions.

The only period in which the data do not seem to be consistent with the hypothesis is the period of the most recent upswing in net in-migration, from 1948 on. If this upswing was induced by relatively more favorable job opportunities in California than in the nation, how explain the higher unemployment rate that prevailed in California in 1948 and 1949, as well as at the time of the 1950 Census, and how explain the fact that, during the Korean War period itself the unemployment rate in California tended to be slightly higher than that in the nation?

First of all, had it not been for the outbreak of the Korean War, there might have been very little rise in net in-migration between 1948 and 1953.

---

[16] For California indices, see D. McEntire, *The Labor Force in California* (Berkeley: University of California Press, 1952), p. 87.

Furthermore, there is a real question as to whether the upswing of these years will prove to have marked the beginning of a new migration wave. This problem will be discussed more fully at the end of the next chapter, after the relationship between waves in migration to California and waves in other streams of migration has been considered. So far as the differences in unemployment rates during the Korean War period itself are concerned, they were so narrow that they may have been explained by differences in statistical methods.

In no earlier period, so far as has been discovered, did the unemployment rate in California exceed that in the nation by as wide a margin as prevailed during the five years following the end of World War II. This may conceivably be attributable to the complete absence of usable data for certain earlier periods (for example, the middle 'twenties) when a somewhat similar relationship might have been expected on the basis of our general hypothesis. On the whole, however, it seems unlikely that more complete statistical information for earlier periods would reveal a situation comparable to that of the late 'forties, in view of the fact that there was no earlier episode in which temporary changes in the structure of employment imposed readjustments on the California economy comparable with those which occurred during and after World War II. The question as to whether the California economy has become more susceptible to periods of relatively severe unemployment than was the case before World War II will be discussed in the concluding chapter.

VIII. MIGRATION WAVES AND
"SECONDARY SECULAR MOVEMENTS"

THE TWO preceding chapters have traced the relationship between waves in migration to California and fluctuations in economic activity in the state. A good deal of evidence was found that indicated that changes in the rate of net in-migration tended to be closely related to changes in the rate of economic expansion in the state relative to that in the nation. The analysis would be incomplete, however, if it failed to take account of the fact that waves in migration to California are closely related to waves in other streams of migration and in the rate of growth of the American economy.

WAVES IN IMMIGRATION TO THE UNITED STATES

A number of writers have observed that there have been long and pronounced waves in immigration to the United States. As figure 13 indicates, these waves have been somewhat similar in amplitude and duration to those observed in net migration to California. The timing of fluctuations during the present century has clearly been influenced by the two world wars, and the volume of immigration fell off sharply after the enactment of the Immigration Act of 1924. Nevertheless, between 1842 and 1933, there were five long cycles in immigration, of wide amplitude and some fifteen to twenty years in duration.[1] During the present century, moreover, the timing of these immigration waves—apart from the interruption of immigration during World War II—agreed quite closely with the timing of cycles in net migration to California.

Several attempts have been made to determine what factors have been responsible for these long waves in immigration. In his classic study of migration and business cycles, Jerome did not especially concern himself with the problem of these long waves but showed that *cyclical* fluctuations in immigration tended to correspond to cyclical variations in employment opportunities in the United States, with fluctuations in immigration usually lagging from one to five months behind variations in employment opportunities.[2] Silberling, who did concern himself with the long waves and especially with their relation to building cycles in this country, concluded

---

[1] Data for the early part of this period are not shown in figure 13, but may be found in U.S. Bureau of the Census, *Historical Statistics of the United States: 1789–1945* (Washington, 1949), p. 37.

[2] See H. Jerome, *Migration and Business Cycles* (New York: National Bureau of Economic Research, 1926), especially chapter x. A similar conclusion was reached by Dr. Dorothy S. Thomas, in her *Social and Economic Aspects of Swedish Population Movements, 1750–1933* (New York: A. A. Knopf, 1941), pp. 166–169.

that, although Jerome's interpretation of the shorter fluctuations was correct, the longer waves in immigration reflected primarily the influence of

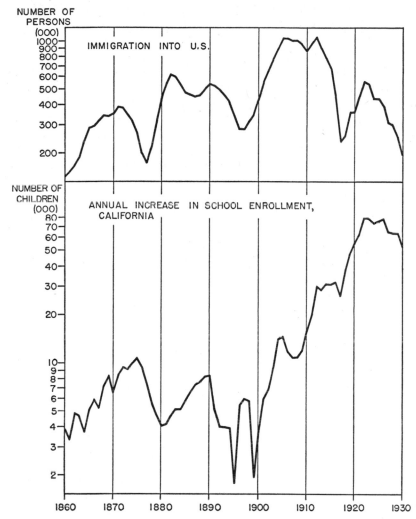

SOURCES: See Appendix B.

Fig. 13. Immigration into the United States and annual change in school enrollment in California, five-year moving averages, 1860–1930.

conditions in foreign countries and were to be regarded (from the point of view of the student of *American* business fluctuations) as "originating factors in the strict sense."[3]

----

[3] N. J. Silberling, *The Dynamics of Business* (New York: McGraw-Hill, 1943), p. 187 n.

Brinley Thomas, who has looked into somewhat the same problem more recently, concludes that in the late 'forties and early 'fifties of the last century, the timing of fluctuations in immigration to the United States (or emigration from Europe) *was* determined by expulsive forces in the Old World, but that after the structural changes of the late 'sixties, the "pull" element was as evident in the long cycles of migration as in the short cycles.[4] According to Thomas, it was primarily fluctuations in railway construction which determined the timing and amplitude of these long cycles. Emigration from Britain to the United States, as well as British capital exports, tended to move in the wake of American activity in railway construction but to precede changes in building activity.[5] In other words, there were major investment cycles with a span similar to those of immigration and building cycles, akin, Thomas believes, to the "secondary secular movements" which Kuznets found in the rate of growth of the gross national product in the United States.[6]

These findings are of interest primarily because there may very well be important similarities between the manner in which changes in the volume of immigration and of internal migration respond to changes in economic conditions. It must be remembered, however, that immigration from abroad constituted an important direct source of migration to California through the first decade of the present century.[7] Some of these foreign-born persons, of course, had lived in other states before coming to California, but, though there is no way of measuring how many persons came directly to the state from abroad, the annals of the period suggest that their numbers were substantial.

WAVES IN FARM TO CITY MIGRATION

During the period when immigration was heavy, the growing needs of the urban centers of the East for manual workers were in very considerable

---

[4] Cf. B. Thomas, "Migration and the Rhythm of Economic Growth, 1830–1913," *The Manchester School of Economic and Social Studies*, XIX (1951), 215–271.

[5] Thomas points out that the period he was able to study may not have been long enough to form a basis for firm generalization about these relationships. He qualifies his conclusions, moreover, by pointing out that the emigration of young adults from European countries was related to the level of the birth rate at the time the emigrants were born and that fluctuations in the rate of population growth may conceivably have constituted the initiating factor in bringing about waves of emigration. On the whole, however, he appears to feel that the timing of the turning points was determined by changes in economic conditions in the United States, rather than by European population changes.

[6] See the reference in footnote 13, below. Thomas also points out, interestingly enough, that the British home investment cycle was inverse to that of the United States in the late nineteenth century, showing major periods of upswing when capital exports and emigration to the United States fell off.

[7] See Appendix, table A-1.

part being met by the stream of foreign-born immigrants. When the volume of immigration from abroad was sharply cut back by World War I—and later by the Immigration Act of 1924—the character of internal migration changed somewhat. From about 1915 on, migration from the South to the North assumed increased proportions, doubtless partly in response to expanding job opportunities which were not being met by immigrants. Migration from the West to the East also began to play a more important role, though the net movement was still westward.

In part, these shifting regional currents of migration reflected the fact that farm-to-city migration, which had long been taking place to some extent, was beginning to assume more decisive proportions as a major factor in supplying the needs of urban centers for an expanding labor force. But the volume of farm-to-city migration, like that of other streams of migration, has been highly variable, as the estimates of net farm-nonfarm migration published by the Department of Agriculture for the years from 1920 to 1948 clearly indicate (see fig. 14). Interestingly enough, moreover, these variations show a rather marked resemblance, in their broad outlines though not as to precise turning points, to fluctuations in net migration to California—the marked rise in the early 'twenties and tapering off thereafter, the increase after the depression, the sharp rise during the war, and the lower level in the postwar period. The fact that movements into and out of the Armed Forces are reflected in these data during the 1940's helps to account for the sharp rise in 1942 and the net back-to-the-farm movement in 1945, but there was an estimated net movement of 2,930,000 civilians from farms to nonfarm areas during the war.[8]

Farm-to-city migration does not represent a very important direct source of interstate migration to California, nor do migrants from California farms represent an important percentage of the migrants to California cities, as they do in Midwestern cities. But the correspondence between the variations in net farm-nonfarm movement and in net migration to California suggests the possibility that similar economic forces act upon both types of movement. It is therefore of some interest to us to inquire briefly into the factors responsible for fluctuations in farm-nonfarm movement.

Broadly speaking, it is known that the most important secular forces which have stimulated the farm-to-city movement have been: (1) the more rapid increase in demand for goods and services produced in urban areas, (2) the higher incomes earned in urban employment, (3) mechanization and improved efficiency on the farm, and (4) the higher birth rate in rural areas. Thus, there have been both "push" and "pull" factors behind the farm-to-city movement, as in the case of all migratory movements, and for

[8] See U.S. Bureau of the Census, *Population*, Series P-S, No. 6, October 29, 1945.

any given individual the decision to migrate has undoubtedly represented the result of a complex interaction of both sets of forces. But the available evidence seems to indicate that, for the most part, the fluctuations in the volume of net farm-nonfarm movement have reflected changes in employment conditions in urban centers—probably the most important "pull" factor—rather than changes in the income position of the farmer—the chief "push" factor. On the whole, urban employment opportunities and cash farm income have changed in the same direction and with approximately the same timing. When urban job opportunities improved, the net movement from farm to city increased, although cash farm income was also increasing, and the net movement from farm to city fell off when urban unemployment increased, although the income position of the farmer was likewise deteriorating. The experience of the 1920's constitutes something of an exception to this generalization. The marked rise in net farm-nonfarm migration from 1920 to 1922 was probably at least partly attributable to the sharp drop in cash farm income (32 per cent) in this period, rather than to unusually favorable employment conditions in urban areas, for non-agricultural employment was 4 per cent lower in 1922 than in 1920, and unemployment has been estimated at nearly 3,000,000 in 1922 as compared with 558,000 in 1920.[9] On the other hand, between 1922 and 1929, when net farm-nonfarm movement showed, on the whole, a tendency to decline, cash farm income increased 31 per cent and nonagricultural employment 20 per cent.

Of special interest to anyone concerned with migration problems are the data on gross movement between farm and nonfarm areas in figure 14. These data show that net movement from farm to nonfarm areas has represented, not a single stream of migration in one direction, but the difference between substantial flows in both directions, with the relationship between the two streams changing somewhat from time to time, when economic conditions changed or when, as in the war and immediate postwar periods, there was substantial movement into or out of the Armed Forces. To a greater or lesser degree, this type of relationship appears to hold for all migration, including movement into and out of California.

WAVES IN MIGRATION TO SELECTED STATES

In seeking to determine to what extent waves in migration to California have conformed with waves in other streams of migration, it is worth while looking into the fluctuations in net movement to other states in which net

---

[9] See the National Industrial Conference Board estimates of annual average employment and unemployment in U.S. Bureau of the Census, *Historical Statistics of the United States: 1789–1945* (Washington, 1949), p. 65. Farm income data may be found in the same volume, p. 99.

in-migration has represented an important component of population growth. Actually, states are not the most appropriate geographic units with which to work, since they represent complex composites of economic

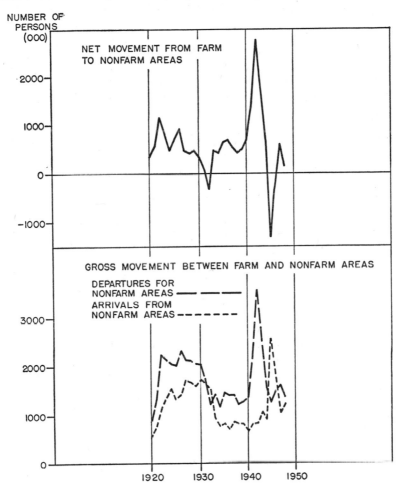

SOURCES: U.S. Bureau of the Census, *Historical Statistics of the United States: 1789–1945*, p. 31 and *Statistical Abstract of the United States: 1950*, p. 21. (Estimates prepared by U.S. Bureau of Agricultural Economics.)

Fig. 14. Estimated farm-nonfarm migration, United States, 1920–1948.

activity with varying degrees of urbanization and industrialization, but they are the only areas (other than a few cities) for which continuous annual population estimates are readily available for a considerable period. As in California, however, annual estimates of net in-migration cannot

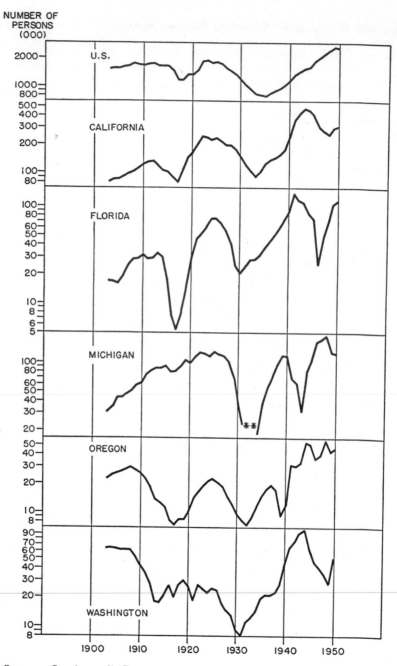

NUMBER OF
PERSONS
(000)

2000 — U.S.

1000
800

500
400
300 — CALIFORNIA

200

100
80

100
80 — FLORIDA
60
50
40

30

20

10
8

6
5

MICHIGAN
100
80
60
50
40

30

20 **

50
40 — OREGON

30

20

10
8

90
70
60
50
40

30

20

WASHINGTON

10
8

1900   1910   1920   1930   1940   1950

SOURCES: See Appendix B.

Fig. 15. Estimated annual population growth of the United States and selected states, five-year moving averages, 1903-1950.

Michigan's total resident population (five-year moving average) showed an increase of less than 1,000 in each of these years.

easily be made, even for states, for years before 1920, when births were not adequately reported, or for the decade of the 'forties, when movements into and out of the Armed Forces exercised a dominant influence on annual population changes in many states.

Figure 15 brings together estimates of annual population growth since 1900 for the United States and for four states, in addition to California, for which net in-migration has represented an important component of population growth during a large part of the period. The states selected were all predominantly urban, at least by 1950.[10] Preferably, of course, estimates of net in-migration, rather than of total population increase, should be considered, but such estimates are available only for a considerably shorter period, and it can readily be demonstrated that, for these states, in the period for which there are adequate birth and death statistics, fluctuations in total population growth have primarily reflected changes in net migration. In order to eliminate irregular fluctuations, which tend to obscure similarities in broader movements, the data are presented in the form of five-year moving averages.

The series for three of the states show marked similarities in their broader fluctuations, at least up to 1940. Variations in annual population growth in California, Florida, and Oregon conformed in broad outline to variations in annual population growth for the country as a whole, though they were more pronounced, and precise turning points differed somewhat. The same statement also applies to some extent to the data for Washington on the second page of the chart. The Michigan data showed only a very slight decline in 1915–1916, probably because of the impact of the rapid growth of the automobile industry, followed by a boom in military production during World War I.

Similarities in the various series were less marked from 1940 on, partly because of the distorting effect of military movement of varying proportions into and out of the various states. If members of the Armed Forces overseas are included, as in figure 15, the annual gain in total population for the country as a whole tended to increase steadily during the 1940's. Net civilian in-migration into each of the five states has been estimated by the Census Bureau for the 1940–1942, 1942–1945, and 1945–1950 periods. These estimates show that, for all five states, net civilian in-migration was somewhat lower, on an average annual basis, in the postwar period than during the first half of the decade.[11] In the case of Washington, in fact, there

---

[10] Predominantly rural states which have grown largely through in-migration, for example, Arizona, show a somewhat different pattern of fluctuations, as we should be inclined to expect in the light of what we know about farm-nonfarm migration.

[11] See U.S. Bureau of the Census, *Current Population Reports*, Series P-25, No. 72, May, 1953. The estimates for California included in this publication agree closely with the earlier estimates prepared by the California State Department of Finance, which are cited in chapter vi. (See chapter vi, footnote 1.)

was net out-migration of civilians between 1945 and 1950. In Florida, on the other hand, net civilian in-migration was almost as high (on an annual average basis) in the postwar period as from 1942 to 1945. Nevertheless, although there were pronounced differences in the extent of the change, the data for all five states indicate a peak in net civilian in-migration some-time between 1940 and 1945.

Nation-wide migration surveys also indicate that the internal migration rate tended to decline somewhat in the postwar period. In the year immediately following V-J Day, 15.7 per cent of the civilian population (four-teen years old and older) participated in intercounty migration, but the proportion was only 6.7 per cent if men who were in the Armed Forces at the beginning of the period are excluded.[12] In the three years from April, 1947, through March, 1950, the civilian migration rates gradually fell from 6.4 per cent to 5.6 per cent. In the following year, probably as a result of the Korean crisis, the rate moved up again, to 7.1 per cent. In 1951–1952, however, and again in 1952–1953, the rate was 6.6 per cent.[13] Approximately half of the migrants moved between states, whereas the remainder moved within their respective states, but these proportions varied slightly from survey to survey.

On the whole, the data examined strongly suggest that the long waves which show up so prominently in net migration to California are part of a much broader phenomenon. There have been similar waves in immigration (at least before World War I), in farm-nonfarm migration, and in net migration (as roughly indicated by annual population increments) to a group of predominantly urban states, but the dates of turning points in these various streams of migration have varied slightly.

Although the relationship between each of these migration waves and changes in economic activity have not been analyzed in detail, there is a good deal of evidence to suggest that in all these cases, the "pull" of relatively rapidly expanding employment opportunities in the areas of in-migration played an important role in explaining the upswings in migration, and a weakening of the relative strength of these pulls helped to explain the downswings.

For the nation as a whole, the fact has already been mentioned that the swings in immigration and in total population growth may be related to secondary swings in the rate of increase in the gross national product. In his studies of the growth of the national economy since 1870, Kuznets has

[12] Cf. U.S. Bureau of the Census, *Population*, Series P-S, No. 24, June 6, 1947.

[13] See U.S. Bureau of the Census, *Current Population Reports*, Series P-20, No. 49, December 1, 1953. The percentages refer to the percentage of the civilian population (one year old and older) participating in intercounty migration. They are thus not precisely comparable with the percentage cited for the year following V-J Day.

found that there have been three long swings, and a partial fourth swing, in the rate of increase in the gross national product (in constant prices) during the period. The peak of the first swing was reached about the late 1870's and its trough about the early 'nineties; the second peak occurred about the early 1900's and a second trough about 1910–1912; the third upswing reached a peak about the middle 'twenties, with a trough following approximately a decade later. At the time these findings were published (1952), the peak of the fourth upswing which began in the middle 'thirties could not be dated with any degree of confidence.[14] It is doubtful if it could be dated any more confidently today (1954).

These peaks and troughs are dated on the basis of data for overlapping decades. It is quite possible that, when Kuznets has completed his analysis of the annual data on gross national product that he has been developing, he may arrive at somewhat different turning points. In any event, these long swings appear to bear a rough relationship to the immigration and migration waves which have been discussed in the present chapter. A precise comparison of turning points will not be justified until Kuznets' annual data become available.

It should be noticed that these secondary secular movements, averaging more than twenty years in length from peak to peak or trough to trough, are distinct from the fifty-year Kondratiev cycles or the nine-to twelve-year Juglar cycles, both of which play important roles in Schumpeter's cyclical scheme.[15]

What accounts for these swings in the rate of economic growth of the United States? Kuznets himself is extremely cautious in interpreting his data, and it is clear that more detailed studies are needed before it can be determined (1) whether these secondary secular movements are truly cyclical, in the sense that they are self-generating and may be expected to recur, and (2) what forces are responsible for them. No conclusions can be attempted on this range of problems within the context of a study of employment expansion in California. Yet, if these swings in the rate of growth of the American economy are closely related to the swings which have been observed in the rate of growth of the California economy, they are obviously of great interest to anyone who is concerned with the state's economic problems.

Kuznets points out that there appears to have been a sequence in which a change in the rate of flow of goods to consumers induced, with some lag,

---

[14] See International Association for Research in Income and Wealth, *Income and Wealth of the United States: Trends and Structure*, Income and Wealth Series II, Papers by Simon Kuznets and Raymond Goldsmith (Cambridge, England, 1952), p. 49.

[15] See J. A. Schumpeter, *Business Cycles* (New York: McGraw-Hill, 1939), Vol. I, especially chapters iv and v.

a change in the rate of population growth of the United States, which in turn led to a change in the volume of construction.[16] But this sequence seems to have been somewhat condensed in recent decades. Even if it is possible to establish a sequence of this kind, moreover, it is still a question why swings of this type occur. The best that can be done here is to set forth a number of hypotheses which might conceivably explain these secondary secular movements, stressing the fact that these are possible alternative explanations, none of which has been clearly demonstrated to be valid. The reader will observe that, since some of the hypotheses are mutually exclusive, they could not *all* be supported. Among the more important of these possible explanations are the following:

1. Innovations and other structural changes play a strategic role in generating major swings in economic activity. After a major depression, there is likely to be a period of increasingly intensive exploitation of investment opportunities associated with such changes. Since the economic expansion generated by this investment stimulates the rate of population growth of the country as a whole and of individual regions, and these effects in turn lead to an upswing in construction activity, the cumulative expansionary effect of the initial stimulus may be spread over several ordinary business cycles.[17] Of special interest in connection with studies of regional economic development is the probability that young industries (whose growth is stimulated by innovations) are not likely to follow the same patterns of industrial location as older industries and may well contribute to spurts of growth in particular areas (consider the impact of the growth of the automobile industry on Detroit, of the rubber industry on Akron, and of the aircraft industry on Los Angeles).

2. Innovations in the transport industry (canals, railroads, automobiles, airplanes) have led to intensive periods of relocation of industry and population, which in turn have been responsible for building cycles.[18]

3. Secondary secular swings have their origins in major wars, which result in a major displacement of normal growth relationships in the economy. Certain types of activity are stimulated during the war—others (including marriages, births, and residential and commercial construction) tend to be held back during the period of most intense hostilities, but to be stimulated immediately following the war. A displacement of serious magnitude may generate a series of secular swings of diminishing intensity, until a new major war introduces a new set of relationships.

[16] See International Association for Research in Income and Wealth, *op. cit.*, p. 189.

[17] Schumpeter (*op. cit.*) stresses the role of innovations but does not link their effects with a twenty-year cycle. For some suggestive discussion of the exploitation of investment opportunities, see R. A. Gordon, "Investment Opportunities in the United States before and after World War II," paper presented at a meeting of the International Economics Association, Oxford University, September, 1952 (to be published in a forthcoming volume recording the proceedings of the meeting).

[18] See W. Isard, "Transport Development and Building Cycles," *Quarterly Journal of Economics*, LVII (1942), 90–112; and other articles by the same author. Silberling (*op. cit.*, especially chapter x) also stresses the importance of the relationship between fluctuations in the transport and building industries in attempting to explain major swings in the economy.

4. Major swings in economic activity are generated by the changes in the rate of population growth which result from major wars.[19] This hypothesis, it will be observed, differs from the others in assigning the *initiating* role to changes in the rate of population growth.

Periods of rising internal migration, then, are apparently related to major periods of upswing in economic activity in the nation as a whole. In view of the primary interest in employment trends in this study, it is interesting that during the initial stages of these major periods of upswing in migration, employment (in the United States) has tended to increase more rapidly than the labor force, but this relationship has tended to be reversed in the later stages of migration waves.[20] In other words, it would appear that migration was encouraged in periods when employment was increasing more rapidly than the labor force and tended to decline in periods when employment was increasing less rapidly than the labor force.

Conclusions

The evidence assembled in the present chapter suggests that waves in migration to California cannot be explained solely in terms of developments which accelerated or retarded the rate of change of economic activity in the state relative to that in the nation. These waves have tended to coincide roughly with waves in other streams of migration and to be related, apparently, to secondary secular swings in the rate of growth of the American economy.

It is for this reason that the question was raised, at the end of the preceding chapter, as to whether the upswing in migration to California from 1948 to 1953 represented the early stages of a new wave in migration, or perhaps a temporary rise associated with the Korean War, which is likely to be followed, at some point, by a substantial downswing in the rate of net in-migration. Clearly, it will be many years before there will be a definite answer to this question, but if the relationships discussed in the present chapter continue to work themselves out in the future as they have in the past, there are a number of reasons for holding that the most recent upswing in net migration to California probably does *not* represent the beginning of a new migration wave.

1. The early 1950's probably represented either the late stages of an upswing of a secondary secular movement or some phase of a downswing. The gross national product (in constant dollars) reached an all-time high in 1953, according to

---

[19] This view is held by August Lösch, who, unlike most economists and population experts, regards changes in the rate of population growth as the *initiating* factor bringing about changes in the rate of economic activity. See his "Population Changes as a Cause of Business Cycles," *Quarterly Journal of Economics*, LI (1937), 649–662, and, for a more detailed exposition, *Bevölkerungswellen und Wechsellagen* (Jena: G. Fischer, 1936).

[20] See Appendix, table A-25.

Department of Commerce estimates, but the rate of increase between 1944 (the wartime peak) and 1953 was much less pronounced than between 1933 and 1944.[21] We may find, when figures for later years become available, that after an adjustment has been made for trend, the peak of the upswing which began after the Great Depression was reached toward the end of World War II. What seems unlikely is that the rise in the early 'fifties represented the beginning of a new upswing.

2. The annual increase in the number of households was tending to decline in the early 'fifties. From an annual increase of about 1,500,000 in the period from 1947 to 1950, it had fallen to an estimated 956,000 in the year ending April, 1953, though the latter figure represented a slight increase over the estimate for the previous year.[22] A further decline in the middle and late 'fifties was anticipated. In view of this, a downswing in the building cycle seemed likely, *unless* income and employment levels remained so high that the replacement demand for housing became a much more important factor in the situation than it had been in previous decades.

[21] See U.S. Department of Commerce, *Survey of Current Business*, February, 1954, p. 5, and earlier issues.

[22] See U.S. Bureau of the Census, *Current Population Reports*, Series P-20, No. 48, October 4, 1953, and No. 53, April 11, 1954. It should be kept in mind that these estimates are subject to sampling variability.

IX. CONCLUSIONS

PERHAPS the most important conclusion emerging from the present study is that California's economic development during the present century has been subject, not only to ordinary cyclical fluctuations, but also to alternating phases of rapid and slower growth, of longer duration than the usual business cycle. These longer variations in the rate of growth have had a wavelike character and have been similar, in timing and duration, to the "secondary secular movements" which have been observed by some investigators in the economic development of the country as a whole.

During at least part of the expansion phase of each of these waves, California's rate of economic growth has tended to be more rapid than that of the country as a whole, and it has been during these spurts of rapid growth that the greatest influxes of migrants have occurred. On the other hand, the contraction phase of these secondary secular movements has not necessarily tended to be more pronounced in the state than in the nation, though there has been evidence of somewhat more serious unemployment in California following a peak in the rate of in-migration.

It is not clear that these waves in California's rate of growth are cyclical in character, in the sense that they are self-generating and likely to recur in the future. In fact, it would be rash to attempt to reach a definite conclusion on this point, in view of the evidence that they are related to nationwide and, possibly, to world-wide movements. Yet this study has served to draw attention to the possibility that large-scale internal migration to areas which are in a relatively immature stage of economic growth may well tend to be an accompaniment of the expansionary phase of secondary secular movements, and it does not seem unreasonable to infer that a period of unusually heavy migration to such areas must be followed by a period of "absorption" before economic conditions are favorable for a new influx of migrants. But it must be recognized that these waves of alternating heavy influx and absorption may be expected to vary considerably in length, particularly in view of the very obvious fact that wars have influenced their timing and duration. Furthermore, in the light of the evidence that the heaviest influxes of population have occurred during periods of rapid spurts in the rate of economic growth in California and that the spurts have been associated in large part with the growth of young industries, it is conceivable that a particular state might go through an entire period of upswing in a secondary secular movement without experiencing any very marked rise in in-migration.

The evidence that net migration to California has been sensitive to changes in the rate of economic expansion in the state suggests that a prolonged maladjustment between the rate of population growth and the rate of employment expansion is unlikely. In other words, if a secular decline in the rate of employment expansion should develop, we should also expect a secular decline in the rate of in-migration, which has tended to be the most important determinant of the rate of population growth.

On the other hand, as might be expected, net migration has not been so sensitive to changes in the rate of economic expansion that short-run maladjustments have been altogether avoided. It was not only in the period following World War II, but also in certain earlier periods, that the unemployment rate was relatively high in California a few years after a peak in net in-migration. In no earlier period for which there are any data, however, was the difference between the unemployment rate in the state and in the nation as wide (in percentage terms) as in the years following World War II.[1] The evidence suggests that a serious maladjustment, even of a short-run nature, between the rate of in-migration and the rate of employment expansion is not likely to occur except as a result of the abrupt changes in the level of employment which can be brought about, for example, by a sharp expansion and subsequent contraction of the level of defense spending. Even then, whether the unemployment rate is higher in California than elsewhere, will depend on a complex combination of factors.

Throughout most of this discussion, the fact has been emphasized that a rise in the volume of migration to California tends to come about in *response* to an increase in the rate of employment expansion in the state. Although on the whole, this is true, it will not suffice as a generalized description of the relationship between economic conditions in the state and the rate of in-migration. There has been *some* net in-migration even in seri-

---

[1] It may well be that in certain periods, the unemployment rate in rural areas in California has been unusually high. It has not been possible, on the basis of the available data, to determine to what extent the higher rural unemployment in California which showed up in each of the last three decennial censuses, was attributable to differences in the timing of seasonal variations in agricultural employment or to other factors. It seems reasonable to suppose that a maladjustment between the rate of in-migration of farm laborers and the rate of employment expansion in California agriculture in the middle and late 'thirties may have resulted in a relatively high unemployment rate, particularly in off-seasons, among farm laborers in the state, but available statistical data do not shed much light on this question. Furthermore, there has been a tendency for workers to migrate from California cities to farm areas in periods of serious urban unemployment, but there is very little available information on the question as to whether this tendency has been *more* pronounced here than in other states. A reverse movement has tended to occur in periods of rising urban employment opportunities. See L. V. Fuller, *The Supply of Agricultural Labor as a Factor in the Evolution of Farm Organization in California*, printed as Exhibit 8762A in Hearings, U.S. Senate Committee on Education and Labor, 76th Congress, 3d Sess., Part 54, *Agricultural Labor in California* (Washington, 1940).

ous depressions, and the available evidence suggests that these depression migrants have probably included relatively more elderly persons and relatively fewer young adults of working age than the migratory streams of more prosperous periods. Second, so far as can be judged for somewhat limited data, there has been a tendency for the rate of net migration to California to rise as soon as the nation's economy began to recover from a severe depression, even though recovery proceeded no more rapidly in California than in the country as a whole. Third, it is obvious that a substantial (though immeasurable) proportion of the expansion in employment has come about as a *result* of the increase in population, since more people mean higher demand which, of course, means more jobs. But it remains true that the big spurts in net in-migration have apparently occurred in response to economic developments which accelerated the rate of employment expansion.

The emphasis throughout the discussion on the relationship between changes in economic activity and fluctuations in the volume of net migration to California may have led the reader to conclude that I consider economic considerations to be of overwhelming importance among the various factors motivating the decisions of workers to migrate to California. Actually, this does not necessarily follow. There is little doubt that noneconomic considerations play a highly important role in connection with decisions to migrate to California.[2] But a worker in, say, Ohio, who would like an opportunity to escape freezing winter weather and to spend his summer vacations fishing in the Sierra, is likely to postpone actual migration to California until such time as he feels reasonably confident that he will find a job without inordinate difficulty when he arrives there. If he owns a house in Ohio, moreover, he will prefer not to attempt to sell it in the midst of a depression but will wait until real estate prices have recovered somewhat before putting his house on the market.

In other words, it can be argued that, though noneconomic considerations play an important role in connection with decisions to migrate to California, economic considerations play the leading role in relation to the *timing* of actual migration, that is, in relation to migration *waves*. Nevertheless, the fact that noneconomic motivation is important helps to explain the strength of the secular tendency to migrate to California.

If this is true, may it not follow, after all, that it is the rapid population growth of California that has accounted for its rapid economic develop-

---

[2] For an interesting recent discussion of this question, see E. L. Ullman, "Amenities as a Factor in Regional Growth," *The Geographical Review*, XLIV (1954), 119–132. For an earlier analysis, in which the authors conclude that noneconomic factors have been of primary importance in explaining the heavy volume of migration to California, see M. L. Bright and D. S. Thomas, "Interstate Migration and Intervening Opportunities," *American Sociological Review*, VI (1941), pp. 773–783.

ment, rather than the reverse? In other words, whereas economic developments accounted for the *fluctuations* in the rate of growth, the high secular rate of economic growth must be explained largely as a response to the high secular rate of population growth, which in turn must be explained largely as a response to the attractions of the California climate and way of living.

This argument has a certain plausibility, particularly when it is taken into account that the growth of Western manufacturing, as well as of trade and service industries, is dependent to a considerable extent on the growth of the Western market. But in its most extreme form it reduces to an absurdity, namely, that the Western states could absorb unlimited additions to their populations without experiencing a marked reduction in their relative standards of living. Even in a less extreme form, the argument has its limitations. Is it not likely, for example, that California's population growth would have been substantially less spectacular than it actually was in the last twenty years if the aircraft industry had not developed in southern California? (In weighing this question, the stimulating effect of aircraft employment on employment in a wide variety of other industries must be remembered.) And yet the development of the southern California aircraft industry came about, not primarily in response to population growth in the area, but rather as a result of a combination of technological developments and the discovery that the climate had certain specific advantages in relation to production problems in the industry.

It must certainly be conceded that population growth *per se* has a stimulating effect on the growth of many industries, but California's population growth would probably have been considerably less rapid during the first half of the present century in the absence of certain specific economic developments which stimulated the growth of new or young industries. At the same time, of course, it must be recognized that here is a problem of the chicken-and-egg variety, in which cause and effect cannot be fully disentangled.

In emphasizing the extent to which in-migration has responded to changes in the rate of expansion of employment opportunities, relatively little attention has been paid to the possibility that changes in the rate of in-migration may have come about in response to changes in wage differentials between California and the nation, as orthodox economic analysis would suggest. It has proved impossible to explore this problem fully within the compass of the present study, although the behavior of both per capita income and wage differentials over the course of migration waves have been briefly discussed. There is evidence that, when employment opportunities were expanding more rapidly in California than in the nation as a whole, wage differentials between state and nation tended to widen, whereas a reverse movement occurred as soon as the rate of expansion of employment opportunities fell to the national level or below it. But this leaves unsettled the question as to whether the increase in net in-migration occurred in response to the relatively rapid expansion of employment opportunities or in response to the increase in wage differentials. On the whole, it could be argued that differential changes in employment opportunities appear to have played a relatively more important role in explaining short-run variations in migration, although the whole question of short-run changes in wage differentials deserves more careful study. In the *long run*, as pointed out in chapter v, a decline in the relative rate of expansion of employment opportunities in the state would tend to be accompanied by a decline in wage differentials.

Another problem that deserves further investigation is the relationship of gross to net migration to California. There is evidence that, at least in recent years, the volume of migration both into and out of the state has been considerably larger than the net in-migration figure.[3] It may very well be that the sensitivity of net migration to changes in employment conditions in the state is in part explained by changes which occur in the relationship between gross in-migration and gross out-migration. In other words, the number of workers who migrate to California in search of employment may always exceed, by some margin, the net in-migration figure for any given year, but the degree of success or failure experienced by inmigrant workers in finding jobs in the state will determine how many of them will elect to remain and how many will decide to return to their former places of residence or, alternatively, to seek employment in other states. This is not to deny that the volume of gross in-migration, as well as the volume of net in-migration, probably fluctuates considerably with changing economic conditions. The reports received by job seekers in other states on employment conditions in California through (1) letters from friends or acquaintances in California, (2) recruiting activities of business firms or other organizations, and (3) public and private employment agencies undoubtedly affect the decisions of workers to migrate to California in the first place. Their experience in finding jobs, once they have arrived in the state, affects their decision as to whether or not to remain. The tremendous rise in automobile ownership has undoubtedly made it easier for workers from other states to "try their luck" at finding a job in California, even while on vacation from jobs in other states, but there is evidence that, long before the day of the automobile, large numbers of in-migrants some-

[3] See California, Department of Employment, *A Sourcebook on Unemployment Insurance in California* (Sacramento, 1953), p. 24. See also the data on in-migration and out-migration in 1949–50 in *1950 Census of Population: Advance Reports*, Series PC-14, No. 17, July, 1953, pp. 23–24.

times left the state if employment conditions appeared to be unfavorable here.[4]

If population growth has been stimulated to a considerable extent by specific economic developments, what can be said about the relationship between population growth and the industrial *pattern* of employment expansion? Are there not many sectors of the California economy—those that cater primarily to the local market—in which changes in the rate of employment expansion have come about largely in *response* to changes in the rate of population growth? (Among local market industries should be included large and important sectors of construction, manufacturing, transportation, communications, utilities, and service, as well as some branches of agriculture and mining.) The answer here seems to be that, although population growth is the chief determinant of the *secular* rate of employment expansion in such industries, the short-run relationship between population growth and employment expansion in these industries is subject to a variety of disturbing influences and is not necessarily predictable.

As the analysis in chapters iii and iv clearly indicated, there has been no consistent relationship between the rate of population growth and the industrial pattern of employment expansion from decade to decade. Each decade has been characterized by its own particular pattern of employment expansion, which can be fully interpreted only in the light of a thorough understanding of economic developments in that decade, and each broad industry group has had its own peculiar pattern of response to economic developments.

Now, it can certainly be argued that a decade-by-decade analysis— which was undertaken largely because it was necessary to rely heavily on census data for years before 1940—has serious limitations in this connection. If monthly or annual employment data during the entire period had been available, short-run relationships between employment expansion and population growth could have been analyzed much more satisfactorily and different conclusions might have been reached. Actually, however, the behavior of the various annual economic series which have been examined does not suggest that the conclusions would have been markedly different, though they might have had to be modified to a certain extent. In chapter vi, it was found that each major period of economic expansion in California since 1900 has been dominated by a somewhat distinctive combination of economic developments. The evidence strongly suggests that the industrial pattern of employment expansion from 1900 to 1913 probably

[4] Population estimates assembled by Dumke show a substantial decline in the population of many of the larger Southern California cities and counties between 1887 or 1888 and 1890. See G. S. Dumke, *The Boom of the Eighties in Southern California* (San Marino: Huntington Library, 1944), p. 278.

differed considerably from that which prevailed between 1919 and the late 'twenties or between 1935 and 1944. The behavior of the local market industries was probably somewhat more consistent from period to period than that of the industries serving a national market, but it is clear that there were a variety of factors in each period which would have accounted for differences in the patterns of response even of the local market industries to a rise in the rate of population growth. Among such factors would be included not only the labor market developments associated with the two world wars, but also the differing impact of minor cyclical disturbances and other influences in each period.

Analysis of developments during the last fifty years strongly suggests that both employment expansion and population growth will tend to be considerably slower in the second half of the present century if no new situations develop which provide the impetus to rapid spurts of growth. It has been emphasized that these spurts have been associated in large part with the development and growth of new or young industries. It must be recognized, also, that the spurts of the early 'forties and early 'fifties were stimulated by war or defense spending.

It goes without saying that an all-out war would provide the impetus for a new spurt in growth, but must it be assumed that there will be no new periods of spectacular growth in the absence of a major war?

It must be admitted at the outset that it is impossible for anyone to foresee precisely what industrial innovations are likely to have the greatest impact on the course of economic development, either in California or in the nation as a whole, during the next three or four decades. Those who indulge in this type of speculation tend to point to atomic energy, electronics, chemicals, and light metals as fields in which significant developments may be expected. The possibility that helicopters or other types of light aircraft may some day be widely purchased for individual transportation should not be left out of account, and it is possible to indulge in some entertaining speculation about the patterns of "suburban" development that might result. There would seem to be a reasonable probability that California will share in at least some of these developments, but, as was pointed out in the introductory section, it is not the purpose here to appraise the technical factors which may affect the future growth of California industry. More appropriate to the general purpose is a comment to the effect that, judging from the experience of the past, employment in new or young industries is likely to grow most rapidly during some part of an upswing in a "secondary secular movement."

In the absence of new industrial developments which provide a strong impetus to growth, and in the absence of an all-out war, a moderate long-run decline in the rate of both employment expansion and population growth seems likely. The analysis in the first four chapters of the present study called attention to certain factors which might be expected to contribute to a long-run decline in the rate of growth, but, on the whole, they were factors which would bring about only a very gradual rate of retardation or the direction of their influence in recent decades was somewhat uncertain. In the first of these categories, for example, is the fact that it will require a rising rate of out-migration from other states to maintain a given rate of in-migration to California. In the second is the long-run decline in wage differentials between California and the nation, which seems to have occurred chiefly before the end of World War I.

Analysis of employment trends suggests that the industrial structure of employment will continue to change somewhat in the future, along the lines of the changes that have occurred in the past, but probably at a less rapid rate. A continued long-run decline in the relative importance of the extractive industries may be expected, and also a continued rise in the proportion of workers employed in the distributive and service industries (broadly defined), particularly in the professional services and in public administration. On the whole, this analysis suggests that continued industrialization is not likely to bring with it a *marked* change in the percentage of workers employed in manufacturing, although, as pointed out at the end of chapter iv, the continued growth of the Western market may conceivably create a situation conducive to markedly accelerated growth of manufacturing as compared with the average rate of growth (in *relation* to population growth) in the first half of the century. As for construction, the data provide little basis for prediction, but there are some grounds for supposing that a declining rate of population growth, as well as technological changes in the industry, may result in a long-run decline in the relative importance of employment in this industry. All these changes, however, may be expected to occur in an irregular manner, as the industrial distribution of employment responds to fluctuating economic developments from decade to decade.

One broad question which a study of this kind might be expected to answer has to do with the relationship of a rapid rate of population growth to the stability of employment conditions. Has California's rapid rate of population growth tended to make employment in the state more or less stable than that in the country as a whole? This is a complex question, and no attempt has been made to explore fully every facet of the problem. Furthermore, in relation to *this* question, historical statistical data are particularly inadequate.

On the whole, the empirical data examined—spotty as they are—indicate that unemployment in California has sometimes been slightly more severe and sometimes slightly less severe than in the nation. Only in the period following World War II was it substantially more serious than in the country as a whole. In other words, there has been no *persistent* tendency for the state to be relatively susceptible to unemployment. The danger periods, so far as have been determined, have been those following shortly after a downturn in net in-migration.

The type of unemployment to which California seems to be particularly susceptible may be characterized as *frictional* unemployment. The short-run maladjustments which may sometimes arise between the rate of in-migration and the rate of employment expansion may be regarded as a particular form of frictional unemployment. The whole analysis suggests that this type of unemployment is most likely to present a problem in the early stages of a downswing in a migration wave. Frictional unemployment may also tend to be relatively important in California because of the high business and labor turnover rates which appear to be associated in large part with the rapid growth of the state. This whole problem, however, deserves more careful study, particularly in view of the fact that turnover rates tend to fluctuate with the business cycle.[5] It may not be at all accurate to say that the high turnover which is associated with the rapid growth of California persistently tends to give rise to more frictional unemployment, regardless of fluctuations in business conditions.

On the other hand, there is no clear evidence that *cyclical* unemployment has invariably tended to be more severe in California than in the nation, although we have not been in a position to study this problem specifically.[6] The high percentage of employment in the distributive and service industries, which are relatively less vulnerable cyclically than the commodity-producing industries, would tend to make for relatively more moderate cyclical unemployment rates in the state. It might be argued that the high secular rate of growth of economic activity in the state would also tend to result in reduced susceptibility to cyclical unemployment. This may be true. Yet the data indicate that the higher rate of expansion of economic activity in California during a fifty-year period was explained in large part by spurts of rapid growth in particular groups of years, rather than by a consistent tendency for California's rate of economic growth to exceed the nation-wide rate *throughout* the first half of the century. If a downswing oc-

---

[5] See, for example, W. S. Woytinsky and associates, *Employment and Wages in the United States* (New York: Twentieth Century Fund, 1953), pp. 383–384.

[6] Kidner has shown that the Great Depression was about equally severe in California and in the nation but that some of the minor recessions of the 'twenties and 'thirties were apparently somewhat less severe in the state than in the country as a whole. In the absence of adequate employment and unemployment data, however, he was not in a position to analyze specifically the problem of the relative severity of unemployment in state and nation. See F. L. Kidner, *California Business Cycles* (Berkeley: University of California Press, 1946), especially chapter iii.

curred, however, during one of these spurts of rapid growth, as in 1920–1921, it was relatively mild in California.

One characteristic of California's industrial structure that might tend to give rise to greater susceptibility to a particular type of cyclical unemployment is the relatively high proportion of workers employed in the construction industry, which is associated with the rapid rate of population growth. As was pointed out in chapter vi, this could contribute to relatively serious unemployment in the downswing of a building cycle, not only on the part of construction workers themselves but also on the part of workers in industries producing and distributing construction materials and equipment (for example, the lumber industry). It may well be, however, that, if a peak in construction activity occurs in a period of relatively prosperous business conditions (as in the 1920's), many of these workers may shift to other industries before a serious cyclical downswing gets under way. Labor mobility studies, as well as employment statistics, provide evidence of a good deal of movement into and out of the construction industry in response to changes in the the level of activity in the industry.

Although available data suggest that seasonal variations in total employment have tended to be slightly wider in California than in the nation in recent years, the difference may be attributable to differences in statistical methods. So far as total nonagricultural employment is concerned, seasonal variations tend to be almost identical in state and nation. In this particular respect, California's situation probably compared less favorably with that in the nation fifty years ago. The widest seasonal fluctuations in employment are found in some of the extractive industries and in the manufacturing industries which process their products. These industries occupied a position of far greater relative importance in the state at the turn of the century than they do today. The decline in the relative importance of, for example, employment in fruit and vegetable canning and in the lumber industry constituted a sharper change in the structure of manufacturing employment in California than in the nation in the intervening period.

The most important factor making for potentially serious instability in California's industrial structure today is the heavy concentration of employment in the aircraft and parts industry. The lesser concentrations in military and naval installations, particularly in government shipyards, are also potential sources of instability. In other words, California's economy has become rather markedly dependent on the level of defense spending. This does not necessarily mean, however, that a downswing in business conditions would inevitably be accompanied by more serious unemployment in California than in the nation as a whole.

Whether, in any given business recession in the future, the unemployment rate would turn out to be higher or lower in California than in the nation would depend, probably, on the particular combination of factors contributing to the downswing. If the recession developed (1) shortly after the upper turning point in a wave of migration to California, (2) involved a sharp decline in residential construction activity, and (3) involved sharp cutbacks in military spending, and particularly in aircraft procurement, the chances would be strong that the rise in the unemployment rate would be relatively marked in California. If, on the other hand, the downswing were to be characterized chiefly by (1) a sharp decline in farm income, particularly affecting the corn, wheat, and cattle-raising areas, (2) a fairly sharp decline in private investment, and (3) a substantial drop in the demand for consumers' durable goods, and at the same time the level of military spending and of aircraft procurement was sustained, then there would be a strong probability that other areas would be more severely affected by unemployment than California. This would be particularly likely if the recession began after net in-migration had been declining for some years.

It is not the purpose of this study to arrive at a forecast of employment conditions in California for the next several years or even for the next several decades. Much of the analysis, however, has tended to emphasize the importance of certain relationships which need to be kept in mind by those who *are* concerned with forecasting business and employment conditions. The data indicate that the waves of rapid and less rapid expansion in California's economic development in the present century—and probably earlier—have tended, on the whole, to be related to similar waves in (1) the growth of the nation's economy, (2) the population growth of the nation as a whole, and (3) net migration to the state and other streams of migration. There has also been some tendency in the past for these waves to coincide, roughly, with the building cycle, but the interruption of construction activity in World War I and the much longer interruption in World War II interfered with the response of construction activity to population movements. Although I have cautiously refrained from concluding that the waves in California's economic development have a cyclical character —much less that they may be expected to display uniformity of amplitude and duration—there are both theoretical and empirical grounds for anticipating that the rate of economic expansion in the state will continue to be quite closely related to this group of variables. Thus, their movements should be carefully analyzed and taken into account by those who are concerned with the problem of forecasting, together with fluctuations in income, production, and similar variables which normally receive the chief attention of forecasters.

APPENDICES

APPENDIX A: STATISTICAL TABLES

TABLE A-1

PERCENTAGE DISTRIBUTION OF CALIFORNIA RESIDENTS BY PLACE OF BIRTH,
SELECTED CENSUS YEARS, 1860–1950

Place of birth	1860	1880	1900	1930	1950
Total population of California....	100.0	100.0	100.0	100.0	100.0
Born in the state...............	20.4	37.7	44.5	34.1	36.9
Born in other states.............	41.0	28.4	30.5	45.4	51.4
Americans born outside U.S.[a].....	...[b]	...[b]	0.3	1.6	1.6
Foreign-born..................	38.6	33.9	24.7	18.9	10.0

SOURCES: U.S. Bureau of Agricultural Economics, Population Committee for the Central Valley Project Studies, *California Migration*, Statistical Memorandum No. 6, by C. N. Reynolds and S. Miles (mimeographed report, Berkeley, California, July, 1944), p. 21; and *United States Census of Population: 1950, Special Report*, P-E, No. 4A, p. 14.

[a]Includes, for 1930 and 1950, persons for whom state of birth was not reported, persons born in Territories, possessions, and so on, and persons born abroad of American parents. For earlier years, it includes only persons born in outlying possessions and American citizens born abroad or at sea.

[b]Less than 0.05 per cent.

TABLE A-2

PERCENTAGE DISTRIBUTION OF CALIFORNIA RESIDENTS BORN IN OTHER STATES, BY GEOGRAPHIC DIVISION OF BIRTH, SELECTED CENSUS YEARS, 1860–1950, AND FOR WHITES AND NONWHITES, 1940–1950

Geographic division	Total					Whites		Nonwhites	
	1860	1900	1930	1940	1950	1940	1950	1940	1950
Total persons born in other states (in thousands)	155.7	452.6	2,600.2	3,382.0	5,538.5	3,280.3	5,154.7	101.7	383.8
Per cent[a]	100.0	100.0	100.0	100.0	100.0	100.0	100.0	100.0	100.0
New England	21.1	11.5	4.3	3.3	3.3	3.4	3.5	0.5	0.5
Middle Atlantic	27.4	19.2	11.2	9.4	9.8	9.7	10.4	1.8	1.7
South Atlantic	7.8	4.4	3.3	3.2	3.8	2.9	3.5	10.5	6.6
East North Central	19.4	28.2	24.1	20.2	18.1	20.7	19.2	4.3	3.4
East South Central	9.5	4.8	4.4	4.1	4.4	3.8	3.8	13.5	12.7
West North Central	10.9	20.7	26.5	27.7	24.7	28.3	26.2	8.4	4.7
West South Central	3.5	3.5	10.3	15.7	21.1	14.5	17.7	52.7	65.8
Mountain	...[b]	4.3	11.3	11.7	10.8	11.9	11.4	5.5	3.4
Pacific, other than California	0.4	3.4	4.7	4.7	4.1	4.7	4.3	2.8	1.2

SOURCES: 1860–1930, U.S. Bureau of Agricultural Economics, Population Committee for the Central Valley Project Studies, *California Migration, Statistical Memorandum No. 6*, by C. N. Reynolds and S. Miles (mimeographed report, Berkeley, California, July, 1944), pp. 1–8; 1940, *Sixteenth Census of the United States: 1940, Population, State of Birth of the Native Population*, pp. 15–39; and 1950, *United States Census of Population: 1950, Special Report, P–E, No. 4A*, pp. 19–43.

[a] The small numbers of persons who did not report state of residence were excluded in computing percentage distributions.

[b] A small number of persons residing in California in 1860 had been born in territories, but they could not be allocated accurately by regions.

TABLE A-3

PERCENTAGE DISTRIBUTION OF INCREASE PER DECADE IN NUMBER OF CALIFORNIA
RESIDENTS BORN IN OTHER STATES, BY GEOGRAPHIC DIVISION OF BIRTH, 1900–1950

Geographic division	1900–1910	1910–1920	1920–1930	1930–1940	1940–1950
Increase in number of residents born in other states (in thousands)...	426.4	500.3	1,220.9	781.8	2,156.5
Per cent......................	100.0	100.0	100.0	100.0	100.0
New England.................	3.9	2.3	2.6	0.2	3.2
Middle Atlantic..............	13.4	9.7	8.1	3.7	10.3
South Atlantic...............	3.9	2.9	2.8	2.7	4.7
East North Central...........	31.5	25.6	19.5	7.2	14.9
East South Central...........	5.3	4.7	3.8	3.2	4.9
West North Central...........	26.5	27.7	28.1	31.9	19.7
West South Central...........	6.3	10.5	14.0	33.5	29.8
Mountain....................	6.6	11.5	15.5	12.9	9.4
Pacific, other than California.....	2.7	5.3	5.6	4.7	3.0

SOURCES: See source reference for table A-2.

TABLE A-4

PER CENT OF POPULATION LIVING IN URBAN AREAS, CALIFORNIA
AND UNITED STATES, 1850–1950

Year	California	United States	Ratio of California to United States
1850...........................	7.4[a]	15.3	0.48[a]
1860...........................	20.7	19.8	1.05
1870...........................	37.2	25.7	1.45
1880...........................	42.9	28.2	1.52
1890...........................	48.6	35.1	1.38
1900...........................	52.3	39.7	1.32
1910...........................	61.8	45.7	1.35
1920...........................	67.9	51.2	1.33
1930...........................	73.3	56.2	1.30
1940...........................	71.0	56.5	1.26
1950...........................	67.1	59.0	1.14
1950 (new definition)[b]..........	80.7	64.0	1.26

SOURCE: *16th Census of the United States: 1940, Population* Vol. II, Part 1, pp. 18 and 515, and *United States Census of Population: 1950*, Vol. II, Part 1, p. 87 and Part 5, p. 57.
[a]See table 1, footnote a, for discussion of undercount of California's population in 1850.
[b]For new definition of urban areas, see chapter ii, footnote 17.

TABLE A-5
PER CENT OF POPULATION OF CALIFORNIA LIVING IN
SOUTHERN COUNTIES,[a] 1850–1950

Year	Per cent	Year	Per cent
1850	6.5	1900	23.0
1860	7.6	1910	34.3
1870	7.5	1920	41.8
1880	9.5	1930	53.8
1890	19.0	1940	55.7
		1950	54.5

SOURCE: Computed from decennial census population data.
[a]Imperial, Inyo, Kern, Los Angeles, Orange, Riverside, San
Bernardino, San Diego, San Luis Obispo, Santa Barbara, and
Ventura counties.

TABLE A-6
PERCENTAGE DISTRIBUTION OF NET EFFECTIVE MIGRATION INTO CALIFORNIA
BY AGE GROUP (ESTIMATED), 1880–1940

Age at end of decade	1880–1890	1890–1900	1900–1910	1910–1920	1920–1930	1930–1940
Total	217,466	156,875	718,622	795,411	1,757,738	992,078
Per cent	100.0	100.0	100.0	100.0	100.0	100.0
10–19 years	23.8	31.9	17.1	19.2	13.8	16.4
20–29 years	42.5	38.0	33.1	28.7	27.7	35.9
30–39 years	21.3	17.2	24.5	20.8	29.0	20.4
10–39 years	87.6	87.1	74.7	68.7	70.5	72.7
40–49 years	6.6	5.0	12.9	13.2	14.9	9.1
50–59 years	0.5	−0.7	5.7	8.2	9.1	6.5
60–69 years	4.2	7.2	4.8	6.3	2.6	6.7
70 years and older	1.1	1.4	1.9	3.6	2.9	5.0
40 and older	12.4	12.9	25.3	31.3	29.5	27.3

SOURCE: U.S. Bureau of Agricultural Economics, Population Committee for the Central Valley Project
Studies, *California Migration*, Statistical Memorandum No. 6, by C. N. Reynolds and S. Miles (mimeographed
report, Berkeley, California, July, 1944), pp. 94 and 115–117.

TABLE A-7

PERCENTAGE DISTRIBUTION OF POPULATION OF CALIFORNIA BY RACE, SELECTED CENSUS YEARS, 1860–1950

Year	Total population	White	Nonwhite					
			Total	Negro	Indian	Japanese	Chinese	Other
1860	100.0	85.0	15.0	1.1	4.7	...	9.2	...
1880	100.0	88.7	11.3	0.7	1.9	..[a]	8.7	...
1900	100.0	94.5	5.5	0.7	1.0	0.7	3.1	...
1920	100.0	95.3	4.7	1.1	0.5	2.1	0.8	0.2
1930	100.0	95.3	4.7	1.4	0.3	1.7	0.7	0.6
1940	100.0	95.4	4.6	1.8	0.3	1.4	0.6	0.5
1950	100.0	93.6	6.4	4.4	0.2	0.8	0.6	0.4

SOURCES: *Sixteenth Census of the United States: 1940, Population*, Vol. II, Part 1, p. 516; and *United States Census of Population: 1950*, Vol. II, Part 5, p. 57.
[a]Less than 0.05 per cent.

TABLE A-8

NUMBER OF CHILDREN LESS THAN FIVE YEARS OF AGE PER 1,000 POPULATION, WHITE AND NONWHITE, CALIFORNIA AND UNITED STATES, 1870–1950

Census year	All races			White			Nonwhite		
	California	United States	Ratio of California to U.S.	California	United States	Ratio of California to U.S.	California	United States	Ratio of California to U.S
1870	122	143	0.85	...	...	...	...	...	...
1880	108	138	0.78	118	134	0.88	30	165	0.18
1890[a]	88	122	0.72	93	120	0.78	28	138	0.20
1900	85	121	0.70	87	119	0.73	43	136	0.32
1910	81	116	0.70	83	114	0.73	56	128	0.44
1920	80	109	0.73	78	109	0.72	121	110	1.10
1930	71	93	0.76	70	92	0.76	91	104	0.88
1940	66	80	0.82	66	78	0.85	65	98	0.66
1950	104	107	0.97	103	105	0.98	118	126	0.94

SOURCES: *Sixteenth Census of the United States: 1940, Population*, Vol. II, Part 1, pp. 28, 523; and *United States Census of Population: 1950*, Vol. II, Part 1, pp. 93 and 94, and Part 5, pp. 61–62.
[a]1890 figures for California exclude persons on Indian reservations.

       Employment Expansion and Population Growth

TABLE A-9

Number of Children Less Than Five Per 1,000 White Women 15 to 49 Years
of Age, 1850 to 1950, and for Urban and Rural Women, 1910,
1940, and 1950, California and United States

Census year and area	Cali- fornia	United States	Ratio of California to U.S.	Census year and area	Cali- fornia	United States	Ratio of California to U.S.
1850.......	484[a]	613	0.79[a]	1920.......	294	425	0.69
1860.......	764	627	1.22	1930.......	258	349	0.74
1870.......	643	562	1.14	1940.......	234	278	0.84
1880.......	513	537	0.96	Urban....	201	221	0.91
1890.......	379	473	0.80	Rural			
				nonfarm.	331	347	0.95
1900.......	338	465	0.73	Rural farm	318	397	0.80
1910.......	297	426	0.70	1950.......	400	411	0.97
Urban ...	250	336	0.74	Urban....	380	371	1.02
Rural				Rural			
nonfarm	409	499	0.82	nonfarm	507	499	1.02
Rural farm	386	551	0.70	Rural farm	448	492	0.91

Sources: *Twelfth Census of the United States: 1900, Special Reports, Supplementary Analysis and Derivative Tables,* pp. 415–416; *Sixteenth Census of the United States: 1940, Population, Differential Fertility: 1940 and 1910, Fertility for States and Large Cities,* pp. 21–22, 175, and 191; and *United States Census of Population: 1950,* Vol. II, Part I, pp. 90 and 93–94, and Part V, pp. 58 and 61–62. (Fertility rates for the years 1920, 1930, and 1950 have been computed from census data on age by sex, color, and urban-rural residence.)

[a] See footnote a, text table 1, for a discussion of the undercount of California's population in 1850.

TABLE A-10

NUMBER OF CHILDREN LESS THAN FIVE PER 1,000 WHITE WOMEN 15 TO 49 YEARS OF
AGE, URBAN AND RURAL, BY AGE, CALIFORNIA AND UNITED STATES, 1910 AND 1940

Year and urban or rural residence	All ages	15–19 years	20–24 years	25–29 years	30–34 years	35–39 years	40–44 years	45–49 years
California								
1910................	297	39	335	522	467	348	179	53
Urban.............	250	33	274	450	390	285	139	38
Rural nonfarm.......	409	66	520	686	619	446	231	80
Rural farm..........	386	28	408	699	680	569	323	88
1940................	234	56	384	470	344	200	83	21
Urban.............	201	42	310	414	310	173	64	13
Rural nonfarm.......	331	102	604	609	444	256	127	36
Rural farm..........	318	64	555	715	475	358	154	65
United States								
1910................	426	53	457	748	696	545	316	92
Urban.............	336	33	340	601	558	415	226	62
Rural nonfarm.......	499	87	601	860	757	579	318	90
Rural farm..........	551	62	588	991	952	793	500	151
1940................	278	51	385	544	441	283	138	40
Urban.............	221	35	289	444	367	217	95	26
Rural nonfarm.......	347	79	529	654	500	319	155	41
Rural farm..........	397	67	560	795	656	488	277	88
Ratio of California to United States								
1910................	0.70	0.74	0.73	0.70	0.67	0.64	0.57	0.58
Urban.............	0.74	1.00	0.81	0.75	0.70	0.69	0.62	0.61
Rural nonfarm.......	0.82	0.76	0.87	0.80	0.82	0.77	0.73	0.89
Rural farm..........	0.70	0.45	0.69	0.71	0.71	0.72	0.65	0.58
1940................	0.84	1.10	1.00	0.86	0.78	0.71	0.60	0.52
Urban.............	0.91	1.20	1.07	0.93	0.84	0.80	0.67	0.50
Rural nonfarm.......	0.95	1.29	1.14	0.93	0.89	0.80	0.82	0.88
Rural farm..........	0.80	0.96	0.99	0.90	0.72	0.73	0.56	0.74

SOURCE: *Sixteenth Census of the United States: 1940, Population, Differential Fertility: 1940 and 1910, Fertility for States and Large Cities*, pp. 21–22, 175, and 191.

TABLE A-11

Age Distribution of the Population, California and United States, Selected Census Years, 1870–1950

Age	1870	1900	1920	1930	1940	1950
California						
Total.........................	560,247	1,485,053	3,426,861	5,677,251	6,907,387	10,586,223
Percent.....................	100.0	100.0	100.0	100.0	100.0	100.0
Less than 5 years...........	12.2	8.5	8.0	7.1	6.6	10.4
5–14 years..................	20.2	17.7	15.8	15.7	13.2	14.2
15–24 years.................	16.0	17.8	15.1	16.0	16.2	13.2
Less than 25 years..........	48.4	44.0	38.9	38.8	36.0	37.8
25–34 years.................	20.5	17.7	17.9	17.2	17.3	17.1
35–44 years.................	18.8	15.3	16.7	16.4	15.6	15.4
25–44 years.................	39.3	33.0	34.6	33.6	32.9	32.5
45–64 years.................	10.8	17.0	20.4	20.9	23.0	21.3
65 and older................	1.1	5.2	5.9	6.4	8.0	8.5
45 and older................	11.9	22.2	26.3	27.3	31.0	29.8
Not reported................	0.1	0.7	0.3	0.2	....	....
United States						
Total.........................	39,818,449	75,994,575	105,710,620	122,775,046	131,669,275	150,697,361
Per cent....................	100.0	100.0	100.0	100.0	100.0	100.0
Less than 5 years...........	14.3	12.1	10.9	9.3	8.0	10.7
5–14 years..................	24.9	22.3	20.9	20.1	17.0	16.2
15–24 years.................	20.2	19.6	17.7	18.3	18.2	14.6
Less than 25 years..........	59.4	54.0	49.5	47.7	43.2	41.5
25–34 years.................	14.6	15.9	16.2	15.4	16.2	15.7
35–44 years.................	11.0	12.1	13.4	14.0	13.9	14.3
25–44 years.................	25.6	28.0	29.6	29.4	30.1	30.0
45–64 years.................	11.9	13.7	16.2	17.5	19.8	20.3
65 and older................	3.0	4.1	4.7	5.5	6.9	8.2
45 and older................	14.9	17.8	20.9	23.0	26.7	28.5
Not reported................	....	0.3	0.1	0.1	....	....

Sources: *16th Census of the United States: 1940, Population*, Vol. II, Part 1, pp. 26 and 523; and *United States Census of Population: 1950*, Vol. II, Part 1, p. 89, and Part 5, p. 59.

TABLE A-12

CRUDE BIRTH RATE,[a] CALIFORNIA AND UNITED STATES, 1919–1950

Year	California (1)	United States (2)	Ratio of (1) to (2)	Year	California (1)	United States (2)	Ratio o (1) to (2)
1919	16.9	22.4	0.75	1935	13.0	16.9	0.77
1920	18.9	23.7	0.80	1936	13.3	16.7	0.80
1921	19.1	24.2	0.79	1937	14.5	17.1	0.85
1922	18.4	22.3	0.83	1938	15.3	17.6	0.87
1923	18.8	22.1	0.85	1939	15.3	17.3	0.88
1924	19.2	22.2	0.86	1940	16.3	17.9	0.91
1925	18.0	21.3	0.85	1941	17.8	19.1	0.93
1926	16.8	20.5	0.82	1942	21.2	21.5	0.99
1927	16.4	20.5	0.80	1943	23.0	23.0	1.00
1928	15.6	19.7	0.79	1944	22.2	22.1	1.00
1929	14.7	18.8	0.78	1945	21.6	21.4	1.01
1930	14.8	18.9	0.78	1946	23.5	23.8	0.99
1931	14.0	18.0	0.78	1947	25.0	25.8	0.97
1932	13.3	17.4	0.76	1948	23.9	24.2	0.99
1933	12.6	16.6	0.76	1949	23.7	23.9	0.99
1934	12.9	17.2	0.75	1950	23.1	23.6	0.98

SOURCES: U.S. National Office of Vital Statistics, *Vital Statistics of the United States: 1949*, Part I, pp. 2–3; and *Vital Statistics-Special Reports*, Vol. 37, No. 7, May 19, 1953, p. 161.

[a]Births are classified by place of occurrence, 1919 to 1939, and by place of residence, 1940 to 1950. Rates are computed on the basis of the estimated civilian population, 1941 to 1946, and on the basis of the estimated total resident population for all other years.

TABLE A-13

GAINFUL WORKERS BY MAJOR INDUSTRY GROUP, CALIFORNIA AND UNITED STATES,
1870–1930 (IN THOUSANDS)

	1870	1880	1890	1900	1910	1920	1930
California							
Total gainful workers[a]	239	377	544	644	1,092	1,513	2,501
Commodity producing industries	159	241	318	352	534	728	1,021
Agriculture	70	108	158	161	196	261	332
Forestry and fishing	4	8	9	9	13	12	13
Extraction of minerals	37	39	25	30	31	25	40
Building trades workers	14	20	35	39	98	112	187
Manufacturing and mechanical workers (exc. building trades)	34	66	91	114	195	318	450
Distributive and service industries	78	130	210	273	490	651	1,226
Transportation and communication	16	26	40	54	104	125	199
Trade	22	41	59	88	152	209	437
Public service (n.e.c.)	3	5	7	10	24	46	61
Professional service	7	14	28	40	69	116	235
Domestic and personal service	28	44	76	82	140	155	294
Clerical workers	2	6	16	19	68	133	253
United States							
Total gainful workers[a]	12,506	17,392	22,736	29,287	37,371	42,434	48,830
Commodity producing industries	9,434	12,901	15,456	19,193	23,487	25,674	25,817
Agriculture	6,539	8,596	9,376	11,000	11,621	11,466	10,472
Forestry and fishing	47	92	170	202	242	270	250
Extraction of minerals	184	296	435	702	965	1,090	984
Building trades workers	637	831	1,316	1,599	2,300	2,206	2,960
Manufacturing and mechanical workers (exc. building trades)	2,027	3,086	4,159	5,690	8,359	10,642	11,151
Distributive and service industries	2,988	4,327	6,788	9,325	12,148	13,633	18,986
Transportation and communication	559	848	1,437	1,990	2,638	3,071	3,843
Trade	774	1,284	1,888	2,907	3,165	4,243	6,081
Public service (n.e.c.)	90	138	201	284	459	770	856
Professional service	333	550	883	1,202	1,664	2,144	3,254
Domestic and personal service	1,232	1,507	2,379	2,942	3,772	3,405	4,952
Clerical workers	83	164	492	768	1,737	3,127	4,025

SOURCES: *Ninth to Fifteenth Censuses of the United States* (adjusted data). For a description of the adjustments, see Appendix B.

[a] Includes all gainful workers 10 years of age and older. The total for 1910 has been adjusted for the census overcount of agricultural workers (see source reference for text table 5). Individual items may not always add to totals because of rounding.

TABLE A-14

EMPLOYED WORKERS BY MAJOR INDUSTRY GROUP, CALIFORNIA AND
UNITED STATES, 1930–1950

(IN THOUSANDS)

Major industry group	California			United States		
	1930[a]	1940	1950	1930[a]	1940	1950
Total employed workers[b]...............	2,320	2,476	3,902	46,036	44,888	56,239
Commodity producing industries........	925	888	1,391	24,455	22,053	25,950
Agriculture........................	319	266	287	10,168	8,391	6,885
Forestry and fishing.................	13	8	11	250	105	120
Mining............................	48	46	30	1,067	914	929
Construction......................	151	153	299	2,580	2,075	3,440
Manufacturing.....................	394	416	764	10,390	10,568	14,576
Durable goods..................	.....	204	422	......	5,116	7,757
Nondurable goods..............	.....	206	338	......	5,268	6,697
Not specified..................	.....	5	4	......	184	122
Distributive and service industries........	1,338	1,552	2,465	20,564	22,108	29,450
Transportation communication, and other public utilities..................	187	198	319	3,412	3,108	4,368
Transportation.....................	.....	128	194	......	2,186	2,941
Communication.....................	.....	29	60	......	369	646
Utilities and sanitary services.........	.....	42	65	......	553	782
Trade.............................	403	552	873	6,053	7,546	10,548
Wholesale trade..................	.....	108	183	......	1,205	1,976
Retail trade.....................	.....	444	689	......	6,341	8,572
Finance, insurance, and real estate.......	121	120	179	1,393	1,472	1,916
Service industries....................	553	588	848	8,522	8,576	10,129
Business and repair services.......... }	} 311	70	130	} 5,173	891	1,411
Personal services.................		238	263		3,975	3,489
Entertainment and recreation services..	51	64	77	419	420	554
Professional and related services.......	191	217	378	2,930	3,290	4,675
Public administration................	73	94	246	1,184	1,406	2,409
Industry not reported..................	57	35	46	1,017	728	840

SOURCES: *15th Census of the United States: 1930, Unemployment,* Vol. I, pp. 53 55 and 145 146; and *United States Census of Population: 1950,* Vol. II, Part 1, pp. 103–104, and Part 5 pp. 70–71.
[a]1930 data have been adjusted but are not precisely comparable with 1940 and 1950 data. For methods of adjustment, see Appendix B.
[b]Includes all employed workers, 14 years of age and older. Individual items may not always add to totals because of rounding.

TABLE A-15

PERCENTAGE INCREASE PER DECADE IN POPULATION AND IN NUMBER OF WORKERS
BY MAJOR INDUSTRY GROUP, CALIFORNIA, 1870–1950

Employment status and major industry group	1870–1880	1880–1890	1890–1900	1900–1910	1910–1920	1920–1930	1930–1940	1940–1950
Total population............	54.3	40.3	22.4	60.1	44.1	65.7	21.7	53.3
Gainful workers[a]........	57.8	44.5	18.4	69.6	38.6	65.3	....	....
Civilian labor force.....	....	....	....	....	....	....	16.8	46.2
Employed workers[a].....	....	....	....	....	....	....	6.7	57.6
Agriculture.............	53.6	45.9	2.0	21.7	33.2	27.4	−16.6	7.8
Other extractive industries.................	13.8	−27.4	16.0	14.2	−16.7	42.3	−12.5	−21.9
Building trades workers..	49.8	73.9	9.3	152.9	14.6	66.1	....	....
Construction employment................	....	....	....	....	....	....	1.3	94.8
Manufacturing and mechanical workers.....	93.3	37.8	24.7	72.0	62.8	41.4	....	....
Manufacturing employment............	....	....	....	....	....	....	5.5	83.7
Transportation and communication workers....	58.2	54.7	34.1	93.5	19.7	59.6	....	....
Transportation, communication, and other public utilities......	....	....	....	....	....	....	5.8	60.9
Trade[b]...............	81.3	46.2	47.5	72.9	38.1	108.5	28.2	56.5
Service industries.......	62.5	78.1	17.5	72.5	29.4	95.2	6.3	44.4
Public administration...	54.6	42.5	41.1	140.3	86.2	33.3	28.7	161.1
Clerical workers........	198.2	173.0	16.9	260.0	96.9	88.9	....	....

SOURCES: Text table 1 and Appendix tables A-13 and A-14. The civilian labor force for 1930 has been estimated from 1930 census data, and, for 1940 and 1950, may be found in *United States Census of Population: 1950*, Vol. II, Part 5, p. 67. All computations are based on unrounded data.

[a] Number of gainful workers, aged 10 years and older, 1870–1930, and number of employed workers, aged 14 years and older, 1930–1950.

[b] Includes finance, insurance, and real estate.

TABLE A-16

RATIO OF PERCENTAGE INCREASE IN NUMBER OF WORKERS TO PERCENTAGE INCREASE
IN POPULATION PER DECADE, BY MAJOR INDUSTRY GROUP, CALIFORNIA, 1870–1950

Employment status and major industry group	1870–1880	1880–1890	1890–1900	1900–1910	1910–1920	1920–1930	1930–1940	1940–1950
Total population.......	1.00	1.00	1.00	1.00	1.00	1.00	1.00	1.00
Gainful workers[a].......	1.06	1.10	0.82	1.16	0.88	0.99	.....	.....
Civilian labor force.....	.....	.....	.....	.....	.....	.....	0.77	0.87
Employed workers[a].....	.....	.....	.....	.....	.....	.....	0.31	1.08
Agriculture...........	0.99	1.14	0.09	0.36	0.75	0.42	−0.76	−0.15
Other extractive industries................	0.25	−0.68	0.71	0.24	−0.38	0.64	−0.58	−0.41
Building trades workers..	0.92	1.83	0.42	2.54	0.33	1.01	.....	.....
Construction employment................	.....	.....	.....	.....	.....	.....	0.06	1.78
Manufacturing and mechanical workers.....	1.72	0.94	1.10	1.20	1.42	0.63	.....	.....
Manufacturing employment...........	.....	.....	.....	.....	.....	.....	0.25	1.57
Transportation and communication workers...	1.07	1.36	1.52	1.56	0.45	0.91	.....	.....
Transportation, communication, and other public utilities......	.....	.....	.....	.....	.....	.....	0.27	1.14
Trade[b]...............	1.50	1.15	2.12	1.21	0.86	1.65	1.30	1.06
Service industries.......	1.15	1.94	0.78	1.21	0.67	1.45	0.29	0.83
Public administration...	1.01	1.05	1.83	2.33	1.95	0.51	1.32	3.02
Clerical workers........	3.65	4.29	0.75	4.33	2.20	1.37	.....	.....

SOURCE: Appendix table A-15.
[a]Number of gainful workers, aged 10 years and older, 1870–1930, and number of employed workers, aged 14 years and older, 1930–1950.
[b]Includes finance, insurance, and real estate.

TABLE A-17

PRODUCTION WORKERS IN MANUFACTURING BY INDUSTRY GROUP, CALIFORNIA, 1899–1949

Industry group	1899	1909	1919	1929	1939	1949
Total production workers	72,014	102,386	215,534	263,057	271,290	507,312
Nondurable goods	35,363	43,133	89,229	136,011	145,384	228,800ᵃ
Food and kindred products	17,243	22,549	51,297	66,290	70,466	99,133
Fruit and vegetable canning and preserving	7,669	7,477	21,294	28,186	26,626	28,900ᵃ
Textile mill products	463	542	2,039	7,008	4,581	3,714
Apparel and related products	5,140	3,519	7,660	15,878	22,307	42,062
Paper and allied products	296	936	2,155	4,209	5,424	10,560
Printing and publishing industries	5,101	7,774	10,561	17,099	15,999	27,161
Chemicals and allied products	2,926	3,403	6,250	7,892	9,813	17,312
Petroleum and coal products	53	930	5,388	8,681	9,504	14,397
Rubber products	21	74	431	6,576	4,865	9,800ᵃ
Leather and leather products	4,120	3,406	3,448	2,368	2,425	4,600ᵃ
Durable goods	28,666	52,378	120,268	121,531	119,556	262,200ᵃ
Lumber and wood products	14,413	25,553	29,959	42,089	33,886	49,508
Lumber and wood products, excluding furniture	13,695	23,853	26,982	34,158	24,082	38,150
Furniture and fixtures	718	1,700	2,977	7,931	9,804	11,358
Stone, clay, and glass products	2,127	8,282	6,897	14,205	11,062	25,589
Metal and metal products	10,171	15,304	30,606	51,558	48,243	106,900ᵃ
Primary metal industries	. . . . .	. . . . .	. . . . .	. . . . .	12,810	25,927
Fabricated metal products	. . . . .	. . . . .	. . . . .	. . . . .	18,939	37,668
Machinery (non-electrical)	. . . . .	. . . . .	. . . . .	. . . . .	12,616	32,400ᵃ
Electrical machinery	238	435	2,008	4,353	3,878	10,940
Iron and steel products (exc. foundry and machine shop)	773	1,722	10,649	17,537	. . . . .	. . . . .
Non-ferrous metal products	3,402	4,108	3,664	5,524	. . . . .	. . . . .
Foundry and machine shop products	5,173	8,377	9,827	17,186	. . . . .	. . . . .
Other machinery (non-electrical)	585	662	4,458	6,958	. . . . .	. . . . .
Transportation equipment	1,955	3,239	52,806	13,679	26,365	80,241
Motor vehicles, bodies, and parts	. . . . .	478	3,008	7,613	6,284	14,500ᵃ
Aircraft and parts	. . . . .	. . . . .	. . . . .	1,277	16,800ᵃ	57,400ᵃ
Shipbuilding and repair	885	1,844	47,530	4,178	4,022	6,100ᵃ
Miscellaneous and unclassified	7,985	6,875	6,037	5,525	6,350	n.a.

SOURCES: U.S. Bureau of the Census, *Census of Manufactures*, and, for 1949 data, *Annual Survey of Manufactures: 1949 and 1950.* Data for 1899–1929, originally published in unclassified form, have been classified by our research staff, drawing in part on earlier tables prepared by the California State Chamber of Commerce and by the regional office of the former National Resources Planning Board. Data for 1949 are based on a sample survey and are subject to sampling variability. For a discussion of classification problems and adjustments, see Appendix B.

ᵃNot disclosed by the Census Bureau; data published by California, Department of Industrial Relations (or estimated on the basis of its estimates of wage and salary workers) have been substituted. The totals for production workers in durable and nondurable goods industries in 1949 are based on Census data, except to the extent that subtotals had to be estimated partly on the basis of data published by the state agency.

TABLE A-18

PERCENTAGE DISTRIBUTION OF PRODUCTION WORKERS IN MANUFACTURING BY
INDUSTRY GROUP, CALIFORNIA, 1899–1949

Industry group	1899	1909	1919	1929	1939	1949
Total production workers[a]	100.0	100.0	100.0	100.0	100.0	100.0
Nondurable goods	49.1	42.1	41.4	51.7	53.6	*45.1*[b]
Food and kindred products	23.9	22.0	23.8	25.2	26.0	19.5
Fruit and vegetable canning and preserving	10.6	7.3	9.9	10.7	9.8	*5.7*[b]
Textile mill products	0.6	0.5	0.9	2.7	1.7	0.7
Apparel and related products	7.1	3.4	3.6	6.0	8.2	8.3
Paper and allied products	0.4	0.9	1.0	1.6	2.0	2.1
Printing and publishing industries	7.1	7.6	4.9	6.5	5.9	5.4
Chemicals and allied products	4.1	3.3	2.9	3.0	3.6	3.4
Petroleum and coal products	0.1	0.9	2.5	3.3	3.5	2.8
Rubber products	...[c]	0.1	0.2	2.5	1.8	*1.9*[b]
Leather and leather products	5.7	3.3	1.6	0.9	0.9	0.9
Durable goods	39.8	51.2	55.8	46.2	44.1	*51.7*[b]
Lumber and wood products	20.0	25.0	13.9	16.0	12.5	9.8
Lumber and wood products, excluding furniture	19.0	23.3	12.5	13.0	8.9	7.5
Furniture and fixtures	1.0	1.7	1.4	3.0	3.6	2.2
Stone, clay, and glass products	3.0	8.1	3.2	5.4	4.1	5.0
Metal and metal products	14.1	14.9	14.2	19.6	17.8	*21.1*[b]
Primary metal industries	....	....	....	....	4.7	5.1
Fabricated metal products	....	....	....	....	7.0	7.4
Machinery (nonelectrical)	....	....	....	....	4.7	*6.4*[b]
Electrical machinery	0.3	0.4	0.9	1.7	1.4	2.2
Iron and steel products (excluding foundry and machine shop)	1.1	1.7	4.9	6.7	....	....
Nonferrous metal products	4.7	4.0	1.7	2.1	....	....
Foundry and machine shop products	7.2	8.2	4.6	6.5	....	....
Other machinery (nonelectrical)	0.8	0.6	2.1	2.6	....	....
Transportation equipment	2.7	3.2	24.5	5.2	9.7	15.8
Motor vehicles, bodies, and parts	....	0.5	1.4	2.9	2.3	*2.9*[b]
Aircraft and parts	....	....	....	0.5	*6.2*[b]	*11.3*[b]
Shipbuilding and repair	1.2	1.6	22.1	1.6	1.5	*1.2*[b]
Miscellaneous and unclassified	11.1	6.7	2.8	2.1	2.3	n.a.

SOURCE: Appendix table A-17.
[a]Individual items may not always add to totals because of rounding.
[b]See footnote a, Appendix table A-17.
[c]Less than 0.05 per cent.

TABLE A-19

PERCENTAGE DISTRIBUTION OF PRODUCTION WORKERS IN MANUFACTURING BY
INDUSTRY GROUP, UNITED STATES, 1899–1949

Industry group	1899	1909	1919	1929	1939	1949
Total production workers[a]	100.0	100.0	100.0	100.0	100.0	100.0
Nondurable goods	47.3	47.1	45.0	46.8	52.0	46.4
Food and kindred products	8.0	8.0	9.0	8.8	10.3	9.8
Fruit and vegetable canning and preserving	1.0	0.8	0.9	1.2	1.5	n.a.
Textile mill products[b]	16.0	15.4	13.3	14.1	13.9	9.7
Apparel and related products[b]	7.0	8.1	6.1	6.6	9.6	9.2
Paper and allied products	2.2	2.4	2.6	2.9	3.5	3.4
Printing and publishing industries	4.6	4.3	3.5	4.3	4.1	4.2
Chemicals and allied products	2.4	2.5	3.4	3.3	3.5	4.0
Petroleum and coal products	0.7	0.7	1.1	1.3	1.4	1.5
Rubber products	0.8	0.8	1.9	1.8	1.5	1.6
Leather and leather products	5.6	5.0	4.2	3.8	4.2	3.1
Durable goods	47.4	47.3	50.1	49.1	42.7	47.9
Lumber and wood products	15.7	15.1	10.0	10.3	7.8	7.9
Lumber and wood products, excluding furniture	n.a.	n.a.	n.a.	n.a.	5.4	5.5
Furniture and fixtures	n.a.	n.a.	n.a.	n.a.	2.4	2.4
Stone, clay, and glass products	5.3	5.6	3.8	4.1	3.4	3.5
Metal and metal products	22.0	22.6	26.1	27.6	24.4	28.0
Primary metal industries	....	....	....	....	8.6	7.9
Fabricated metal products	....	....	....	....	5.8	6.4
Machinery (nonelectrical)	....	....	....	....	6.9	9.1
Electrical machinery	0.9	1.4	2.5	3.9	3.2	4.6
Iron and steel products (exc. foundry and machine shop)	8.2	9.5	10.2	10.5	....	....
Nonferrous metal products	3.7	3.7	3.6	3.8	....	....
Foundry and machine shop products	7.4	6.2	5.7	5.4	....	....
Other machinery (nonelectrical)	1.8	1.8	4.1	4.0	....	....
Transportation equipment	4.4	4.1	10.2	7.0	7.0	8.5
Motor vehicles, bodies, and parts	....[c]	1.2	4.1	5.4	5.1	5.2
Aircraft and parts	....	....	....[c]	0.2	0.6	1.8
Shipbuilding and repair	1.0	0.6	4.6	0.7	0.9	0.8
Miscellaneous and unclassified	5.3	5.6	4.9	4.1	5.3	5.6

SOURCES: 1899–1929, *Census of Manufactures* data, as classified by S. Fabricant in *Employment in Manufacturing: 1899–1939* (New York, 1942), pp. 182–214. 1939 data are from U. S. Bureau of the Census, *Census of Manufactures: 1947*, and 1949 data are from U. S. Bureau of the Census, *Annual Survey of Manufactures: 1949 and 1950*. Since the 1949 data are based on a sample survey, they are subject to sampling variability.
[a]Individual items may not always add to totals because of rounding.
[b]Textile mill products and apparel, which were classified in one "textile products" category by Fabricant, have been separated by our research staff for the years, 1899–1929.
[c]Less than 0.05 per cent.

TABLE A-20

RATIO OF PERCENTAGE OF MANUFACTURING PRODUCTION WORKERS IN EACH INDUSTRY
GROUP IN CALIFORNIA TO THAT IN UNITED STATES, 1899–1949

Industry group	1899	1909	1919	1929	1939	1949
Total production workers.......	1.00	1.00	1.00	1.00	1.00	1.00
Nondurable goods.............	1.04	0.89	0.92	1.10	1.03	0.97[a]
Food and kindred products....	2.99	2.75	2.64	2.86	2.52	1.99
Fruit and vegetable canning and preserving..........	10.60	9.12	11.00	8.92	6.53	n.a.
Textile mill products........	0.04	0.03	0.07	0.19	0.12	0.07
Apparel and related products..	1.01	0.42	0.59	0.91	0.85	0.90
Paper and allied products.....	0.18	0.38	0.38	0.55	0.57	0.62
Printing and publishing industries....................	1.54	1.77	1.40	1.51	1.44	1.29
Chemicals and allied products.	1.71	1.32	0.85	0.91	1.03	0.85
Petroleum and coal products..	0.14	1.29	2.27	2.54	2.50	1.87
Rubber products............	...	0.13	0.11	1.39	1.20	1.19[a]
Leather and leather products..	1.02	0.66	0.38	0.24	0.21	0.29
Durable goods...............	0.84	1.08	1.11	0.94	1.03	1.08[a]
Lumber and wood products...	1.27	1.66	1.39	1.55	1.60	1.24
Lumber and wood products, excluding furniture......	n.a.	n.a.	n.a.	n.a.	1.65	1.36
Furniture and fixtures......	n.a.	n.a.	n.a.	n.a.	1.50	0.92
Stone, clay, and glass products.	0.57	1.45	0.84	1.32	1.21	1.43
Metal and metal products....	0.64	0.66	0.54	0.71	0.73	0.75[a]
Primary metal industries.....	...	...	...	...	0.55	0.65
Fabricated metal industries...	...	...	...	...	1.21	1.16
Machinery (nonelectrical)....	...	...	...	...	0.68	0.70[a]
Electrical machinery.........	0.33	0.29	0.36	0.44	0.44	0.48
Iron and steel products (excluding foundry and machine shop)	0.13	0.18	0.48	0.64	...	...
Nonferrous metal products....	1.27	1.08	0.47	0.55	...	...
Foundry and machine shop products.................	0.97	1.32	0.81	1.20	...	...
Other machinery (nonelectrical)..................	0.44	0.33	0.51	0.65	...	...
Transportation equipment....	0.61	0.78	2.40	0.74	1.39	1.86
Motor vehicles, bodies, and parts.................	...	0.42	0.34	0.54	0.45	0.56[a]
Aircraft and parts.........	...	...	...	2.50	10.33[a]	6.27[a]
Shipbuilding and repair....	1.20	2.67	4.80	2.29	1.67	1.50[a]
Miscellaneous and unclassified...	2.09	1.20	0.57	0.51	0.43	n.a.

SOURCES: Appendix tables A-18 and A-19.
[a]See footnote a, Appendix table A-17.

TABLE A-21

PERCENTAGE INCREASE IN NUMBER OF PRODUCTION WORKERS IN MANUFACTURING
PER DECADE, BY INDUSTRY GROUP, CALIFORNIA, 1899–1949

Industry group	1899–1909	1909–1919	1919–1929	1929–1939	1939–1949
Total population................	59.4	46.3	65.6	22.7	52.4
Total production workers in manufacturing....................	42.1	110.5	22.0	3.1	87.0
Nondurable goods..............	22.0	106.9	52.4	6.9	57.4[a]
Food and kindred products......	30.8	127.5	29.2	6.3	40.7
Fruit and vegetable canning and preserving................	−2.5	184.8	32.4	−5.5	8.5[a]
Other food products.........	57.4	99.1	27.0	15.1	60.2
Textile mill products...........	17.1	276.2	243.7	−34.6	−18.9
Apparel and related products....	−31.5	117.7	107.3	40.5	88.6
Paper and allied products.......	216.2	130.2	95.3	28.9	94.7
Printing and publishing industries	52.4	35.8	61.9	−6.4	69.8
Chemicals and allied products....	16.3	83.7	26.3	24.3	76.4
Petroleum and coal products.....	1,654.7	479.4	61.1	9.5	51.5
Rubber products..............	252.4	482.4	1,425.8	−26.0	101.4[a]
Leather and leather products....	−17.3	1.2	−31.3	2.4	89.7[a]
Durable goods.................	82.7	129.6	1.1	−1.6	119.31
Lumber and wood products.....	77.3	71.2	40.5	−19.5	46.1
Stone, clay, and glass products...	289.4	−16.7	106.0	−22.1	131.3
Metal and metal products.......	50.5	100.0	68.5	−6.4	121.6[a]
Transportation equipment......	65.7	1,530.3	−74.1	92.7	204.3
Motor vehicles, bodies, and parts....................	.....[b]	529.3	153.1	−17.5	130.7[a]
Aircraft and parts...........	......	.....	.....[b]	1,215.6[a]	241.7[a]
Shipbuilding and repair.......	108.4	2,477.5	−91.2	3.7	51.7[a]
Miscellaneous and unclassified.....	−13.9	−12.2	−8.5	11.5	n.a.
Total production workers, exc. shipbuilding and repair...........	41.4	67.1	54.1	3.2	87.5
Total production workers in durable goods industries, exc. shipbuilding and repair..................	81.9	43.9	61.3	−1.6	121.7

SOURCE: Table A-17. The percentage increase in population was computed on the basis of Census Bureau annual population estimates. The population in 1899 was estimated by assuming that the percentage increase from 1899 to 1900 was the same as from 1900 to 1901.

[a]See footnote a, Table A-17.

[b]Percentages could not be computed, since employment in base year was zero.

TABLE A-22

RATIO OF PERCENTAGE INCREASE IN NUMBER OF PRODUCTION WORKERS
IN MANUFACTURING TO PERCENTAGE INCREASE IN POPULATION PER
DECADE, BY INDUSTRY GROUP, CALIFORNIA, 1899–1949

Industry group	1899–1909	1909–1919	1919–1929	1929–1939	1939–1949
Total production workers in manufacturing	0.71	2.39	0.34	0.14	1.59
Nondurable goods	0.37	2.31	0.80	0.30	1.05[a]
Food and kindred products	0.52	2.75	0.45	0.28	0.74
Fruit and vegetable canning and preserving	−0.04	3.99	0.49	−0.24	0.16
Other food products	0.97	2.14	0.41	0.67	1.15
Textile mill products	0.29	5.97	3.71	−1.52	−0.35
Apparel and related products	−0.53	2.54	1.64	1.78	1.62
Paper and allied products	3.64	2.81	1.45	1.27	1.73
Printing and publishing industries	0.88	0.77	0.94	−0.28	1.28
Chemicals and allied products . . .	0.27	1.81	0.40	1.07	1.40
Petroleum and coal products	27.86	10.35	0.93	0.42	0.94
Rubber products	4.25	10.42	21.73	−1.15	1.85[a]
Leather and leather products	−0.29	0.03	−0.48	0.11	1.64
Durable goods	1.39	2.80	−0.02	−0.07	2.18
Lumber and wood products	1.30	0.37	0.62	−0.86	0.84
Stone, clay, and glass products . . .	4.87	−0.36	1.62	−0.97	2.40
Metal and metal products	0.85	2.16	1.04	−0.28	2.22[a]
Transportation equipment	1.11	33.05	−1.13	4.08	3.73
Motor vehicles, bodies, and parts	. . . .[b]	11.43	2.33	−0.77	2.39[a]
Aircraft and parts	. . . .	. . . .	. . . .[b]	44.05[a]	4.42[a]
Shipbuilding and repair	1.82	53.51	−1.39	−0.16	0.95[a]
Miscellaneous and unclassified	−0.23	−0.26	−0.13	0.51	n.a.
Total production workers, excluding shipbuilding and repair	0.70	1.45	0.82	0.14	1.60
Total production workers in durable goods manufacturing, excluding shipbuilding and repair	1.38	0.95	0.93	−0.07	2.22

SOURCE: Appendix table A-21.
[a]See footnote a, Appendix table A-17.
[b]See footnote b, Appendix table A-21

TABLE A-23

Changes in Per Capita Income, California, Geographic Regions, and United States, 1919–1952

Area	Per capita income					Percentage change in per capita income					
	1919	1929	1939	1949	1952	1919–1929	1929–1939	1939–1949	1949–1952	1919–1949	1929–1952
United States	603	680	539	1,325	1,639	13	−21	146	24	120	141
New England	687	838	680	1,419	1,749	22	−19	109	23	107	109
Middle East	713	926	709	1,548	1,874	30	−23	118	21	117	102
Southeast	425	344	303	884	1,121	−19	−12	192	27	108	226
Southwest	551	464	386	1,166	1,416	−16	−17	202	21	112	205
Central	609	720	565	1,417	1,773	18	−22	151	25	133	146
Northwest	578	534	418	1,267	1,549	−8	−22	203	22	119	190
Far West	784	865	692	1,560	1,969	10	−20	125	26	99	128
California	827	946	741	1,602	2,032	14	−22	116	27	94	115

SOURCES: 1919 income data are from National Industrial Conference Board, *The Economic Record*, September 8, 1939, pp. 84–85; Census Bureau population estimates were used in computing per capita income, and regional data were adjusted to conform to the regional classification used by the U.S. Department of Commerce. Per capita income data for all other years are from U.S. Department of Commerce, *Survey of Current Business*, August, 1953, p. 13.

TABLE A-24

RATIO OF PER CAPITA INCOME TO U.S. PER CAPITA INCOME, CALIFORNIA AND
GEOGRAPHIC REGIONS, 1919–1952

Area	1919	1929	1939	1949	1952
United States...................	1.00	1.00	1.00	1.00	1.00
New England...................	1.14	1.23	1.26	1.07	1.07
Middle East...................	1.18	1.36	1.32	1.17	1.14
Southeast.....................	0.70	0.51	0.56	0.67	0.68
Southwest.....................	0.91	0.68	0.72	0.88	0.86
Central.......................	1.01	1.06	1.05	1.07	1.08
Northwest.....................	0.96	0.79	0.78	0.96	0.95
Far West......................	1.30	1.27	1.28	1.18	1.20
California....................	1.37	1.39	1.37	1.21	1.24

SOURCE: Appendix table A-23.

TABLE A-25

PERCENTAGE CHANGE IN THE LABOR FORCE AND EMPLOYMENT, AND FLUCTUATIONS
IN UNEMPLOYMENT RATES, BY FIVE-YEAR PERIODS, UNITED STATES, 1900–1950

	Percentage change in		Unemployment rate at end of period
	Labor force[a]	Employment	
1900–1905...............	15.9	20.7	1.8
1905–1910...............	13.3	13.8	1.4
1910–1915...............	5.1	0.4	5.9
1915–1920...............	4.5	9.6	1.3
1920–1925...............	7.4	6.9	1.8
1925–1930...............	8.9	4.3	5.9
1930–1935...............	6.1	−7.1	20.1
1935–1940...............	5.2	12.4	14.6
1940–1945...............	−3.2	11.1	1.9
1945–1950...............	17.2	13.5	5.0

SOURCES: 1900–1930, National Industrial Conference Board estimates as published in U.S. Bureau of the Census, *Historical Statistics of the United States: 1789–1945* (Washington, 1949), p. 65; 1930–1940, U.S. Bureau of Labor Statistics estimates, as published in U.S. Bureau of the Census, *Statistical Abstract of the United States: 1952*, p. 178; and 1940–1950, Census Bureau estimates, *ibid.* The National Industrial Conference Board estimates are not precisely comparable with later estimates because of differing methods; the differences are particularly important in the interpretation of unemployment rates.

[a]For years before 1940, the data refer to the number of gainful workers; from 1940 on, to the civilian labor force.

APPENDIX B: EXPLANATORY NOTES ON STATISTICAL PROCEDURES AND SOURCES

1. *Appendix Table A-13. Gainful Workers by Major Industry Group, 1870–1930*

Strictly speaking, the Bureau of the Census did not collect employment statistics in the decennial censuses before 1940. Nor did it gather information on the number of persons in the "labor force," as currently defined. Beginning with the census of 1870, however, all persons who *usually* worked at gainful labor were asked to report their occupations.[1] The tables on gainful workers which were published in the decennial census reports from 1870 to 1930 apply to all persons, ten years of age and older, who reported that they usually worked at a gainful occupation.

The occupations reported by these workers were classified within a broad industrial framework. Before 1910, a detailed classification of occupations by industry was impossible, since no provision was made for careful reporting of a worker's industrial affiliation. From 1910 on, since two columns were provided on the schedule for separate reporting of a worker's occupation and industry, a more detailed classification scheme could be developed. The published statistics for the census years, 1910 to 1930, present no serious problems of noncomparability, but many difficulties are encountered in any attempt to adjust the statistics for 1870 to 1900 so that they are at least reasonably comparable with those for 1910 to 1930.

Dr. Alba M. Edwards, who undertook to develop a comparable set of statistics on gainful workers by occupation and broad industry group for the years 1870 to 1930, had access to detailed tabulations, for the nation as a whole, which are not available for individual states.[2] On the basis of this information, he was in a position to develop ratios for allocating some of the occupation groups reported in the earlier censuses among the more detailed categories used in later census years. One possible method of approaching the problem of reclassifying the California data might have been to apply these same ratios, wherever feasible, to the published census figures for the state. For the most part, this method was rejected, on the ground that the ratios used by Edwards were not necessarily appropriate for California, in view of the many differences in the occupational and industrial structure of the state and nation. The method which was actually decided upon involved, chiefly, the transferring of occupation groups, in their entirety, from one broad industry group to another, or from a broad category to a more refined category. For example, all "carpenters and joiners," as well as other groups of workers who are employed chiefly in the building trades, were transferred from "manufacturing and mechanical workers," under which they were originally classified, to "building trades workers." Similarly, all "draymen, hackmen, and teamsters" were transferred from "transportation and trade" to "transportation." Where it seemed necessary to split groups into more refined categories, published California data (usually for later census years) were used to develop allocation ratios for the state, and U.S. data for the nation. Results, for the United States, actually differ very little from the final figures derived by Edwards on the basis of his more refined methods.

The most difficult problem arose in the handling of the large group of "laborers, not specified," which appears in the census reports for the years 1870 to 1900, classified

---

[1] For a more detailed discussion of problems encountered in interpreting census statistics, see *Sixteenth Census of the United States: 1940, Population, Comparative Occupation Statistics for the United States: 1870 to 1940*, by Alba M. Edwards (Washington, 1943).

[2] *Ibid.*, Part II.

under domestic and personal service. Because of the lack of information in the census returns on the industrial affiliations of these laborers, they were lumped together under one broad industrial category, even though they should properly have been divided among a number of industry groups. After experimenting with various alternatives, it was finally decided to allocate the California laborers in accordance with the ratios which Edwards had developed for the United States,[3] because of a lack of sufficient statistical information to develop appropriate independent allocation ratios for California. It is probable that some error was involved in this procedure, especially for the years 1870 and 1880, when the miscellaneous group of laborers represented a considerably larger percentage of all gainful workers in California than in the United States. In 1870, for example, 37,586, or 15.7 per cent, of the gainful workers in California were classified by the census as "laborers, not specified," as compared with 1,032,666, or 8.2 per cent, of the gainful workers in the nation as a whole. Probably a good many of the California laborers were among the 10,000 or more Chinese workmen who were dismissed from construction work on the transcontinental railroad in 1869. This group of Chinese laborers is frequently mentioned in the annals of the period, and it is known that many of them later found seasonal employment as agricultural laborers, but there is little quantitative information that would serve as a guide to their allocation among broad industry groups in 1870.

Another troublesome problem arose in connection with the treatment of "clerical workers." This group of workers was classified separately in the census reports for 1910 to 1930, although, unlike the other major categories used in these reports, it was more occupational than industrial in character. The ideal solution would have been to allocate these workers among broad industry groups, as was done by Palmer and Ratner in their reclassification of 1910 census data for the country as a whole.[4] An attempt to apply the allocation ratios developed by Palmer and Ratner to the California data, however, yielded results which were quite inconsistent with other available data for California.[5] This was not surprising, in view of the marked differences in industrial structure between California and the country as a whole, but the detailed industry by occupation data which would have been needed to develop suitable allocation ratios for California alone were unavailable.[6] Hence, it was necessary to fall back on the less desirable alternative of creating a "clerical workers" category for the census years 1870 to 1900, to which were transferred those groups of workers who could be identified as corresponding to the groups classified as "clerical workers" in the census reports for 1910 to 1930.

The other problems encountered in reclassifying the gainful workers data were of relatively minor importance and require no special comment.

The percentages of California workers in certain industry groups in 1870 and 1890 differ somewhat from those appearing in a table in Kidner's *California Business Cycles*.[7]

[3] *Ibid.*, p. 144.

[4] See G. L. Palmer and A. Ratner, *Industrial and Occupational Trends in National Employment: 1910–1940, 1910–1948*, Research Report No. 11, Industrial Research Department, University of Pennsylvania (Philadelphia, 1949).

[5] More specifically, the results were inconsistent with a table included in the 1930 Census reports in which, for the first time, workers were classified by industrial affiliation, rather than occupationally within a broad industrial framework. This table is discussed more fully below.

[6] In reclassifying the 1910 Census data, Palmer and Ratner had access to tabulations which are not available for individual states.

[7] F. L. Kidner, *California Business Cycles* (Berkeley: University of California Press, 1946), p. 15.

Kidner's table is based on an unpublished report prepared by the former National Resources Planning Board, Region 8. The differences are apparently explained by the fact that the staff of the National Resources Planning Board did not undertake all the adjustments which were made in the preparation of table A-13. In particular, the fact that they did not attempt to distribute the "laborers, n.e.c." group among the various major industry groups clearly accounts for the largest differences.

   2. *Appendix Table A-14. Employed Workers by Major Industry Group, 1930–1950*

In 1940, a sweeping change was made in census procedures. The former concept of gainful workers was abandoned, and the more carefully defined concept of participation in the labor force was substituted. Persons in the labor force were classified as employed, on public emergency work, or unemployed.[8] In addition, separate tables were published on the occupational and industrial affiliations of workers, and many modifications were made in the classification system. A few minor changes were also made in 1950. As a result of all these changes, it is impossible to make meaningful comparisons between 1940 or 1950 and earlier census years without undertaking elaborate adjustments.

   Fortunately, the 1930 Census reports included tables in which gainful workers were classified by industrial affiliation rather than by occupation within a broad industrial framework. In addition, the questions relating to the employment status of workers which were included on the 1930 schedule made possible the publication of detailed tables relating to seven classes of "unemployed" workers. Among the groups of "unemployed" persons, Class A includes persons who clearly would be classified as unemployed under the currently used census definition. Tables were published, moreover, on the industrial affiliations of these classes of the unemployed. Thus, it is possible to estimate employment by major industry group in 1930 by subtracting Class A of the unemployed from total gainful workers in each industry group. In addition, the 1930 figures may be made more nearly comparable with 1940 and 1950 data by undertaking some reclassification and by eliminating children aged ten to thirteen and members of the Armed Forces. The resulting estimates for 1930, as presented in table A-14, though not strictly comparable with 1940 and 1950 statistics, are probably sufficiently satisfactory for use in connection with an analysis of long-run trends.[9] They have the advantage of providing a kind of link between the employment data for 1940 and 1950 and the gainful worker data for earlier census years.

   If the industrial distribution of employed workers in 1930, as presented in text table 7, for both state and nation is compared with the industrial distribution of gainful workers for the same year, as presented in table 6, the differences appear to be largely explained by the classification of "clerical workers" as a separate group in table 6. The only sizable differences appear in the total percentages of workers in the distributive and service industries, in which most of the "clerical workers" were undoubtedly employed. Furthermore, the changes in the industrial distribution of employed workers from 1930 to 1950 appear to represent, for the most part, a continuation of long-run changes reflected in the earlier gainful workers data. On the whole, although the data in tables 7 and A-14 are not comparable with those in tables 6 and A-13, the differences do not seem to be so great as to make the data useless for analysis of long-run trends.

---

   [8] For definitions of these concepts, see *Sixteenth Census of the United States: 1940, Population*, Vol. III, Part 1, pp. 3–5.

   [9] It should be noted that the 1940 data in table A-14 are taken from the 1950 Census reports and have been revised, by the Census Bureau, to conform with 1950 data.

3. *Appendix Table A-17. Production Workers in Manufacturing by Industry Group, California, 1899–1949*

In reclassifying *Census of Manufactures* data for 1899 and 1909, the 1937 Census classification was used as a guide. For the years 1919 and 1929, it was possible to utilize the results of earlier work undertaken by the former National Resources Planning Board (Region 8), as published in Kidner, *California Business Cycles*, p. 29. In addition, series for more detailed categories in some cases (apparel and related products, furniture, foundry and machine shop products, and electrical machinery) were developed. The data on employment in "fruit and vegetable canning and preserving" are based on a series published in California State Chamber of Commerce, *Economic Survey Report No. 7: 1932–33.*

To make the earlier data more nearly comparable with those for more recent years, it was necessary to eliminate certain categories which were originally classified under manufacturing but were later dropped from the *Census of Manufactures*. These categories included "railroad repair shops, electric and steam," automobile repairing, and gas (illuminating and heating).

4. *Sources for Figures* (except where indicated on the figure itself)

Figure 3. For the years 1919 to 1939, *Census of Manufactures* data, as reclassified by the former National Resources Planning Board (Region 8), the State Chamber of Commerce, and our research staff were used. (See the note relating to Appendix table A-17.) Data for 1947 are from the *Census of Manufactures* for that year (except for aircraft). For the years 1949 to 1951, the data from U.S. Bureau of the Census, *Annual Survey of Manufactures* for the relevant years (except for those items not disclosed by the Census Bureau) were used. All other figures are based on estimates published by the California State Department of Industrial Relations in *Estimated Employment, Total Wages, and Average Earnings and Hours Worked, Production and Related Workers, Manufacturing Industries, California and Los Angeles and San Francisco Bay Industrial Areas: 1940–1948* (San Francisco, 1949) and in *Estimated Number of Wage and Salary Workers in Nonagricultural Establishments, by Industry, California, 1953* (San Francisco, 1953). (Final 1953 figures were furnished by the agency.)

The estimates of average annual employment of production workers for the years 1940 to 1948 were subjected to minor upward or downward adjustments to bring them into line with *Census of Manufactures* figures for 1947. (In other words, the state estimates were adjusted to *Census of Manufactures* benchmarks.) After 1948, the state agency discontinued its production worker series and substituted a series giving the estimated number of wage and salary workers in manufacturing. The annual percentage changes in employment from 1951 on, as shown by the wage and salary worker data, together with the production worker figures from the *Annual Survey of Manufactures* for 1951, were used as a basis for estimating production worker employment in 1952 and 1953.

Figure 5. Annual population estimates for California for 1900 to 1929 are from *Sixteenth Census of the United States: 1940, Vital Statistics Rates in the United States: 1900–1940* (Washington, 1943); for 1930 to 1939, from U.S. Bureau of the Census, *Current Population Reports*, Series P-45, No. 4, April 9, 1945; for 1940 to 1949, from *ibid.*, Series P-25, No. 72, May, 1953; and for 1950 to 1953, from *ibid.*, Series P-25, No. 70, March 24, 1953 and Series P-25, No. 89, January 25, 1954. Estimates for the United States for 1900 to 1939 are from U.S. Bureau of the Census, *Historical Statistics of the United States: 1789–1945* (Washington, 1949); for 1940 to 1949, from U.S. Bureau of the Census, *Statistical Abstract of the United States: 1950;* and for 1950 to 1953, from U.S. Bureau of the Census, *Current Population Reports*, Series P-25, No. 79, September 16, 1953.

Figure 6. The sources for California population estimates are those used for figure 5. The annual natural increase in California has been computed from birth and death data in California, Department of Public Health, *California Public Health Report: 1951– 1952, Statistical Supplement*, and *Births, Deaths, Marriages*, March, 1953. "Net migration and military movement" represents the difference between the annual increase in the total resident population and the annual natural increase.

Figure 7. For sources of income data, see the source note to Appendix table A-23. Bank clearings data have been compiled from the annual volumes of the *Statistical Abstract of the United States*.

Figure 8. Bank clearings data for principal cities outside New York are from *Historical Statistics of the United States: 1789–1945*. For sources of income data, see the source note to Appendix table A-23. Average annual earnings in manufacturing were computed from *Census of Manufactures* data on total annual wages and average annual employment of wage earners in manufacturing, for Census years. Average hourly manufacturing earnings data for California are from California, Department of Industrial Relations, *Handbook of California Labor Statistics: 1951–1952* and, for the United States, from the annual volumes of the *Statistical Abstract of the United States* (U.S. Bureau of Labor Statistics data). Data on the per cent of industrial and commercial firms failing are from *ibid*. (Dun and Bradstreet data.)

Figure 9. Annual estimates of the value of agricultural products for California for 1899 to 1939 are from U.S. Bureau of Agricultural Economics, Population Committee for the Central Valley Project Studies, *Income*, by E. V. Eggers, Statistical Memorandum No. 7 (mimeographed report, Berkeley, California, December 2, 1944). The estimates (to 1923) were originally prepared by the California State Chamber of Commerce. Data on the value of agricultural products for 1940 to 1952 are from U.S. Bureau of Agricultural Economics, *The Farm Income Situation*. Data on the value of California mineral products and crude petroleum production for 1887 to 1920 are from California, Department of Natural Resources, Division of Mines, *Bulletin No. 139*, April, 1948; for 1921 to 1924, from the *Statistical Abstract of the United States* for the relevant years; and for 1925 to 1950, from U.S. Bureau of Mines, *Minerals Yearbook: 1950*. Data on value added by manufacture are from U.S. Bureau of the Census, *Census of Manufactures: 1947* and *Annual Survey of Manufactures* for the years 1949 to 1951. Data on the value of foreign trade through principal California ports are from the annual volumes of the *Statistical Abstract of the United States* and from Federal Reserve Bank of San Francisco, *Monthly Review*, February, 1953. The customs districts of San Francisco, Los Angeles, and San Diego are included. The index of department store sales in California has been supplied by the Federal Reserve Bank of San Francisco.

Figure 10. The sources of California data (except on electric power) are those used for figure 9. U.S. data on the annual value of farm products for 1910 to 1952 are from U.S. Bureau of Agricultural Economics, *The Farm Income Situation*, September-October, 1953. For 1899, I used, for both California and the United States, the data on value of farm products "not fed to livestock" from the *Twelfth Census of the United States: 1900*. Since comparable annual data on the value of farm products for state and nation were not available for 1900 to 1909, no percentages were computed for those years. U.S. data on the value of mineral products for 1887 to 1920 are from *Historical Statistics of the United States: 1789–1945;* and, for later years, from the sources used for the corresponding California series. U.S. data on value added by manufacture are likewise from the sources used for the corresponding state series. U.S. data on the value of foreign trade are from the annual volumes of the *Statistical Abstract of the United States*. U.S. and California data on electrical output generated are from U.S. Bureau of the Census, *Central Electric Light and Power Stations: 1912* and *Census of Electrical Industries: 1922*. The series on electric power production are from U.S. Federal Power Commission, *Electric Power Statistics* (Washington, 1941), annual issues of the same agency's *Production of Electric Energy and Capacity of Generating Plants*, and the *Statistical Abstract of the United States* for 1951 and 1952. The index of department store sales in the United States is from Board of Governors of the Federal Reserve System, *Federal Reserve Bulletin*.

Figure 11. For the United States, 1895 to 1939, Long's index of the value of building permits, as published in *Historical Statistics of the United States: 1789–1945* was used. For California, an index from data on the value of building permits in California cities was computed. As in the case of Long's U.S. index, the number of cities included in the index varies for different parts of the period, depending on the availability of data. For the years, 1902 to 1906, only Los Angeles and San Francisco are included; Oakland is added in 1907 (data for these early years are from the relevant volumes of the *Statistical Abstract of the United States*); for the years 1913 to 1932, all incorporated areas of California are included (data for these years are from California State Unemployment Commission, *Report and Recommendations*, November, 1932 [Sacramento, 1933]); and for the years 1932 to 1939, 25 major California cities are included (data for this period are from California State Chamber of Commerce, *Economic Survey Report*, for the relevant years). Although the number of cities included in the California index is very small for the earlier years, it compares favorably with the number included in Long's U.S. index (30 to 35 cities for the entire nation during the same period). The indices for both California and the United States from 1939 on relate to the estimated total value of construction expenditures, from U.S. Department of Commerce, *Construction and Building Materials*.

Figure 13. Immigration data are from *Historical Statistics of the United States: 1789–1945*. California school enrollment data are from the annual reports of the State Superintendent of Public Instruction.

Figure 15. The sources of annual population estimates for California and the United States are those used in figure 5. Annual estimates for other states are from the same sources as the California estimates.

INDEX

Agriculture: employment in, 26–29, 32–35, 37, 39, 170–173; income in, 73–74, 76, 78–82; size of farm, 32; value of products, 100, 104–105, 107; unemployment in, 125; wages in, 83–85
Aircraft industry, employment in, 1, 50–51, 60–61, 68–69, 102, 106, 109–111, 149, 174–179
Allen, Arthur D., 130
American Federation of Labor, unemployment in unions, 127
Apparel industry, employment in, 50–57, 59, 63, 67, 103, 174–179
Arizona, construction employment in, 117
Automobile industry. See Motor vehicles industry

Bain, J. S., 98 n., 103 n.
Bank clearings, 92–95
Barber, C. L., 40 n.
Barger, H., 41 n.
Barnet, M., 99 n.
Bauer, P. T., 30 n.
Belloc, Nedra B., 73 n., 97 n.
Benedict, M. R., 33 n.
Block, J. W., 83 n.
Blythe, S. O., 106 n.
Breimyer, H. F., 74 n.
Bright, M. L., 149 n.
Buckley, K. A. H., 117 n.
Building. See Construction
Burns, A. F., 112 n., 115 n.

California: Department of Employment, 3 n., 33 n., 34 n., 106 n., 111 n., 121 n., 128 n., 130 n., 131, 151 n.; Department of Finance, 5 n., 90 n., 141 n.; Department of Industrial Relations, 1 n., 42 n., 45 n., 102 n., 106 n., 107 n., 111 n., 128 n., 129 n., 132, 186–187; Department of Public Health, 187, Division of Mines, 98 n., 187; Reconstruction and Re-employment Commission, 1, 36 n.; State Agricultural Society, 98 n., State Chamber of Commerce, 81 n., 186–188; Superintendent of Public Instruction, 188; Unemployment Commission, 188
Canning industry. See Food industry
Chemicals industry, employment in, 50, 52, 59, 63, 67, 69, 110, 174–179
Clark, Colin, 30 n.
Clark, J. M., 115 n.
Colean, M. L., 112 n., 117 n.

Commercial and industrial failures, 95–96
Commonwealth Club of California, 4 n., 9 n., 12 n.
Communications industry. See Transportation, communication and utilities
Construction: building cycles in California and United States, 111–119; building trades workers, 26–29; employment in, 2, 28, 32, 37, 39–41, 44, 108–110, 170–173; income in, 80–81; residential, 115; wages in, 83–84
Cunningham, W. G., 102 n.

Davis, J. S., 23 n.
Department store sales. See Trade
Domar, E. D., 40 n.
Dorn, H. F., 23 n.
Dumke, G. S., 95 n., 152 n.

Edwards, A. M., 24 n., 26 n., 183 n.
Electrical industry: electric power production, 99, 103–105; use of electric power in manufacturing, 99
Electrical machinery. See Metal industries
Employment: by major industry group, 26–47, 107–111, 170–174; in California and United States, 26–36, 170–171; in manufacturing, 26–29, 32, 35–37, 44, 49–70, 102–103, 105–111, 174–179; in New York, 28–31; longrun trends, 26–47; rate of growth, 181. See also individual industry headings

Fabricant, S., 44 n., 103 n., 176 n.
Fabricated metal products. See Metal industries
Federal Reserve Bank of San Francisco, 106 n., 187
Federal Reserve System, Board of Governors of, 188
Fellner, W., 40 n.
Finance, insurance, and real estate: income in, 80; employment in, 108–109
Florida: employment in construction, 117; employment in wholesale trade, 30; migration to, 138–141
Food industry, employment in, 50–52, 55–57, 61, 63, 66–67, 69, 174–179
Foreign trade, value of, through California ports, 101, 104–105, 110
Forest products. See Lumber industry